STIENNON ON SECURITY

RICHARD STIENNON

IT-HARVEST PRESS

IT-Harvest Press is an imprint of IT-Harvest, LLC, Birmingham, Michigan, USA

Stiennon on Security: Collected Essays, Volume 1. 2010-2020

ISBN 978-1-945254-06-2

Printed in the United States of America

CONTENTS

INTRODUCTION

During the enforced isolation and "social distancing" of March 2020, I began to post more often to sites such as Forbes.com, Peerlyst, (where I am an advisor), LinkedIn, and The Analyst Syndicate. In doing so, and with a recent mindset of recording history, thanks to the February 2020 publication of *Security Yearbook 2020: A History and Directory of the IT Security Industry*, it occurred to me that, taken as a whole, my writing of the past 15 years has some value as a historical record. Choosing topics to write about is invariably flavored by current events and certainly reflective of my own thinking at the time.

I decided to quickly compile these essays into book form. It would be far too onerous to expect a reader who may be interested in these topics to wade through all those web pages with their constant popup ads and eye-distracting images appearing in the margins.

I hope my essays prove valuable. Some have aged well. Others have set in motion formative events in my own life.

The greatest impact to my career occurred when I published a column in Network World Magazine, October 26,

2006. It was titled *Wake up call: An Open Letter to Gil Shwed, CEO of Check Point Software.* At the time, Check Point had lost considerable market share to Cisco and was under pressure from Wall Street to make big moves. Within hours of the piece being published I received a call from Ken Xie, founder and CEO of Fortinet. He wanted to discuss hiring me as Chief Marketing Officer. By November 2006 I had wound down IT-Harvest, my industry analyst firm, to join Fortinet. That column is not included in this collection, but will be saved for Volume 2.

I left Fortinet in 2008 and spun up IT-Harvest again. Writing and publishing is a critical part of being an independent analyst, so that was the first thing I concentrated on, first for my blog, ThreatChaos, which I had started while at Webroot, then ZDNET, where they paid a penny per page view. Finally, Andy Greenberg at Forbes reached out and asked me to become a contributor.

Look at my April 2010 criticism of the proposed Rockefeller-Snowe cybersecurity regulation. That piece earned me a call from Rockefeller's staff. I went to DC to attempt to sway them on my position. I stand by my recommendations for federal government measures first proposed in an open letter to President Obama in 2008, which will also be included in Volume 2, but is summarized nicely in this volume.

My writing in 2010 focused on measures being discussed by the US government on the executive and legislative side. I guess I was on a crusade that in light of later breaches (OPM) and failings could be deemed a failure. I did not move the needle at all. This is probably why I don't write about government proposals very much today, unless they enact substantive measures.

My June 16, 2010, column memorialized the raging debate at the time over the use of the terms "cyberwar" and "cybersecurity." There are still technologists that tune out if they hear "cyber" appended to anything, but I think the world has fully embraced these terms.

My first industry commentary to appear in Forbes was a call for Intel to back out of its plan to acquire McAfee. I believe history has proven me very right on this one.

I stepped in to critique William Lynn's famous "Wake up Call" published in Foreign Affairs. Lynn's article marks the beginning of the transformation of the NSA and the creation of US CYBERCOM.

I cover technologies often. My critique of DHS' Einstein and IDS in 2010 is worth reflecting on. I introduce my thoughts on reputation services and beaconing detection in May 2011. I was transitioning to doing video interviews at the time so these articles were mere introductions to the videos. Because I charged the vendors a nominal fee to cover production, Forbes soon decided these violated its terms, so eventually I had to move them to IT-Harvest.com.

In May of 2011 I wrote about leaving Facebook because of its security challenges. While they fixed those issues for the most part, and I am on Facebook every day now, this article foreshadows, unwittingly on my part, the abuse of Facebook for spreading disinformation. In an upcoming column I am going to review the amazing book, *Mind F*ck*, by Christopher Wylie, which covers the attack on the US elections 2016.

You will find one of my common themes over the years is that network security vendors should not attempt to get into endpoint security and vice versa. I remember advising Symantec not to do that when I was at Gartner. I advise against the Sophos-Astaro merger in a May 2011 column.

After a flurry of posts in 2011 inspired by interviews with industry executives, I dip back into the cyberwar debate by critiquing the Clausowitzian thinking in a paper by Thomas Rid. You can start to see the influence of my academic period as I had gone back to school to study military history.

On November 7, 2011, I took a stab at criticizing Microsoft. Much of delving into the licensing structure for Windows products came from a white paper I wrote for several anti-virus vendors that wanted someone to make the argument that Microsoft's "free" security offerings were in fact more expensive than using an independent product.

In April of 2012 I posted a critique of Palo Alto Networks just prior to its IPO. That was my most-read column up to that time. It also caused PAN's executives to shun me forever.

I had to report on David Sanger's front page NYT article on Stuxnet on June 4, 2012. This first evidence that the US engaged in cyber attacks ushered in a new world of cyber conflict.

On July 25, 2012, Symantec's board sacked Enrique Salem, arguably the last "security guy" to be CEO. It was the beginning of the Demise of Symantec, which I cover in March 2020 and is the last essay reproduced in this volume.

There is a back story to my July 30, 2012, post *Let's Be Clear on Ethical Hacking.* After calling out the two founders of AlienVault in this post, first Forbes banned guest blogging on its platform, and then these two engaged in some heated Tweeting. Eventually the executives at AlienVault had to step in to smooth things over.

On September 19, 2012, I wrote an open letter to Senator Rockefeller. It was in response to a letter he sent out to Fortune 500 CEOs asking them to provide a report on their cyber readiness. I hope someday to see a FOIA request that reveals what those letters said.

By February 2013 I tackled the just-announced Presidential Policy Directive 21 (PPD21). I did not like it. And then on February 19, Mandiant published its famous APT1 report, the first public report of a nation hacking that included indicators of compromise (IoCs). In several of my books I point to this report as a turning point.

Following the usual flurry of writing inspired by the interviews I conducted at RSAC 2013 we entered a new phase of the cybersecurity world, what could be called the post-Snowden era. My June 7, 2013, column on how the surveillance state will threaten the US technology industry, and the next day's post about a Crisis of Confidence in US tech, was noticed by Tom Gjelten and led to my first NPR interview.

I took a break from writing about Snowden, privacy, and the surveillance state in March 2014 to address the turmoil in Ukraine and predict various methods that Russia would use if they planned an invasion. Then I wrote about what to do about the rush to create more university programs for cybersecurity in *STEM Stinks for Cybersecurity.*

Then back to Symantec with some pointed advice, which they never took.

In April 2014 I wrote *Why Network Security Vendors Should Stay Away From Endpoint Security, and Vice-Versa*, a theme I get to return to whenever a network security vendor acquirers an endpoint company. I get to write about that again; as this book goes to press, WatchGuard, a firewall vendor, announced the acquisition of Panda, an AV company in Spain.

In May of 2014 I attempted to point out that vendors of sandbox tools were violating Microsoft's terms of use policies by shipping multiple licenses of Windows on each appliance. The industry reaction was underwhelming. Microsoft never pursued anybody and eventually adjusted its terms.

I had gone back to school in 2011 to study War in The Modern World at King's College, London. I hoped the understanding of post-WWII history would inform my writing. It certainly slowed down my output as I was struggling with academic research reports until I graduated in July of 2014. I repurposed my Master's dissertation as a book, *There Will Be Cyberwar.*

In July 2015 I wrote *How PowerPoint Kicked Off A Revolution In Military Affairs.* It recounts the story of how Admiral Archie Clemins introduced the concept of net-war to the US military.

I also called for Intel to spin off McAfee on July 21, 2015, something they finally did in April of 2017.

Thinking about all the things the military did wrong I pointed that out in *Fixing the Pentagon.* I must get around to writing Part 2 where I use my experience from the automotive industry to provide advise on how to take on large projects in a rapidly evolving environment.

By August of 2016 I was working as Chief Strategy officer of Blancco Technology Group, so my writing focused on data erasure, privacy, and of course Hillary Clinton's emails, which were effectively overwritten.

In December 2017, just after leaving Blancco, I wrote about 5G. This was the first time I addressed the impact of 5G and my thinking informed the book *Secure Cloud Transformation*, which I started working on in January 2018 and published in time for the RSA Conference 2019.

The effort to write *Secure Cloud Transformation: The CIO's Journey* slowed down my posts dramatically. It was almost a year before I published *The Three Stages of Cloud Transformation: Application, Network, Security*, which reflected the theme of the book as it launched.

I end this volume with *The Demise of Symantec*, written March 16, 2020. This column received over 85,000 views on Forbes.com, the most for any of my posts. It was derived from the history of Symantec in *Security Yearbook 2020*.

By mid-March 2020 the world was plunged into a global pandemic. For a writer, being required to shelter at home means it is time to get serious about writing.

BEST OF SHOW RSA CONFERENCE 2010

MARCH 11, 2010

One thing is evident from this year's mega-security conference in San Francisco: the security industry is back with a vengeance. The show was packed with attendees and the expo floor was busier than I can remember in the last seven years I have attended.

The reason? While economic downturns can curtail general IT spending and investments in upgrades and new technology deployments, they have little impact on the need for securing existing infrastructure. Cyber criminals prey on companies in good times and bad. Add to that the newfound interest in security from governments as they discover that they are under attack from their adversaries and you have a formula for a boom.

Although I had an exhausting RSA this year (I met one-on-one with 48 vendors), my survey of the industry was not exhaustive. But I saw much to commend at RSA Conference 2010. Here are my choices for Best of Show RSA Conference 2010.

1. Astaro's Red Box is the single most innovative product I

saw. It is a little appliance that is drop-shipped to a remote office. Once it is plugged in to the network behind the router it creates an SSL tunnel back to headquarters. It extends the corporate network to as many locations as desired. This leverages the investment in security at one location by extending it to many. It is simple and inexpensive at MSRP of $299.

2. F5's new enterprise Big-IP edge gateway is based on SSL as well. It uses the web application acceleration features that F5 usually deploys in front of web servers to allow faster access to those applications in a secure manner.

3. PhoneFactor, a young company based in Kansas, has introduced strong authentication via SMS to add to their existing product that used voice authentication. The idea is not new, Estonia has been doing phone-based authentication for years, but the timing is right. Imagine a transaction authentication solution for your bank account. Every time you transfer funds or pay a bill online you would acknowledge a text message sent to your phone.

4. GreenSQL. While not officially exhibiting at RSA, the founder of this Israeli startup, David Mamam, was making the rounds. He introduced a database firewall that has been downloaded 75,000 times in its free form. The commercial version is a powerful solution that is affordable for the small to medium business.

5. Secunia, the premier vulnerability research company, announced an integration with Microsoft WSUS, making patching of critical vulnerabilities possible in quick and painless fashion.

6. Damballa has found that they are in the right place at the right time. Their focus on fighting botnets turns out to be just what people are looking for post Google-Aurora.

While cloud computing was the most hyped subject at RSA 2010, I saw the most development in authentication and extensions of protective capabilities in UTM solutions. Privileged access management is gaining momentum with several vendors, including last year's IT-Harvest Best of Show, Xceedium, present.

The industry breathed a sigh of relief last week as they saw evidence that 2009 is behind us. I look forward to a busy RSA 2011.

A SIMPLE SOLUTION FOR GOOGLE IN CHINA

MARCH 15, 2010

.

The Wall Street Journal reported over the weekend that:

A top Chinese minister warned Google Inc. "will have to bear the consequences" if it stops filtering its search results in China, suggesting there is little room for compromise in the high-profile showdown over censorship.

Here is an idea for Sergey, Larry, and Eric , and it may provide an option that allows them to continue to operate from China while avoiding the onus of censoring Google search results. The idea stems from a village in Turkey. If you have been to Istanbul (not Constantinople), you will have noticed the many Internet cafes, a situation born of high connect charges from home. In 2004 the government of Turkey imposed censorship on these Internet cafés, making them responsible for blocking objectionable content that included pornography and anti-Ataturk writings. The owners of Internet cafés in a small city not far from Istanbul found that the local police would make frequent spot checks and were always able to discover illegal sites that led to high fines, even though the cafés had invested in web filtering solutions to comply with the law. Their solution was simple and elegant. The café owners banded together and invested in the equipment and software needed to filter censored content at a point in the network that could cover them all: their ISP. Then they turned control over to the police. The café owners avoided the fines, the police stopped harassing them, and the letter of the law was enforced.

What if Google were to take the same route? Create a separate control interface to Google search that could be handed over to censors. The result would be:

1.   Google would no longer be in the censorship business. They could focus on their core business and not worry about every new dissident group and what must be continuous demands from the Chinese Communist rulers for imposing more and more granular controls.

2.   The ire of Chinese citizens would be more focused than before on those ultimately responsible for restricting their free access to information: their government.

While the moral high ground might be to completely exit the China market, you have to admit that Google search, by providing effective access to the world's information, provides benefits that weigh in favor of staying in China. By decoupling censorship from that benefit, Google may have a chance to continue to operate in China while sidestepping the moral implications.

KEEP AUSTIN WEIRD, BUT USE GOOD PASSWORD CONTROLS

MARCH 18, 2010

Wired's ThreatLevel reports that a disgruntled ex-employee of a car dealership in Austin, Texas, used a black box lock-out device on over one hundred vehicles to disable them or make their horns sound. The service he used, provided by Payment Technologies in Cleveland, is well thought out with safety features and back up batteries. If a car owner fails to make a payment the car will not start. There is a one-time emergency code to use once per pay period and other safeguards. (Read how it works on Paytek's site, and read Daniel Kennedy's excellent Firewall post on measures everyone should take regarding terminated employees and password controls. My thoughts are from the perspective of the service provider.)

But one little issue is the lack of access controls on the web-based service provided to the dealer. Like so many web-based services (think Twitter 18 months ago) the login is a simple web page that asks for username and password. Since the publishing of Wired's article, it is easy to predict that that login page is getting hammered by brute force password guessing tools already. It is only a matter of time before a cracker gets access to the system with some other dealership's credentials.

The lesson learned is simple. Do not ever provide a service over the web that controls something critical (house lights, surveillance cameras, bank accounts, car lock-out devices, street signs, traffic lights, bank accounts, stock trading accounts, etc.) without having at least rudimentary controls in place. Those controls are:

1.   Lock out the user after four failed attempts. (Works great when you do not have a lot of users and their usernames are not easily guessable. If you have millions of users like Facebook or Twitter, you have another problem. The attacker assumes a password (abc123, password, Celtics) and brute forces the username. Twitter has the issue of publicly revealed usernames: the Twitter ID.)

2.   Require CAPTCHAs. As annoying as this is, it stops brute force attempts and assures your customers that you are protecting their accounts.

3.   If large sums of money are involved, use two-factor authentication. (A one-time password token, call back to cell phone, see PhoneFactor.com for one such tool.)

Unfortunately, most new services are rolled out with the simplest login requirements. Do that and you will learn the hard way: a disruptive incident and public exposure in the press.

WHY ROCKEFELLER-SNOWE'S REGULATIONS WON'T PREPARE THE US FOR CYBERWAR

APRIL 5, 2010

Senators. Jay Rockefeller (D-W. Va.) and Olympia Snowe (R-Maine) have formulated a new cybersecurity bill that they described in Friday's *Wall Street Journal*. The bill as proposed will be disruptive to the operations of every business and will do essentially nothing to prepare the US for cyberwar.

Regulations have been tried before. One of the main drivers for investments in IT security has been regulations. California 1386 required the disclosure of data losses that has had a remarkable impact on banks, insurance companies, and schools. HIPAA created an industry of consultants to address potential health records losses. GLBA created a mountain of privacy letters sent to every account holder in the country. And Sarbanes-Oxley, thanks to an off-hand reference to requiring companies to deploy a security framework, has caused mountains of paper work and investment for publicly traded companies.

But regulation is not the primary driver for new technology, new investment, or new training; the threats are. The Payment Card Industry (PCI) standard was created by the credit card industry to protect the viability of their brand. Too much credit card theft was finally hurting them and they now require anyone who handles credit card information to encrypt that data. Aside from progress being made on that front, the threat against networks and data continues unabated.

Rockefeller and Snowe's bill will add nothing to the US's cyber preparedness. It's main points are:

-- Create the position of national cybersecurity adviser to coordinate government efforts and collaborate with private businesses. The person who fills this position would be confirmed by the Senate and answer directly to the president.

This position already exists. It was created in response to Melissa Hathaway's Cybersecurity Policy Review (CPR). Howard Schmidt was appointed by President Obama to be the Cybersecurity Coordinator. If cybersecurity can truly be coordinated by someone with no budget, no authority and dozens of competing factions to corral, Howard is the man for the job. What possible benefit could be derived from having a Senate confirmation of the person selected for this role other than to politicize the process?

-- Launch a new public awareness campaign to make basic cybersecurity principles and civil liberty protections as familiar as Smokey the Bear's advice for preventing forest fires.

The CPR also called for a Smokey the Bear campaign. Just as devastating forest fires still occur despite Mr. Bear's exhortations, debilitating cyber attacks will occur even if a well-intentioned mascot stands up for cybersecurity. A new public awareness campaign would be worthless.

-- Support significant new cybersecurity research and development and triple the federal Scholarship-For-Service program to 1,000 students. This program recruits individuals to study cybersecurity at American universities and then enter public service.

Cybersecurity is probably the most heavily researched endeavor in all of computer science. Tens of thousands of extremely bright people are crouched over their computers around the world every hour of every day tracking the latest cyber threats and countering them in near real-time. If some university applied for a grant to study a particular defense or technology, the threat would have moved on before they were awarded the money they asked for. This is one arena where the government is not needed and to which public research cannot contribute.

-- Create a market-driven process that encourages businesses to adopt good cybersecurity practices and innovate other ways to protect our security. Companies that excel at this will be publicly recognized by the government and companies that fall short in two consecutive independent audits will be required to implement a remediation plan.

There already is a market driven process to encourage good cybersecurity. The repercussions of being attacked successfully far outweigh the expense of defense. Companies are spending billions of dollars on cybersecurity today and growing that investment at a rate of over 20% annually. Public ridicule and recognition from the annual GAO audits of government agencies' cybersecurity has not been very effective in getting them to change their ways. Why should the private sector be subjected to what could only be a massive incursion into the way they do business?

-- Encourage government agencies and private businesses to work together to protect our civil liberties, intellectual property rights and classified information. The bill provides for unprecedented information sharing, including giving cleared private sector executives access to classified threat information.

Any executive who wants access to threat information is welcome to join the FBI's Infragard, where this is already done. The rest of the oft-repeated refrain for more public-private partnership is wasted. The private sector is well-prepared for cyber threats and will react quickly to any changes. It is the government that needs to change its ways.

-- Require the president and private companies to develop

and rehearse detailed cyber emergency response plans in order to clarify roles, responsibilities and authorities in a time of crisis. In a cybersecurity emergency, such as a terrorist attack or a major natural disaster, our country must be prepared to respond without delay.

There have been major earthquakes, floods, power-grid failures, and Internet outages for decades. We are still here and the Internet is alive and well. I can see that government officials want to have proposed legislation on the books so that they can say "I told you so" after the next cyber incident, but preventing the next incident is not only possible, it is easier to accomplish than creating a massive response capability that will be caught off guard anyway.

In my open letter to President Obama published the day before he was elected, I proposed the measures that have to be taken to protect government networks and assets from cyber attack. Cyber preparedness is something the US military and agencies have to take on. They already own and control their networks. They do not need legislation to do their jobs. Here is an abbreviated list of the steps that could be taken today by the US government.

-- Immediately issue a Presidential order that establishes responsibility for cybersecurity with real negative repercussions for those who fail to prevent breaches. For civilians this means being fired; for the military this means court martial, demotion and expulsion for serious security breaches. Do not allow the blame to be foisted off on contractors. The only way that security gets implemented is if someone's job is on the line.

-- While the National Institute of Standards and Technology (NIST) has been responsible for security standards and has created some great documents, it is a stretch to try to make the entire government comply with them during your term as President. Those responsible for locking down government networks and defending data will need to be empowered with a set of strict rules. These rules should include:

- All access must be explicitly authorized.
- All users must be identified and strongly authenticated.
- All applications must be reviewed for security vulnerabilities.
- All network attached systems must be scanned for vulnerabilities on a schedule.
- All network connections must be firewalled.
- All firewalls must be configured to "deny all except that which is explicitly allowed."
- All government networks must be mapped and understood.
- All data needs to be encrypted at rest.
- All communication links need to be encrypted.
- All intrusions need to be aggressively analyzed and appropriate responses executed.

-- Empower OMB to withhold funding to any agency that does not comply in a timely (less than six months) manner with the above.

-- Decentralize security management. One person cannot be effective in overseeing a cybersecurity policy. Security is everyone's responsibility and the system should motivate responsible individuals to take action.

-- Fix the DHS information sharing capability by learning from the recent advance of social networking. Getting members of law enforcement to collaborate effectively is not a task that can be accomplished by rolling out a quick fix technology. In a secure environment, individuals could find the most effective ways to communicate and share critical information.

-- Do not confuse security awareness campaigns with actual security improvements. The time, effort, and money that are spent on publicity campaigns could be better allocated to securing government networks.

-- Do not propose a new massive spending effort or any new departments to oversee cybersecurity. Security should be part of every computing infrastructure purchase and every-one's job.

-- Enhance transparency. Publish the methods of attacks used successfully against the Pentagon and NIPRNet. That is security awareness at its best. If the community knew the types of attacks and the sources it could better prepare for them.

-- Stop spying on citizens of the United States. While discovering terrorist plots is a legitimate function of the FBI, the violation of the privacy and individual rights of the people is too high a price to pay for the dubious information gleaned by snooping on email.

-- While offense cyber techniques will be developed, keep in mind that in cyberspace the best offense is a perfect defense.

Congressional oversight of these points may well be effec-tive, but new legislation is not needed. The executive branch can and should take the lead. The country is getting tired of legislation. Passing a cybersecurity bill would not do anything to better prepare us for cyber attack. Beefing up our defenses with accepted security practices would.

IS CHINA TESTING CYBERNUKES?

APRIL 9, 2010

China has been in the cross hairs of Google and the US State Department recently thanks to the discovery that hackers had used extremely clever espionage techniques to get access to Google's networks (and at least 30 other major corporations). Infiltrating target networks is one thing, but they raise the question of when an Internet superpower will use the big guns: BGP route announcements.

While resilient, the Internet suffers from a glaring vulnerability: the impact of spurious Border Gate Protocol (BGP) routing. Anyone can issue instructions to the basic building blocks of the Internet, the backbone routers, that, if accepted, will seriously disrupt the function of the Internet. This was dramatically demonstrated in the mid-1990s when a neophyte engineer at an Internet service provider (ISP) in Florida entered a new route in his routers that was picked up by his upstream provider and shared with the rest of Internet. For most of a day anyone who attempted to go to AOL.com was routed to his network. This pretty much shut down the Internet in the southeast US.

Similarly, Pakistan took YouTube off the Internet in early

2008, which led to Pakistan being taken off the Internet as well. Now we discover that in March one of China's ISPs leaked routes to one of the top level domain name servers that is maintained within their borders. This had the globally minor, but real, impact of imposing China's censorship of Twitter, Facebook, etc., on those affected. (Inside China, people are redirected to other sites if they attempt to use these services.) For a complete description of this incident look up the excellent report from the network watchdogs at Renesys.

The malicious announcement of BGP routes could temporarily completely disrupt Internet traffic for any network and could have spillover effects that could take an entire country offline, as happened in the Pakistan-YouTube incident. Using BGP route announcements to cause damage is the most powerful cyber-weapon available.

Yesterday, the folks at BGPMon, who monitor such things, discovered that IDC-China Telecom had leaked spurious route announcements for such popular sites as dell.com, cnn.com, www.amazon.de and www.rapidshare.com, causing them to be unreachable for some users.

Thousands of network routes were essentially hijacked yesterday by Chinese ISPs. Was this intentional? BGPMon speculates that it was an accident, which is reasonable since there are no documented cases of anyone *ever* issuing malicious route announcements. They are always user-errors. But if one were to contemplate developing offensive cyber weapons, wouldn't you test them occasionally to see if they worked?

HOW TO WIN—NOT JUST MAINTAIN—A CYBER COLD WAR

APRIL 13, 2010

Perhaps in response to rather vocal criticism of his frantic warnings about cyberwar, Mike McConnell, retired Navy Admiral and one-time Director of National Intelligence, published a position piece in *The Washington Post* in February. He drew on the Cold War to support his thesis that the US must do more to counter cyber threats. Here is my take on his comments.

Deterrence. McConnell describes the need for attribution and the ability to respond in a massive way to cyber threats. Attribution is a slippery subject in the world of cyber attacks. In all the incidents that have been reported, the United States is the *only* government that has admitted to meddling in international cyber affairs. That was when Twitter revealed that the US State Department had contacted the company and asked them to delay a scheduled maintenance on their popular micro-blogging site during the uprising in Iran when protesters were using Twitter to spread news of gatherings and protests in the streets. All other incidents have been vehemently denied by the states involved; specifically China and Russia.

Admirals and generals have often found themselves at odds with the populations of democratic countries. They have devoted their lives and sacrificed the lives of the people under them to protect the property and freedom of those citizens and feel compelled to maintain the military machine that they drive. Yet, in time of peace the populace views war preparation as leading to those very wars, not as a deterrent. The pacifist democracies of Europe and the UK could have easily prevented the carnage of World War II by slapping down Hitler when he first violated the Treaty of Versailles and moved troops and artillery into the Rhineland region in 1936. A quick response would probably have led to Hitler's removal by his general staff as they had advised against his aggressive moves in the first place. They lost credibility as each of Hitler's audacious moves met no resistance. But that is not how democracies work. Do not mistake me, when the enemy is at the gate freedom loving people are the first to stand up and defend their homelands. But no amount of flag waving and dire predictions will change them.

I draw on WWII, McConnell draws on the Cold War. But, by focusing on the balance of power created by the threat of nuclear holocaust, McConnell leaves out how the Cold War was won. Let's be honest. Democracy and freedom and the states that support those principals survived the Cold War. Totalitarianism perished in the end. While there are many theories of how this was accomplished, from the influence of Rock and Roll, to the fax machine, I tend to give the most credence to the economic front. The West outspent the Soviet Union. Technology, innovation and a massive arms buildup forced the Soviets to make parallel investments that, along with the crippled industrial plans that could not work in a modern world, impoverished the country to the point where internal strife pulled it down.

I suggest that rather than focus on creating a balance of mutual assured destruction such as existed during the protracted Cold War, a more appropriate response to cyber threats is to increase the costs for the attackers by improving defenses.

Public Private Partnership. McConnell goes on to make the completely unfounded statement:

"... the lion's share of cybersecurity expertise lies in the federal government..."

I am sure the security researchers at Symantec, Fortinet, McAfee, Bluecoat, Webroot Software, Sourcefire, and hundreds of other security vendors as well as the tens of thousands of security practitioners in the private sector, would be mystified by this claim. Yes, there are cybersecurity experts within the federal government. No way does the "lion's share" reside inside the government. That is why we are in the sorry state we are in today.

McConnell is somewhat conflicted in his call for greater public-private partnership as pointed out by Glenn Greenwald, writing for Salon.

Ever since McConnell created the Comprehensive National Cybersecurity Initiative (CNCI) during the Bush administration, we have heard a lot about public-private partnerships but have seen very little action or reduction in successful cyber attacks. As I have maintained, the private sector does not need the government's help. Certainly, laws requiring Internet service providers to filter attacks are not required and would create a morass of enforcement and oversight. McConnell favors such laws. The private sector is actually way ahead of the Pentagon and federal government when it comes to countering network-based attacks. Akamai, the biggest content delivery network (CDN), recently started to market its security services and is now hosting many of the government sites that were taken down during last July's Denial of Service (DoS) attacks. Verisign has their own DoS defense services, as does Prolexic and dozens of other companies.

I hope Congress realizes the impracticality of trying to

pass laws during a rapidly evolving situation as they engage this week in reviewing the appointment of Lt. Gen. Keith Alexander to head the Pentagon's Cyber Command.

SENATOR LEVIN POSES THREE CYBER SCENARIOS

APRIL 16, 2010

.

Thursday's hearing on the nominations of Keith Alexander to head CYBERCOM (and James Winnefield to head NORAD and NORTHCOM) was the first time that operational responsibilities of CYBERCOM have been discussed in a public forum. The Chairman of the Armed Services Committee, Senator Carl Levin (D-Michigan), began by posing three scenarios to Lieutenant General Alexander:

Scenario 1. A traditional operation against an adversary, country "C". What rules of engagement would prevail to counter cyber attacks emanating from that country?

Answer: Under Title 10, an "execute" order approved by the President and the Joint Chiefs would presumably grant the theater commander full leeway to defend US military networks and to counterattack.

Title 10 is the legal framework under which the US military operates.

Scenario 2. Same as before, but the cyber attacks emanate from a neutral third country.

Answer. Additional authority would have to be granted.

Scenario 3. "Assume you're in a peacetime setting now. All of a sudden we're hit with a major attack against the computers that manage the distribution of electric power in the United States. Now, the attacks appear to be coming from computers outside the United States, but they are being routed through computers that are owned by US persons located in the United States, so the routers are in here, in the United States.

Now, how would CYBERCOM respond to that situation and under what authorities?

Answer: That would be the responsibility of the Department of Homeland Security (DHS) and the FBI.

Alexander: "That's probably the most difficult [scenario] and the one that we're going to spend the most time trying to work our way through."

These were great questions and Alexander's answers are short and to the point. You cannot blame him for not being completely specific, because this is uncharted territory. In his opening remarks, Senator Levin questioned Keith Alexander's suitability because his background has been in military intelligence, not combat command. I for one think this is a good thing for someone leading a military CYBERCOM. Military metaphors can be dangerous when confronting Internet threats.

Keep in mind that CYBERCOM is a joint operation made of many components. I've outlined those components in my forthcoming book *Surviving Cyberwar* and in a post on my own blog, Threatchaos.

SEVEN CYBER SCENARIOS TO KEEP YOU AWAKE AT NIGHT

APRIL 29, 2010

Scenario planning is an important tool in the realm of cyber-security. Stakeholder teams are assembled to create plausible scenarios of possible future threats. Repercussions are predicted to help quantify risk and justify mitigating invest-ments in technology and changes to policy and operations.

Here are several cybersecurity scenarios. The scary thing is, they have already occurred. While the incidents covered may affect adjacent or even unrelated industries, it is advisable that IT security practitioners and other stakeholders are aware of the threats posed by the prior occurrence of these scenarios.

These scenarios are the subject of talks I am giving in Sydney and Melbourne the week of May 10.

1. Collateral damage from cyberwar

The scenario: Widespread attacks in conjunction with hostilities between two or more nation-states leads to network outages that spread beyond the geo-political participants.

The reality: Hosted websites in Atlanta, Georgia, suffer when Russia attacks the country of Georgia, August 8, 2008. Tulip Systems, a hosting provider in Atlanta, graciously offers to host the web sites of President Saakashvlli (president.-gov.ge) and the Georgian television station (rustavi2.com). A fire hose of DDoS attacks points at Tulip, disrupting traffic for all of its US based customers.

2. Political protestors enlist social media to target attacks

The scenario: Activists enlist social media to spread their message and generate crowd-sourced attacks.

The reality: During the 2009 protests over Iranian election results, Twitter users were enlisted in massive denial of service attacks against government webservers. While this was the most abject demonstration of how crowdsourcing over social networks can be effective, it also demonstrated that getting people engaged in such attacks is still hard to do. It is like getting a stadium crowd to do the "wave." It takes constant cheerleading to keep up and the first distraction shuts it down.

3. An insider uses privileged access to steal customer data

The scenario: an authorized user gleans credit and financial information and sells it.

The reality: During the mortgage frenzy of 2006-8 an employee of Countrywide absconds with millions of records and sells the data, loaded on USB devices, to a cyber-criminal.

4. Malicious software updates

The scenario: An attacker delivers software updates that surreptitiously enable a backdoor in critical information systems.

The reality: The Athens Affair. Over a period of months leading up to July 2005, attackers uploaded components of software to Ericsson phone switches that, when complete, gave them backdoor access, which was used to tap the cell phones of 100 officials and diplomats. While the perpetrators were never identified, it was revealed that the Ericsson software was actually developed in Greece. One of the engineers responsible for the switches was found hung in his apartment.

5. Hardware backdoors

The scenario: The supply chain of network equipment is subverted to allow the installation of remote command and control capability.

The reality: Remember the Clipper Chip? For those who don't, it was a Clinton administration attempt to embed back-doors in network equipment that would encrypt traffic but the cryptographic keys would be "escrowed" by the NSA and available for law enforcement. Thanks in part to the EFF, this project died. There are numerous allegations of secret back-doors in various equipment, which have turned out to be just hype. The Chinese vendor, Huawei, has found itself accused of having backdoors in its equipment by India, the US and the UK. No evidence has ever surfaced. Yet you can always find someone who will share scary stories over a couple of drinks about government tampering with equipment. So, while possible, and worth worrying about, the world still awaits the discovery of a wide-spread case of backdooring computer equipment.

6. Insider abuse

The scenario: An insider uses his knowledge of IT opera-tions to subvert them to his own purposes.

The reality: The multi-billion trading losses at Société Générale. In January 2008 it was discovered that Jérôme Kerviel, a securities trader at Société Générale had used his knowledge of back office operations, gained while working as an IT guy, to skirt internal controls and cover his heavy losses ($7.1 billion). The timing of the announcement was devas-tating to the markets just when they were most vulnerable.

7. State-sponsored spying

The scenario: State-sponsored email corruption leads to data loss and even endangers the lives of employees.

The reality: An infiltration of 1,200 networks of foreign offices and State Department facilities implicates diplomats and knowledge workers. As documented in the GhostNet report, the Dalai Lama's office was infiltrated by hackers, apparently from China, who acted on the knowledge gained to harass a Tibetan worker. The deeper the researchers from SecDev dig, the more damaging material they are finding.

What does this mean?

It is hard to propose a cybersecurity scenario that has not already occurred somewhere in the world. While doomsday scenarios of economic devastation and complete loss of critical infrastructure for extended periods is highly unlikely, it is still important to be cognizant of past incidents and thus become better armed to think about how these scenarios could play out in your own organization.

ROCKEFELLER'S CYBERSECURITY ACT OF 2010: A VERY BAD BILL

MAY 4, 2010

There are a bunch of cybersecurity bills trickling through Congress right now; some of them several years in the making. Senator Rockefeller's Cybersecurity Act of 2010 (S.773) is deemed the most likely to get voted on by the Senate as it was just unanimously passed through the Senate Committee that he chairs, Commerce Science and Transportation.

It is time for the security industry to take a closer look at this $1.82 billion bill, as it contains some pretty drastic measures that are going to be very disruptive, and I believe also detrimental.

The preamble, labeled "Findings," sets the stage with the dramatic language we have become familiar with:

As a fundamental principle, cyberspace is a
vital asset for the nation and the United States
should protect it using all instruments of national
power, in order to ensure national security, public
safety, economic prosperity, and the delivery of critical
services to the American public.

Even though there is a section listing definitions, "cyberspace" is never defined in S. 773. And, setting aside the dangling participle, this is a rather broad declaration. *All instruments of national power?*

There are further claims drawn from various cybersecurity experts including the President, Melissa Hathaway (author of *Cyber Policy Review*), Dennis Blair (Director of National Intelligence), Howard Schmidt (Cybersecurity Coordinator), Mike McConnell (former Director of National Intelligence), Paul Kurtz (Good Harbor consultant), James Lewis (Senior Fellow, CSIS), Booz Allen Hamilton, Allan Paller (SANS), and various policy think tanks, supporting the claim that cyberspace is a vital asset, and it is not secure or resilient.

If we stipulate for the moment that cyberspace is a vital asset and the government needs to step in to make it secure and resilient, let's examine the rest of the bill to see, if enacted, it would accomplish both those goals.

Section 4 of the act requires the President to define critical infrastructure. Specifically, within 90 days of enactment:

The President, in consultation with sector coordinating councils, relevant government agencies, and regulatory entities, shall initiate a rulemaking ..., to establish a procedure for the designation of any information system the infiltration, incapacitation, or disruption of which would threaten a strategic national interests as a critical infrastructure information system under this Act.

In other words, the Act requires the President to convene a bunch of meetings with as-yet-undefined groups to define a procedure with no timeline to designate what is and is not critical. Now, there is a tough task. But not to worry about the implications, these amorphous bodies are also instructed to "establish a procedure...by which the owner or operator of an information system may appeal." This will keep a lot of very high priced lawyers busy for years. Imagine if the NYSE or MasterCard-Visa is designated a "critical information resource."

Now comes the great regulatory overlay for IT security professionals, **Title 1 – Workforce Development.**

The President will be required to ask the National Academies (National Academy of Sciences (NAS), the National Academy of Engineering (NAE), the Institute of Medicine (IOM), and the National Research Council (NRC)) to conduct a one year study of existing accreditations and report after one year. From there, within six months, the President will be required to institute accreditation requirements for cybersecurity professionals working within the Federal Government and on *designated critical information systems*. There will be semi-annual audits to make sure each system is in compliance and remediation plans will be worked out if a department or agency is not in compliance for two consecutive audits.

The Director of the National Science Foundation (metallurgist Arden L. Bement) shall establish a **Federal Cyber Scholarship-for-Service** program which will apply to 1,000 students who will receive free-ride scholarships plus stipends and internships. Promising *K-12* students will also be identified for participation in summer work and internships. I am sure the senators do not really mean to include kindergarten students. Funding for the scholarship program will start at $50 million in 2010 and rise to $70 million in 2014. Fifty thousand dollars a year for each student (and program overhead) should do the job.

Next up is the **Cybersecurity Competition and Challenge**. The Director of NIST (physicist Patrick Gallagher) shall establish cybersecurity competitions and challenges with cash prizes not to exceed $5 million. The competitions will include middle school students. $15 million will be appropriated each year through 2014 for NIST to fund this.

Then comes the **Cybersecurity Workforce Plan** that requires every Federal agency to develop a strategic cybersecurity workforce plan with a mind boggling array of requirements for establishing that strategy and measuring its effectiveness.

Title II – Plans and Authority

This section gives the President 180 days to develop a Comprehensive National Cybersecurity Strategy. The President may declare a cybersecurity emergency that invokes a "collaborative emergency response and restoration plan" to be developed as part of the Strategy. Note this is the watered down version of the first proposed legislation, the so-called "kill switch."

Biennial Cyber Review

The President shall complete a review of the cyber posture of the United States every two years.

Cybersecurity Dashboard Pilot Project

Within a year, the Secretary of Commerce (Gary Locke) shall propose and implement a "system to provide dynamic, comprehensive, real-time, cybersecurity status and vulnerability information of all Federal Government information systems managed by the Department of Commerce including an inventory of such, vulnerabilities of such systems, and corrective action plans for those vulnerabilities." Apparently this would include all 15 operating units of the Department of Commerce including the Census Bureau, NOAA, and NIST. A very nice idea but do not underestimate the momentous size of this task or the disruption to the computing environments of the Commerce Department to pull this off within a year.

NIST Cybersecurity Guidance

This section requires NIST to promote auditable, private sector-developed cybersecurity risk management measures. Another laudable goal but I am afraid that cybersecurity risk management solutions that exist today lag behind the threat landscape by a number of years. While the Federal sector has to play catch up, the end result of successfully completing this section of the ACT will result (if completely successful) in agencies that can demonstrate they are in compliance with today's risk management best practices but will still be completely vulnerable to advanced threats. The requirements of this section will also apply to US Critical Infrastructure

Information Systems, creating a huge burden of compliance for an already stressed industry sector.

Joint Intelligence Threat and Vulnerability Assessment

A SMALL SECTION with huge impact reads in total:

"The Director of National Intelligence (Dennis Blair), the Secretary

of Commerce (Gary Locke), the Secretary of Homeland Security (Janet Napolitano), the Attorney General (Eric Himpton Holder, Jr.), the Secretary of Defense (Robert Gates), and the Secretary of State (Hillary Clinton) shall submit to the Congress a joint assessment of, and report on, cybersecurity threats to and vulnerabilities of Federal information systems and United States critical infrastructure information systems."

No timeline is provided for this monumental task.

Federal Secure Products and Services Acquisitions

The Administrator of the General Services Administration (Martha N. Johnson) shall require that requests for proposals will include cybersecurity risk measurement techniques for Federal information systems products. Perhaps the time has come for this measure but it will add tremendous overhead to an already burdensome acquisition process.

Title III -- Cybersecurity Knowledge Development

A new cybersecurity awareness campaign that "calls on a new generation of Americans to service in the field of cybersecurity." The Secretary of Education (basketball pro Arne Duncan) shall establish K-12 curriculum guidelines to address cyber safety, cybersecurity, and cyber ethics.

The Act also provides for the funding of new cybersecurity research into how to design and build secure software, and test and verify it.

The Cybersecurity Research and Development Act will be amended to provide over $150 million in funds each year. And the Computer and Network Security Centers will receive an additional $50 million per year. The Computer and Network Security Capacity Building Grants will be enhanced to the tune of $40 million+ per year. The Scientific and Advanced Technology ACT Grants will be bumped up by $5 million+ per year. The Graduate Traineeships in Computer and Network Security Research will have $20 million+ added. Total new authorization for Title III comes to $1.445 billion through 2014.

Title IV -- Public-Private Collaboration

The first step will be the creation of a Cybersecurity Advisory Panel. This panel will be called on to consult with the President on every other measure in the bill. The members will not be compensated other than for travel expenses.

State and Regional Cybersecurity Centers will be set up to "enhance the cybersecurity of small and medium sized businesses." The Secretary of Commerce is given 120 days to issue a description of the Centers. Note that it has been a year already since Congress passed an Act requiring the Small Business Administration to set up an IT Security Advisory Board. The SBA is already six months late in establishing that board.

Public-Private Clearing House

The government will review how threat information is currently shared between public and private sources and recommend the establishment of a central clearing house for threat and vulnerability information. That is what InfraGard and US-CERT are supposed to do today.

That's it. That is the vaunted public-private partnership that Senator Rockefeller is stumping in his latest public presentations and op-ed pieces.

Repercussions

If passed, S.773 will be an unmitigated disaster for the security industry, security professionals, and the security stance of the US government. Remember Sarbanes-Oxley? There was one tiny reference to "security frameworks" in that bill that caused every security team at publicly traded companies to drop everything they were doing and document their compliance with ITIL and COBIT. Some would argue that is a good thing but the end result was not enhanced security postures, but enhanced record keeping. This bill represents a gargantuan overlay on top of a vibrant industry that is finely tuned to address the rising threats that this bill attempts to address. It will be a windfall for those involved in cybersecurity certification, and academics who have been left in the dust by advances in cybersecurity being developed by entrepreneurial firms. If enacted, it will create a guild of government certified security professionals who have the luxury of taking the time to qualify.

And of course, those who vote for this Act will be able to point to the proactive stance they took when the next cyber embarrassment occurs. They will not have done anything to prevent the next cyber incident. But they will have covered their...backs.

DHS DEPLOYING WRONG WEAPONS IN CYBERWAR

JUNE 16, 2010

Siobhan Gorman, writing at the *Wall Street Journal*, tells us that a report from Richard Skinner, DHS Inspector General, will be presented to Congress today. The report highlights troubles at US-CERT, in particular turnover in leadership and severe understaffing.

But the problem is not with US-CERT's administration. It is with their impossible mission. There appears to be some belief within DHS and the inspector general's office that the secret Einstein project is somehow going to improve cybersecurity. Pointing fingers at slow deployment and lack of information dissemination is ignoring a more fundamental problem.

The Einstein project, authorized under the still classified portions of the Bush Administration's Comprehensive National Cybersecurity Initiative (CNCI), is a plan to deploy Intrusion Detection sensors (IDS) at all of the government's Internet gateways.

Even if US-CERT was fully staffed with three shifts to monitor and report on the alerts Einstein generated, even if all of the sensors were deployed, even if all of the information were distributed to every department and agency within DHS, the US would not be able to fight cyber attacks.

Let's review. IDS is a technology invented over 15 years ago. It is signature-based, which means it relies on a massive collection of snippets of text and code that researchers have discovered over the years are associated with unwanted network traffic, be it worms, port scans, or intrusions. Because the original deployments of IDS were just passive data collectors, there was no impact on network performance from adding new signatures, so the data base grew and grew and the logs IDS generated grew and grew to the point where even a mid-size organization would receive millions of alerts a day. IDS log management became a major problem that gave birth to two industries: Security Event Information Management (SEIM) and Managed Security Service Providers (MSSP). SEIM products from companies like ArcSight attempt to prioritize alerts so that security personnel can focus on just the important events. MSSPs (Symantec, Secureworks, BT) use SEIM products to make it even easier for a customer to handle the flood of alerts their IDS generates. To make the claim that they are effective, MSSPs staff their SOCs (Secure Operations Centers) around the clock. US-CERT has been tasked with becoming the MSSP for DHS.

But do you see the problem here? The only tool in DHS's chest is a monitoring tool. Millions of alerts have to be filtered down. The continuous port scans, the worm traffic, the DDoS attacks, have to be winnowed down to something actionable. And even if that were possible, attacks such as those seen by Google, the Dalai Lama's office, and the Pentagon, would still be effective. I have been beating this drum since 2003 when I visited the Pentagon and in no uncertain terms informed them that they were wasting their money on IDS. The ensuing public debate was well covered by the media but must have been missed by the framers of the CNCI.

Einstein is a waste of money and a distraction. Other than

generating huge reports that highlight the levels of attacks targeting DHS, it will do nothing to protect DHS networks. There have been a lot of advances in network security technology since 2003. It is time for DHS to get serious about security.

THE TEN-YEAR-OLD CYBERWAR DEBATE CONTINUES

JUNE 16, 2010

In 2001 Ralf Bendrath, a German cybersecurity writer and researcher, wrote a report that dug into the efficacy of the use of the term "cyberwar." His report is remarkable in that most of what he covers ten years ago represents today's state of affairs.

Bendrath was writing before 9/11, at the end of the dot-com boom, yet he can cite research into the militarization of cyberspace dating back to the early '90's. Read his opening statement:

"Cyberwar" has become a growth market in the US. While ten years ago the term would hardly have made sense to any expert, in the meantime attacks on computer networks and their implications for national security have received broad coverage in the media. In the broad range of service providers from technical security solutions to policy advisory groups, a whole cottage industry has sprung up. Warnings of an "electronic Pearl Harbor" or a "cyberwar" against the US's infrastructures by "rogue states" or terrorists are part of the standard repertoire in security policy analyses.

Sound familiar? Does it remind you of the debate held

June 8, 2016 to address this proposition: "The Cyber War Threat Has Been Grossly Exaggerated"?

The debate, hosted by Intelligences Squared, featured Bruce Schneier, (chief security technology officer with BT) and Marc Rotenberg (executive director of the Electronic Privacy Information Center) speaking in support of the idea that the threat of cyberwar has indeed been exaggerated. And opposed, we saw Mike McConnell executive vice president and leader of the National Security Business for Booz Allen Hamilton and a member of the firm's Leadership Team, and Jonathan Zittrain, professor of law at Harvard Law School, where he co-founded its Berkman Klein Center for Internet & Society.

The debate was won hands down by McConnell and Zittrain mostly because they stuck to the topic while the Schneier-Rotenberg team attempted to paint a picture of a power and money grab on the part of the defense-industrial base. If you have an hour or so, watch these accomplished thinkers duke it out.

The debate, of course, is not over. There is a disconnect between the IT security industry and policy makers the world over on the topic of cybersecurity. The discord is so great that both sides are not even listening to each other. On several occasions I have heard security geeks brush off Congress' attempts to pass a cybersecurity bill as "silly." In the debate Bruce Schneier even used "silly" to describe the idea of cyberwar.

In 2001 Bendrath's conclusion was that:

"The militarization of cybersecurity policy will be very difficult in a liberal society with private infrastructure providers. From the American experience, we should rather conclude that "cyberwar" is a fundamentally inadequate term that disrupts discussion on useful risk policy more than it contributes."

For that discussion on useful risk policy to occur, security professionals have to learn a new lexicon that includes terms like cyberwar and cybersecurity. Policy makers have to understand that they are dealing with technology that is changing faster than governing bodies can respond. Both sides must continue to engage in debate as well as just talk to and get to know each other.

NEW CYBERSECURITY FOCUS FOR FEDERAL R&D GROUP

JUNE 22, 2010

A few weeks ago I participated in a cyber roundtable pulled together in Washington, DC. This was, in part, a meeting to kick off a new organization that will seek to bring security technologists and policy makers together. (Much more on this at a later date.)

The participants (who met under the Chatham House Rule) included uber security geeks, privacy advocates, Defense Industrial representatives, and policy influencers. There was quick acknowledgement from all of the participants that there are multiple problems in the way the cybersecurity challenge is being met, including technology and R&D investment, information sharing, and a lack of understanding of those problems as evidenced by the bills wending their way through Congress.

So I was heartened to see that the US Networking and Information Technology Research and Development (NITRD) consortium is stepping up to address at least the technology issues. NITRD is supported by 14 federal agencies including the National Science Foundation and DHS. They held a meeting May 19, 2010 to propose three areas of investigation that would lead to game-changing research and development and opened the discussion to public comment. Herewith are my comments that I submitted to their forum. (The comment period ends today, June 18, 2010.)

The first proposed theme is Tailored Trustworthy Spaces. This theme, while at first glance appearing overly academic, is crucially important and is actually evolving on the Internet. It reflects the way we change how we behave and interact depending on the particular forum we are participating in. A Skype conversation with a child away at school, fund transfers between bank accounts, executing stock trades, using a VPN to enter the corporate network, commenting anonymously on blogs, a LinkedIn discussion group, Craigslist, Twitter, and Facebook are all examples of different trust environments we participate in.

We adjust how we interact, who we trust, what information we reveal, and in some case adjust our browsers or even the computer we use to participate. A bank may still require Internet Explorer to access its online accounts but the security-conscious will use Firefox for general web browsing. Some people have even started to use separate computers for some activities. Research should begin with what is working today and what about those solutions is succeeding. The concept of segmentation should be included to provide damage control when a trustworthy space is breached.

As new models are developed they should be deployed and tested quickly to discover their failings. Behavior monitoring should be used to alert when new and unusual behaviors arise. Remember Network News Groups? Initially NNTP (Network News Transfer Protocol) gave rise to vast forums where like-minded people could discuss politics, cats, even knitting. When spammers started spewing postings to the thousands of groups, NNTP died out. Built-in defenses against spam behavior may have saved News Groups. The key point is that all possible attacks on a Trustworthy Space cannot be predicted. Monitoring, reporting, and alerting should be included (along with privacy protections).

The second theme is Research into Moving Target (MT) technologies. This is a great concept and ties into the next theme of economics. Few will disagree that monocultures, thanks to the wide deployment of a single code base, rife with vulnerabilities, is the single biggest cause of the cybersecurity challenge.

Technologies such as Solidcore (just acquired by McAfee) can be installed to make a Windows machine impervious to attack via essentially randomizing memory and system call registries. Other randomizing in the network can add to the investment an attacker must make to be successful. There is one area that is ripe for exploration. The decades-long movement towards platform consolidation should be reversed and R&D efforts should support that reversal. Certain environments (critical infrastructure, DoD, the intelligence community) should move to multiple platforms just to increase the number of systems an attacker must have tools to compromise.

As a start, Windows systems should be limited to desktops only. All servers for DNS, directory services, databases, applications, and cloud computing should be on non-Windows platforms. This would ensure that popular vectors, developed by cyber criminals to attack and control the target-rich consumer space, would not also lead to infections of SCADA controllers, transaction processors, or real-time environments. Certainly handhelds, ships, tanks, airplanes, medical equipment and manufacturing systems should never share a code base with a dominant consumer product. Over time even desktop environments should be transitioned to multiple different platforms. R&D efforts could enhance the management of multi-platform environments. Open source communities could be supported to enhance the protections of Linux variants.

The third proposed theme is Cyber Economic Incentives. In October 2006 I was asked to join a workshop on modern malware hosted by the Santa Fe Institute and co-chaired by Matt Williamson, principal research scientist from Sana Security, and Esther Dyson. I can sum up the overall sense that was shared by the participants at the end of the second day: This is a war.

The enemy is organized, well-financed and smart. Reactive measures such as research and signature generation are falling behind. Most important, when the workshop convenes again, at least half the time and effort should be devoted to understanding the economics of cybercrime. As far as I know, that follow-on meeting never occurred. While the intent of this theme seems focused on providing economic incentive for improving the security practices of the good guys, I would not neglect research into understanding the motivations of the bad guys as well.

NITRD has asked the right questions and proposed valuable avenues of future investment. I applaud this effort and hope that support for it comes from the member agencies. One final suggestion is that international participation should be invited. We are all in this together and only by pulling in the brilliant researchers around the world can cybersecurity challenges be addressed.

BOTTOM LINE: ASSUME THAT YOU'VE BEEN HACKED

JULY 7, 2010

It is increasingly evident that even the most secure environments are compromised. While the successful penetrations might not be targeted in all cases, there are enough incidents now public to indicate the extent of the present danger. Every organization should revisit their security plans based on a new assumption: *that their enterprise is already compromised and that their data is being exfiltrated.*

Consider just these few incidents taken from a Heritage Foundation report published in 2008. (I am not stressing the China factor here, only the loss of data and the methods used.)

Titan Rain. In 2004 Shawn Carpenter discovered significant amounts of data from government research labs, NASA, and defense organizations residing on servers outside the United States.

United Kingdom Government. Throughout December 2005 British Parliament offices were surreptitiously penetrated, also from computers using the Guangdong network. Britain's National infrastructure Security Coordination Center investigators told reporters, "These were not normal hackers...The degree of sophistication was extremely high. They were very clever programmers." Some of the attacks targeted files in British government offices that deal with human rights issues.

The Trojan email attacks targeted specific victims. "One email was targeted at one company in aviation. It was a Word document that had a math/cad component. If you did not have math/cad on your computer, it would not open," said one expert. "The point was to find documents that had been written in that particular program and then send them back." (Check out this McAfee whitepaper on the incident.)

Taiwan. According to an official of Taiwan's Ministry of National Defense, in 2006 Taiwan detected 13 PLA zero-day attacks launched within Microsoft applications and experienced a total of 178 days of vulnerability between notifying Microsoft of the attacks and receiving the appropriate patches. One PowerPoint-based attack was so sophisticated that it took Microsoft engineers over two months to construct a patch.

Foreign Coast Guard Agency. In Spring 2007, a program was discovered at a foreign coast guard agency that systematically searched for documents that had shipping schedules, then forwarded them to an email address in China, according to David Rand, chief technology officer of Trend Micro.

And more recently we have seen the extent of the network of infiltrated machines specifically targeting organizations that impact Tibet-China relations, as documented by research teams at the University of Toronto and SecDev in their GhostNet report. These techniques look remarkably like those used to target Rio Tinto, the Australian mining giant.

The methodologies employed in these widespread attacks is typically the combination of new vulnerabilities and custom Trojan horses delivered over the web or through email. This January's revelation that Google and dozens of other companies had succumbed to such attacks was a wakeup call for industry, the US State Department, and now Congress, which is responding with legislation to address the issue.

What should you be doing to address the presence of compromised internal resources? While Data Leak Prevention attempts to provide an overlay of classification, network monitoring, and endpoint management (for USB devices), there is another approach that uses advanced agents on the desktop that continuously check for abnormal behavior that is indicative of root kits and custom Trojans.

I just posted a white paper on such a technology. By identifying, disabling, and repairing infected machines you will engage in a constant battle against the enemy within. But at least you will have a weapon for that battle instead of flying blind and trusting to ineffective AV, IDS, and firewalls.

LEGISLATING GLOBAL INTERNET FREEDOM

JULY 20, 2010

There is a disturbing tendency on the part of the US Congress to legislate the Internet. A case in point is HR 2271 backed by eleven US Representatives and submitted to review by the House Energy and Commerce and Foreign Affairs Committees last May (2009). Thankfully, there has been no serious deliberation on this proposed measure which intends to somehow regulate the Internet to promote, ironically, freedom of speech. In its preamble the intent is well articulated:

To prevent United States businesses from cooperating with repressive governments in transforming the Internet into a tool of censorship and surveillance, to fulfill the responsibility of the United States Government to promote freedom of expression on the Internet, to restore public confidence in the integrity of United States businesses, and for other purposes.

Reading between the lines you can discern that this bill was proposed in part in a reaction to Google, Yahoo!, and Microsoft engaging in less than ethical collusion with the Chinese government; activities that have led to incarceration of bloggers and restrictions on access to information.

The Bill has sections devoted to:

Creating an annual report that identifies those countries that engage in restrictive Internet activity (105). Would this watch list contain Australia which is setting up a massive filtering infrastructure to protect its citizens from the less tasteful content on the Internet? Would it include Germany which has attempted to ban hacking tools? Or the EU which has considered blocking searches that include certain key words like "bomb"? Would it identify the US which, thanks to widespread eavesdropping on AT&T's network by the NSA, has frightened businesses away from ever hosting data in a country where they perceive that data to be unsafe from snooping?

Setting up the Office of Global Internet Freedom reporting to the Secretary of State and led by a Director (104). I suspect just the name of this department will create additional work for the State Department to smooth ruffled feathers of those that may take umbrage to the US unilaterally setting global policies of any sort. Ironically, the only defined task for this Office will be to "identify key words, terms, and phrases relating to human rights, democracy, religious free exercise, and peaceful political dissent..." an activity that in itself smacks of thought control.

Section 203 requires any US company that imposes changes to their search results at the behest of one of the listed countries must report it to the Director of the Office of Global Internet Freedom (DOGIF). **Section 204** has similar regulatory burdens for any US company that hosts information. This is obviously targeted at Google, Microsoft, and Yahoo!, but there are thousands of online content and search engine companies that could fall under these requirements.

HR 2271 also points out in its preamble:

"A number of United States businesses have enabled the Internet censorship and surveillance of repressive governments by selling these governments or their agents technology or training."

Luckily it stops short of proposing the restriction of sale of that technology. It is hoped that the backers realized the tremendous damage they could inflict on the US's networking industry if they attempted to restrict commerce to the extent necessary to stop the sale of all technology that can be used for restricting access to information. It would include all firewalls, routers, and content inspection technology.

There seems little danger of HR 2271 ever coming to a vote, but we must keep a wary eye on this 111th Congress that has over 40 measures under consideration that bear on highly technical issues. A misstep could be costly and have debilitating consequences for a fragile economy. Global Internet Freedom will be best served by governments of all types avoiding any meddling in the still young Internet.

INTEL SHOULD NOT CONSUMMATE MCAFEE ACQUISITION

AUGUST 19, 2010

Some deals just don't make sense. Some have underlying motivations that are not immediately apparent. Intel's announced intention to acquire McAfee for $7.68 billion is a deal that does not make sense no matter what perspective you take.

Technology acquisition. One argument put forth by analysts so far is that by acquiring a market-leading anti-virus software company, Intel will be able to add security features to their core business: chips. Seven billion dollars is a lot to pay for technology when there are 27 such technology companies that would cost less to acquire (Symantec, of course, being more expensive).

Intel could acquire one of many anti-malware companies that have arguably better technology, better research, and much less baggage.

Brand enhancement. While there is a good argument to be made for technology vendors to acquire security companies to enhance their brands (EMC + RSA a notable example), Intel is not going to accomplish that by acquiring McAfee. Intel already has one of the most recognized brands in all of technology and they have no negative perceptions because of a lack of security association. Intel is highly respected across the board and is rarely faulted for lack of security. This acquisition does not bolster their brand at all. If anything, it dilutes Intel's brand.

Government play. With a tremendous increase in government spending on cybersecurity projected, one could argue that acquiring McAfee gives Intel a piece of the action. McAfee's EPO desktop security suite is already shortlisted within most of the US Defense Department and the firewall business McAfee acquired with their Secure Computing acquisition has a large federal component. But Intel is already entrenched in all aspects of state, local, and federal government in almost every country in the world with their ubiquitous CPUs. Intel needs no help getting government business.

Network play. McAfee has invested considerable time and effort in revamping the Secure Computing line into a credible network security play. They also have one of the largest install bases of Intrusion Prevention (IPS) solutions. Will Intel work to enhance those network security products by supporting multi-core architectures in them? What does that mean to every other networking company that could have been big consumers of Intel CPUs? How will they feel about using chips from a direct competitor? And if the acquisition is a networking play, why would Intel put McAfee in their Software and Services division?

Investment. In the tradition of conglomerates and holding companies, this acquisition could be viewed as an investment in the relatively stable security industry. The plan would be to streamline operations and increase profitability. Is Intel really trying to become the next GE or ITT? Is that its core strength? Did it look at other investment opportunities? I understand beachfront property on the Gulf coast is looking pretty good right now.

At $7.68 billion, this is the biggest acquisition of a pure

play security company ever. It is also the worst. There is no synergy, no channel benefits, marginal revenue enhancement (considering the price), no new markets, and no meaningful strategy.

THE GOOD, THE BAD, AND THE UGLY IN THE PENTAGON'S CYBERSTRATEGY

SEPTEMBER 3, 2010

William Lynn, the US Deputy Secretary of Defense, wrote the most succinct description of the US Pentagon cyberstrategy yet in the September/October issue of Foreign Affairs. Here are the good, the bad, and the ugly components of that strategy.

The good. Lynn begins by acknowledging successful cyber attacks against the US military, in particular the intrusion via USB thumb drives that occurred in the fall of 2008. This intrusion led to the Pentagon making an unprecedented move to ban USB thumb drives from the military; a ban that was only rescinded in February 2010. The cleanup effort to recover from the widespread worm infection, that Lynn claims was initiated in a Mideast base by foreign agents, was dubbed Operation Buckshot Yankee (OBY) in the Defense Department and Operation Rampant Yankee in the Army.

Lynn also states, "To stay ahead of its pursuers, the United States must constantly adjust and improve its defenses." This is an important acknowledgement and reflects the state of cyber defense for every organization. There is no single technology solution to be deployed that will counter all threats and even the latest and greatest technology will not defend against tomorrows attack methodologies.

Deterrence has been the subject of many recent reports coming from think tanks and cyber commissions. Most have taken the view that cyber offensive or retaliatory measures must be in place to deter assailants. I like Lynn's take: "Deterrence will necessarily be based more on denying benefit to attackers than on imposing costs through retaliation."

In other words, a strong defense is the best cyber defense.

Lynn also addresses the issue of international cooperation: "If there are to be international norms of behavior in cyberspace, they may have to follow a different model, such as that of public health or law enforcement." Agree.

I can find no fault with Lynn's summary: "The principal elements of that strategy are to develop an organizational construct for training, equipping, and commanding cyber defense forces; to employ layered protections with a strong core of active defenses; to use military capabilities to support other departments' efforts to secure the networks that run the United States' critical infrastructure; to build collective defenses with US allies; and to invest in the rapid development of additional cyber defense capabilities. The goal of this strategy is to make cyberspace safe so that its revolutionary innovations can enhance both the United States' national security and its economic security."

The bad. Even after highlighting the problems facing the Defense Department, Lynn makes the argument that the Pentagon must leverage its ten years of concerted investment in cyber defense to support broader efforts to protect critical infrastructure. Yet the two areas that he suggests the DoD has made headway in are computer hygiene (keeping anti-virus and firewalls up to date) and "sensors which detect and map intrusions."

As I am the one most often associated with criticism of these sensors (IDS), I must point out that while they sound sexy, the industry has moved way beyond signature-based intrusion detection. There is no argument that a massive government initiative could provide some interesting intelligence about the source and methods used by attackers if they deployed sensors on the 15,000 networks Lynn says they have. But the effort will not do anything to stop those attacks today when there are many technologies that will. If the most that the DoD can offer to protect critical infrastructure is IDS and anti-virus updates, we have a problem.

The ugly. Back to Operations Buckshot and Rampant Yankee. Wired questions the attribution to foreign agents for the attack. If such claims are to be made, the Defense Department is going to have to do more to make visible the results of their forensic work.

There is no question that the cleanup activity truly turned Pentagon resources out in a massive effort. One Army base awarded four IT personnel special medals for the work they did to reimage all of the computers on an entire base. If universal reimaging was the response to a spreading worm, there is much yet to be done within the DoD to update its security practices.

Apparently that military has recognized some of the work needed and even states in the DoD Fiscal Year 2011 IT President's Budget Request dated March 9, 2010:

"The AF (Air Force) Network Action Plan is designed to reinvigorate operational rigor and address lingering systemic issues in the AF Global Information Grid highlighted by the Operation BUCKSHOT YANKEE." Those "lingering systemic issues" apparently include the lack of ability to use networks to communicate effectively that created the widespread use of USB thumb drives.

Barry Rosenberg interviewed Lt. General Jeffrey Sorenson on August 10, 2009:

When the dictate was put out that thumb drives were no longer going to be allowed, it did have some operational implications because this was how different orders, missions and organizational information were transmitted from headquarter to headquarter. Over time, we've had to go back and look at how we transfer data, and, clearly, the use of the thumb drive was one of these expedient methods by which information was passed between computers because we didn't have a system set up properly to transfer the data.

And there is the whole concept of the network service center, by which data can be forward-staged and transmitted via the network as opposed to people picking up their hard drives, or in this case, what used to be thumb drives or servers, and moving them. We're still a number of years in the future before we have a net-centric or net-enabled capability that can be used to share data.

In many cases, as we've learned through the most recent Army "Rampart Yankee" and [Defense Department] "Buck-shot Yankee" exercise — where we had to go off and reme-diate computer systems because of some infected thumb drives — that was a rather laborious, manually intensive effort to essentially achieve a capability that we would like to have, which would be machine-to-machine.

This raises the almost insurmountable prospect of an IT infrastructure stuck in the '90s.

The effort to modernize includes a plan to consolidate Active Directories as well. Lt. General Sorenson states here that 17 trees and 5 rogues (with that number climb-ing) exist within the Air Force alone. User identity directory consolidation was a big issue in 2003. If the military has stan-dardized on Microsoft and is only now moving to a consoli-dated directory structure they have a long road ahead of them in modernizing their IT operations.

Lynn has set the stage for the creation of a concise cyber-strategy for the Pentagon. Now they need to follow through on defending their networks at least up to industry standards.

A BRIEF HISTORY OF CHINESE CYBERSPYING

FEBRUARY 11, 2010

.

A frightening pattern of targeted espionage reports has a new entry provided by McAfee. The *Night Dragon report*, issued Thursday, details a concerted effort to harvest oil and gas reserve information and other highly confidential information from the executives of at least five major oil, gas, and energy companies. Reserve trading and SCADA information was also compromised. McAfee provides strong attribution that the attacks came from China (strong, not conclusive, which would require a believable source taking credit for the attacks).

The pattern indicates that China engages in focused projects that target particular industries or governments. A brief timeline with ever-increasing attribution:

2004 Titan Rain (Slideshare presentation)

2006 British MPs targeted. (*Guardian*, Smash and Grab, the High Tech Way)

2007 German Chancellery compromised and China accused of being the perpetrator. (*Der Spiegel*, Merkel's China Visit Marred by Hacking Allegations)

2007 US Pentagon email servers compromised for an

extended period. Cost to recover: $100 million.(Paul, Ryan. "Pentagon e-mail taken down by hackers." *Ars Technica*. 22 June 2007)

2007 Oak Ridge National Laboratory targeted by Chinese hackers. (Stiennon, Haephratic Technique Used to Crack US Research Lab)

2009 GhostNet report from SecDev on Chinese infiltration of Dalai Lama's office. (Scribd presentation: Tracking GhostNet)

2009 Three largest resource companies in Australia, including Rio Tinto, compromised. (Rio Tinto hacked at time of Hu arrest)

2009 Google Aurora attacks target user data and source code. (McAfee blog)

2010 Corollary Aurora attacks against Marathon Oil, ExxonMobil, and ConocoPhillips (*Christian Science Monitor*, US oil industry hit by cyberattacks: Was China involved?)

2010 *Shadows in the Cloud* report from SecDev on successful attacks against India's military networks. (Scribd report: Shadows in the Cloud)

McAfee *Night Dragon* provides details of attacks against five large energy companies. (McAfee: Globa Energy Cyber Attacks: "Night Dragon")

This trail of increasing attribution should be taken as a critical alert to industry groups that deal with strategic global information including:

- State departments
- Military
- Critical resources including agriculture, oil, gas, building materials, and mining (iron, aluminum, gold, silver, platinum and alloy ingredients such as molybdenum, magnesium, palladium, and chromium).
- Computers and technology

These industries should be on high alert and take extraordinary measures to first determine if they have already been compromised, and then lock down their environments. Tools such as Damballa, FireEye, Guidance Software, and NetWitness should be deployed immediately to detect "beaconing" connections from inside their networks to command and control servers. Web application firewalls from Application Security, F5, or Imperva should be deployed in front of exposed web resources. Whitelisting products from Bit9, CoreTrace, Lumension, or Savant Protection should be trialed immediately on executive laptops.

Adversaries using pernicious methodologies are targeting (see webinar New definition of APT) the data of globally strategic industries. Business as usual based on risk-based methodologies has to be supplanted by an urgent revamping of security deployments to counter a frightening new level of threat.

HOW REPUTATION SERVICES ENHANCE IPS

MAY 3, 2011

Reputation has become an effective and required ingredient for many aspects of security. Using a large database of known suspicious or bad source IP addresses, even URLs, has made dramatic improvements to spam filters and web security gateways. Now reputation is beginning to be used to improve the effectiveness of Intrusion Prevention Systems (IPS). How these systems employ reputation will be the determining factor in the success of any IPS solution.

Anti-spam vendors have long used reputation. Through a series of honeypots, email accounts set up to capture spam samples, it is possible to quickly identify the sources of spam, usually infected hosts belonging to consumers with broad band access. The behavior of such a spam bot is easy to identify as it spews millions of spam messages. Once identified it is simple to quickly update anti-spam solutions with a list of spam sources that are automatically blocked. This saves on processing requirements as the individual messages do not need to be investigated. One of the fastest (and thus lowest stress on network gear) functions is dropping connections from a list of sites.

Secure web gateways also rely on reputation to quickly identify sources of malware and block access to URLs that are known to contain malware.

Discovering malicious URLs, however, needs a different approach. Honeypots, which are passive email accounts, are not effective at discovering sources of malware. Likewise, a web crawling robot that follows links such as Google is not effective. Most reputation services for identifying malicious sites rely on a large install base of deployed appliances that report new URLs and their associated behavior back to a central database for automated inspection, backed up by teams of researchers for those sites that defy automated analysis. Through this technique a real-time list of bad URLs is formed and pushed back out to the secure web gateways for blocking.

IPS solutions have long relied on reduced sets of signatures for worms, Trojans, malware, and targeted attack exploits. As IPS technology evolved, and the number of signatures required for effective blocking grew, many IPS solutions incorporated signatures that are based on vulnerabilities instead of exploit. This meant that defenses against unknown exploits that target new unpatched but known vulnerabilities could be incorporated.

However, signatures that are written to be general purpose and block based on a category of potential exploits against known vulnerabilities can cause false positives and thus block legitimate connections. While IPS vendors strive to reduce these false positives and increase the effectiveness of their signature bases they are also beginning to borrow from the success other solutions have had with reputation.

An example of how reputation services could protect an organization is provided by the recent attack against NASDAQ's Director's Desk service. The Director's Desk is a service that NASDAQ offers to public companies whose stock is traded on the NASDAQ exchange. Director's Desk is a third-party hosting solution for critical documents and communication generated by the boards of over 230 companies. There are over 10,000 users of the service. In February 2011 it was revealed that malware had been inserted into the Director's Desk portal. This is a common way for attackers to target high-value users. In this case the users were high value in that they had access to valuable inside information and from a cyber criminal's perspective were likely to engage in high value transactions on other platforms such as banking and stock trading sites. Infecting their machines to garner additional information on target organizations or steal access credentials would justify the attack. Similar infections through ad-serving sites have been recorded. An IP reputation service, once the NASDAQ site had been identified as compromised through either publication or detection by continual IPS reputation evaluation, would have given system administrators early warning of the attack.

Reputation, if properly executed, can improve both the performance and accuracy of modern IPS solutions. Developing a reliable, scalable, and effective reputation service is the key to effective IPS and will quickly become a required function in next generation IPS.

I had a chance to interview Dan Holden, director of DVLabs at HP TippingPoint. He explains more about how reputation services are implemented in HP TippingPoint's IPS solutions.

Parts of the post were excerpted from a recent IT-Harvest White Paper.

BEACONING DETECTION HEATS UP

MAY 4, 2011

One of the hottest areas in network security is what I term beaconing detection. The success of the vendors in this space is predicated on what is rapidly becoming a common observation: most organizations are infested with surreptitious malware (APT). Examples abound of this type of infection, from GhostNet, to attacks on the Pentagon, Google, RSA, and the McAfee Night Dragon incident. Once a desktop or server is infected, it "phones home" for additional downloads, instructions, and ultimately to exfiltrate stolen data.

I have been conducting a series of video interviews with key security industry leaders. You will see a lot of these over the next several months. Taken in total they provide a great education on the industry and the types of protection technologies available. NetWitness is a pioneer in this space and growing at over 100% a year. Their sensors record network traffic and use a feed of data about threat sources associated with command and control servers. Any communication with a suspect IP address is immediately identified. Having the ability to automatically combine any source of data and compare it to live network flows makes many more things possible, too.

NetWitness was recently acquired by RSA, the security Division of EMC. I had a chance in February to interview both Amit Yoran, the CEO, and Tim Belcher, CTO of NetWitness.

Watch Amit's interview first to understand the threats that NetWitness is targeting. https://vimeo.com/22008294

And here is the interview with Tim who explains Netwitness's approach to beaconing detection: https://vimeo.com/22011548

GOODBYE FACEBOOK, I AM GOING TO MISS YOU

MAY 5, 2011

Facebook is the best way to stay connected with friends, family, and even professional acquaintances. I would hate to sum up all the hours I have spent on Facebook; probably enough to accomplish some amazing project like finally learning to juggle five balls. Its utility and benefit are unquestioned. My problem is with the looming issue of security. This problem has grown to the point where I am forced to sign off Facebook. If they do not fix their security it could be lethal to the service. Here is how.

The history of internet communities is littered with the empty husks of services that saw exponential growth only to be taken down by spammers and criminals. Remember Network News? When I operated an early ISP, Rust.net, this was often the reason people subscribed in the first place. Network News is still around of course. It runs on its own protocol, NNTP. In its early years it provided a home for thousands of separate interest groups. From writers, to home electricians, to cat fanciers, Network News was the daily fix for that sense of community one gets from engaging in conversation with like-minded people. You may not recall the furor caused by two green card processing lawyers who set up a script to post the first spam to every group offering their services. Outrage!

The reason you do not use Network News today is spam. Spammers killed Network News. Email came very close to experiencing the same fate at the hand of spammers. It is only through massive investment on the part of service providers (Google, Yahoo, MSN) and a multibillion-dollar industry that combats spam with ever-increasing sophistication that email has survived.

Twitter has its own spam issue with perhaps half of all Twitter IDs being spammers, marketers, or even command and control dead drops for botnets (see chart). Luckily you can choose to only follow a limited number of people. Twitter took steps early enough to counter the posting of links that led to malware. It is relativity easy to check every link posted for malware or malicious intent. Because of Twitter's restriction on message length there has come about URL shortening services that are great ways to obfuscate the final landing page of a posted link. Now you can just hover over a link from bit.ly or url.ca and Twitter reveals the ultimate destination. Twitter will survive.

In recent weeks the number of compromised Facebook accounts out of only 500 people I "friend" has become too much for this security guy to handle. The risk is too great that in a moment of laxness I will click on one of those enticing posts and get infected myself. Most infections delivered by Facebook are calculated to spread. You just click on something someone has posted and it appears on your Wall as something you "liked." This induces your friends to click on it as well and thus the viral spread.

The damage to your reputation can be immediate. One very well-known security expert and author succumbed to this trick yesterday. I won't add to his embarrassment by identifying him. But therein lies the risk. Even a security guru can be caught out on Facebook. This week's barrage of posts claiming to link to PICTURES OF OSAMA'S BODY is only the latest. I came so close to clicking on those.

Facebook needs to immediately reign in these attacks. They have no choice. They must scrub all posts of links to malicious downloads. There are over a dozen services that can help them do that. Facebook must immediately take steps to protect the user's privacy by default. They must purge abusers. They must enforce stronger authentication. They must fix the Firesheep issue. (Using Facebook on an unencrypted wireless network makes it easy for someone nearby to hijack your account.) They can do this by turning on SSL encryption for everyone or other more sophisticated methods. Failing to react to this crisis that faces them could lead to Facebook joining the legion of failed Internet services.

Facebook is losing a user today. I am signing off right after posting a link to this article. :-) Someone let me know when it is safe to come back.

SOPHOS + ASTARO: GOOD COMPANIES, BAD DEAL

MAY 6, 2011

This morning Sophos, the fourth largest anti-virus company, announced the acquisition of Astaro, the fourth largest
UTM vendor. Both companies are successful in their own
segments of the IT security space. Both are growing. Both are
innovative and arguably have great products. But the combination of two good companies is not always a good thing and
when they bridge separate segments of an industry, the results
rarely meet the expectations of the acquirer.

Sophos is primarily an endpoint anti-virus company
competing with larger vendors like Symantec, McAfee (Intel),
and Trend, as well as several dozen smaller vendors like
Kaspersky Labs, ESET, GFI Sunbelt, and AVG. IT-Harvest
estimates that Sophos will do about $400 million in revenue in
2011. This is not their first acquisition, with past investments
in Utimaco, the German encryption company, and several
others.

Astaro is an open source Unified Threat Management
vendor with appliances and software that provide a full suite
of protections at the gateway including AV (signatures from
Avira), URL filtering, Firewall, and IPS. According to Sophos

they did $56 million in billings in 2010, which puts them clearly in the number four spot after Fortinet (NASDAQ: FTNT), SonicWall (privately held by Thoma Bravo), and WatchGuard (privately held by Francisco Partners and Vector Capital) and ahead of NetASQ in France and Cyberoam in India.

In continuing their purchases of adjacent vendors in the security space Sophos is executing on the one-stop shopping model that relies on brand and channel to succeed. Sophos has a large customer base that is happy with their brand and has been gaining in market share. But their primary strength has been in endpoint protection. Most attempts to sell into both network and host security spaces do not do well. Symantec has the longest history of attempting this crossover strategy, with little success. McAfee attempted to do it as well when they re-entered the firewall/UTM space with the acquisition of Secure Computing. Even the network security vendors get confused about their strategy and invest in host-based protection. Fortinet, the leading UTM vendor, maintains the FortiClient. Cisco attempted to get into the host side with the Cisco Security Agent, now discontinued.

Why do host-plus-network security strategies fail? There are three primary reasons.

1. Separate buying centers. In most organizations there are different staffs for endpoint security and network security and different buying centers. Thus there is little evidence that a company will buy an AV product from their firewall vendor.

2. Separate channels. Because of the separate buying centers there are separate channels for network and host security sales. Sophos will be faced with encouraging VARs with strong host and server markets to get into a new specialty. The Astaro channel will have a mirror challenge.

3. There are no technical synergies between host and network security. As much as dominant vendors like Cisco and Microsoft would like you to believe, there are no security benefits from coupling host and network security. NAC (Net-

work Admission Control) was one such marketecture pushed by Cisco. The idea sounded good: each host checks in with the network and provides its bonafides before being allowed on the network. While some customers use this to overcome problems they have with enforcing vulnerability and patch management policies, it is a cumbersome technology that does nothing to address new threats, zero day vulnerabilities, or insider attacks.

Sophos is a lean security-only company. They have the basic research into threats that is required for a UTM vendor to succeed. That will enhance the Astaro position. The UTM space is growing rapidly and displacing traditional firewalls so, if properly executed, Sophos could benefit from this acquisition. Sophos should avoid the pitfall of trying to couple all of their offerings into an ecosystem. Their only chance to continue growing both aspects of their business is to focus on having the best possible UTM and the best possible endpoint protection.

THE NEW ENTRUST: IS 2011 THE YEAR OF PKI?

MAY 9, 2011

The digital certificate business has gone through several gyrations. Initial forays by Entrust and RSA into Certificate Authority (CA) software and servers were met by Verisign's (now Symantec) hosted model. Entrust went public in 1998 and then was taken private in 2009 by Thoma Bravo, the private equity firm that also owns SonicWall and LANDESK.

IT WAS SURPRISING to see Entrust announce financial results, an unusual move by a private company, in February. I had an opportunity to interview Bill Conner, Entrust's CEO, shortly after they announced $105.6 million in total order bookings and that overall product growth was up 24 percent for 2010.

In addition to the CA business, Entrust has come a long way from its early days. They now provide SaaS services, embed certificates on chip sets, and recently announced a certificate management platform for discovering and cleaning up the plethora of certificates and CAs that most enterprises have accumulated over the years.

Watch this interview with Bill Conner to get to know the new Entrust. https://vimeo.com/25828691

GRANULAR APPLICATION CONTROL DRIVES NEXT-GEN FIREWALLS

MAY 15, 2011

First there was AOL. Remember how hard it was to block access to what most admins considered a trivial time waster? AOL would change their IP addresses on a regular basis which made it hard for firewalls to block access. And then there were the peer-to-peer apps that gave firewalls nervous breakdowns. Skype is still a challenge for many organizations. Because it is peer-to-peer and uses an encryption scheme, it is very hard to write a simple rule for blocking it. Skype detection has become a selling point for UTMs and firewalls that go beyond stateful connections and look into actual traffic. Now application awareness is the defining feature of advanced firewalls.

Web apps in particular have become a nightmare for IT staff. Should users be allowed to use Twitter, URL shorteners like bit.ly or ur1.ca, or even Facebook? And if they do, what should they be allowed to do within the app? Posting updates is one thing. Playing Mafia Wars is another.

I interviewed Chris King, Director of Product Marketing at Palo Alto Networks (PAN to insiders) to find out more about

application control in the network and PAN's Next Generation
Firewalls.

https://vimeo.com/21896964

PERHAPS SONY SHOULD CONSIDER STRONG AUTHENTICATION?

MAY 16, 2011

There is no question that authentication is a hot market. I have seen more start-up activity in this sector since 2008 than any other component of the security industry. There are three drivers: cloud, threats, and mobile platforms that are fueling this growth.

The simultaneous DDoS (Distributed Denial of Service) attack and breach of Sony's PlayStation Network highlights the problem with username/password pairs for authentication. Aside from the relative ease with which attackers guess passwords, once they have stolen the list of usernames and hashed (a one-way algorithm used to hide data) passwords, the attacker just checks a dictionary of hashed words against the hashed passwords to find matches. A recent case involved the theft of 1.2 million records from Gawker.com. The attackers published the list including username, email address, and cracked passwords.

Enterprise networks figured out years ago that some form of two-factor authentication is needed to secure access to their resources. At the current rate of attacks, strong authentication will be needed for services like Sony's PSN, Facebook, Twitter, online banking, and even administrative access to blog accounts. The trouble is that issuing tokens or using biometrics requires a device, and what service can afford to ship and maintain devices for its millions of users?

Along comes the cell phone, something we all have. If used as an authentication device it can be the vehicle for providing a means of strong authentication. It is "out of band" meaning that an attacker that may have access to the network you are on cannot see the authentication process, so he is less likely to intercept it.

PhoneFactor is one company that is gaining traction with two-factor (strong) authentication based on mobile devices. Watch my interview with Tim Sutton, CEO: https://vimeo.-com/22627991

MODERN MALWARE REQUIRES MODERN METHODOLOGIES TO BLOCK

MAY 17, 2011

You may recall the Haephrati Trojan fiasco : several Private Investigation firms in Israel were found to have tricked their targets into installing custom Trojan software which then stole documents and exported them to servers in Germany and the UK. They were using a service developed by Michael Haephrati. He would use a simple toolkit to generate new Trojan software that was not detectable by the common AV solutions. Custom Trojans are as hard for signature-based anti-virus to catch as the dreaded zero-day threats, which exploit previously unknown vulnerabilities.

Ashar Aziz, founder of FireEye, recognized early on that custom malware, zero-day threats, and drive-by downloads could all slip by common defenses that most organizations have deployed (firewalls, IPS, AV). He built the technology needed to take all executables off the wire, and essentially unpack and run them in a mini-cloud of virtual emulators on a hardware appliance. By looking at what the software does in its intended environment (usually Windows), FireEye can determine if it is malicious or not and then allow it through or block it.

Over a year ago, FireEye added beaconing detection to its appliance. This has been the key to their recent fast-track growth.

Once installed on a customer's network they invariably discover previously downloaded malware attempting to "phone home" to command and control servers. The customers get the immediate value of discovering those infections and the ability to prevent future downloads of what Ashar calls modern malware.

Watch my interview with Ashar Aziz to learn more about FireEye: https://vimeo.com/22051058

DEMYSTIFYING NEXT-GEN FIREWALLS AND UTM

MAY 18, 2011

I take a lot of calls from private equity and Wall Street analysts seeking to get educated on various aspects of the IT security industry. One of the benefits of spending ten years researching and analyzing a market is that I have developed a simple high level view of a rapidly changing industry. That change is within a very rigid framework. Understanding the framework provides the insight needed to understand where the market evolved from and where it is going.

There are four segments of the security industry: network, endpoint, data, and users. Not only are these four buckets good for categorizing the 1,200 vendors in the space, but they provide a "red flag" for the analyst. If a particular technology, or even vendor, attempts to encompass more than one of these categories, watch for trouble in their go-to-market and sales strategies.

Network security is primarily gateway security: the firewall. But wait, you say, what about IPS? What about access control? What about URL content filtering and network anti-malware? Aren't those separate products, categories, industries? NO! These are features in the gateway security product.

As always, during times of rapid change in an environment, in this case the rise of targeted attacks and state-sponsored hacking, there are point products that are the first to provide a response. But industry dynamics force the established vendors to add the capabilities of the point products. And customers, overwhelmed by the need to manage multiple solutions from multiple vendors, gravitate towards established vendors that can provide comprehensive protection in a managed platform.

One such vendor is Netasq the leading European UTM (Unified Threat Management) vendor. Born as an IPS solution, Netasq rapidly leveraged their ability to do deep packet inspection (or, as IDC terms it, complete content inspection), to apply policies based not just on source-destination-port, but on content of assembled packet streams.

It is well worth your time to hear Netasq's story as related by its CEO, Francois Lavaste, in this interview. (https://vimeo.com/21557107)

As you listen to Francois, compare his story to that of the so-called Next Generation Firewall vendors who have settled on a subset of network protections to define NGF, namely IPS and application awareness. Yet, UTM encompasses NGF, and indeed most of the NGF vendors also include URL content inspection, and anti-malware features.

When selecting your next gateway security solution, assemble a set of features and capabilities you require (or already maintain), then compare that to the offerings from the vendors regardless of the terminology they choose to describe their product. Next Generation Firewall and Unified Threat Management are two names for the same thing.

LEVERAGING TPM

MAY 19, 2011

Steven Sprague, founder and CEO of Wave Systems, has a vision for trusted computing. Wave Systems is a software company that leverages the Trusted Platform Module (TPM) that is already built into most PCs to essentially enable multi-factor authentication. In other words, the device becomes the "something you have" in the dictum for strong authentication: "something you know, something you have, something you are (biometrics), etc."

In this interview with Steven, he explains how it works. The TPM securely stores digital certificates and keys. The enterprise, using his software, pushes out keys to that TPM on employee laptops. Then when the employee attempts to connect to the corporate network, the device itself is authenticated along with the user. Steven cites my Alma Mater, PricewaterhouseCoopers, as one large enterprise that is standardizing on Wave Systems and TPM to secure the laptops of their 80,000+ road warriors.

In addition to authentication, Wave leverages the TPM to support self-encrypting drives.

This is not a new paradigm, although its time has come for

laptops. The SIM card (Subscriber Identity Module) in cell phones provides the same function. Have you noticed that theft of cell accounts by people hanging out in public places with special scanners has stopped? Thank the SIM card for that. Set-top boxes for satellite and cable also use a hardware module to authenticate devices and bind them to subscribers. There used to be a thriving industry for counterfeit set-top boxes. That dried up when the providers moved to hardware authentication.

Listen to Steven Sprague's well-honed arguments in favor of leveraging TPM for security and authentication: https://vimeo.com/21892060

WHY PORT CONTROL MATTERS

MAY 23, 2011

In 2008 the US DoD was severely crippled by malware that had been introduced via a USB thumb drive. William Lynn, the US Deputy Secretary of Defense, tells us the attack was initiated by "foreign agents" in the Mid-East. It was a targeted attack that compromised the secret DoD network (SIPRNet). Secret networks are supposed to be completely disconnected from the Internet and any other non-secret network. Much of the power grid and many manufacturing networks are disconnected in this way. The trouble is that the preferred way to transfer data from the secure to the insecure networks is via USB thumb drive! So it should come as no surprise that SIPRNet was infected in this manner.

STUXNET IS the other most prominent event that highlights how critical it is to defend against targeted malware being delivered via USB token. An attacker managed to infect at least four sites within Iran with a sophisticated worm that sought out the particular machine controllers that ran centrifuges for making refined uranium. And it succeeded.

There are more mundane threats from USB devices including iPods, hard drives, and memory sticks. They are an excellent way for insiders to take information off your network.

Every USB port within an organization has to be treated like a potential entry point for an attacker. Many endpoint protection solutions have now added port control to their suite of functions. Safend is one company that was early in focusing on port control and has since branched out into other areas of so-called Data Leak Prevention (DLP).

I had a chance to interview Edy Almer, VP Product Marketing at Safend to learn more about their solution. You can watch it here:

https://vimeo.com/22649058

HEIGHTENED THREATS, NEW TECHNOLOGY

JUNE 7, 2011

This has been a tumultuous two weeks in the cyber domain. Hacker attacks on Sony, PBS.org, and Honda Canada fill the news while what is evidently a well-planned and executed attack on the Defense Industrial Base using previously acquired RSA SecureID seeds is underway. Add in the revelation today that attacks against China experts are ongoing and involve more than the report by Google that Gmail accounts of White House officials are targeted and you have an atmosphere of fear that is (finally) causing many executives to question the security of their own networks.

This is a good time to re-look at deployed technologies and to continue my series of video interviews with security vendor executives. I talked to Gord Boyce about the products of Forescout, an IT security firm that first introduced what I called at the time "more better" IPS. That function would recognize a network scan when it was occurring and offer up some fake IP addresses to the attacker—a mini honeynet for the enterprise. Attacks against those fake IP addresses allowed internal cyber defense operatives to discern when they were being actively targeted.

But Forescout has continued to evolve over the years and now their primary offering is a Network Access Control product that can address the introduction of new devices into the enterprise, a major trend as employees purchase iPads, Android devices, and iPhones. Forescout can fingerprint and identify those devices, and as Gord explains in the video below, allow the system administrator to determine what kind of access the employee can get.

Aside from new mobile devices, the other major trend in IT today is virtualization. Forescout introduces their virtual appliance product line today to continue their evolution and address the move to virtualized data centers.

Listen   to   the   complete   interview: https://vimeo.com/22636306

There are mind boggling arrays of security solutions available today. I count over 1,200 vendors. Stay tuned as I continue to conduct video interviews with the top 200 vendors over the next eighteen months.

BATTLEGROUND CYBERSPACE: HACKERS VS. WHITE HATS

JUNE 7, 2011

Spend a few a minutes with a security researcher, someone who works at one of the hundred plus anti-malware companies, and you begin to realize that there is an ongoing battle between the good guys and the bad. Malware researchers are on the front lines. They capture samples via honeypots and customer reports, unpack them, reverse engineer the executables so they can see the source code, and try to figure out what the malware is doing. In the meantime, the creators of malware are organized, sophisticated, and financially motivated—and fully aware of what the defensive tools can do.

I interviewed Etay Maor, Head of Knowledge Delivery at RSA FraudAction Lab, about this battle ground. The story he tells paints a picture of determined adversaries with full-time jobs delving deeper and deeper into business practices to generate the most profits.

One Trojan, Sinowall, existed for over two years before it was discovered and is credited with stealing over 300,000 credentials. Initial infection is with a drive-by download on an otherwise innocent site. The Trojan is location-aware and can be tuned to only affect devices in a target region—Germany, for instance.

Etay also mentions the Nimkey Trojan that infiltrated a Romanian cement company late last year and stole 1.6 million carbon credits from their trading account. The street value at the time was about $30 million. The attackers understood what they were after and laundered the credits across several countries before cashing out.

My own estimate is that there are about 10,000 white hat security researchers working full time to counter malware (100 vendors x 50 average and double that for independents.) I am still working on an estimate of the number arrayed on the other side of this battle ground.

Listen to the interview. See if you had the same reaction I did to Etay's story. https://vimeo.com/22043724

REDUCE POLICY COMPLICATIONS TO ENHANCE SECURITY

JUNE 9, 2011

Complexity introduces vulnerabilities. One of the primary advantages of management tools is that they can help reduce complexity.

Firewalls are the first layer of defense for most organizations. They are deployed at the Internet gateway. They invariably have several physical ports and are backed up by a second firewall that shares the load or comes online if the other one fails for some reason. All firewalls fail closed, meaning that if they crash or suffer a power outage, the network connection is cut off. This is necessary to prevent an attacker from devising an attack that would shut the firewall down. Firewalls are simple in concept but have become increasingly complicated to maintain. Keeping them properly configured, updated with the latest software from the vendor, and monitoring the logs they generate is the primary duty of the network security team. Because of their critical placement at the gateway, the firewall is often the source of a lot of pain for the IT department. Any change to the complex rule set in the firewall could have unintended consequences. When deploying a new internal application, network, or server, several new rules have to be added to the firewall. Often the firewall will break some existing process, requiring the ability to quickly investigate recent changes, back off those changes and fix whatever caused the disruption. This induces a tendency in many organizations to leave old rules in place. Over time firewall rule sets, called policies, tend to grow. Today there are some organizations that have tens of thousands of rules in their firewalls. This makes it difficult to audit the firewall, especially since many of the policies are not well documented, and too many rules can impact performance.

Most organizations have deployed firewalls from multiple vendors at different points in their network. A home office device might be different than the corporate data center. Through M&A there may be entire divisions with different network architectures and products. A central policy management solution can provide a single place to review, optimize, audit, and manage all the devices.

An attacker may attempt to change firewall rules or remove logs to cover their tracks. Because the firewall is so critical, it is important to monitor it continuously for changes and control access to it.

The growth in number of rules and their complexity has given rise to firewall policy management solutions from several vendors. They all provide the following capabilities.

Central management. From a single console, all of the firewalls in an organization can be monitored. Some organizations have hundreds of locations with gateway security devices deployed at each one. The ability to record and control events on each firewall is the primary benefit from central policy management.

Rule optimization. Determine redundant rules, rules that can be collapsed into smaller sets, and rules that are not ordered in the proper sequence. (Firewalls work from the top down applying the first rule in the stack of policies and sequencing down to the last, which is always deny all.) If, for instance, one rule blocked all FTP access and a rule below it in the sequence allowed FTP access to a particular server, that rule would not work. It is out of place and needs to be moved up.

By examining the firewall logs, which are a record of every attempt to connect, those that are dropped and those that are allowed, it is possible to compare them to the firewall policy and discover unused rules. Eliminating those rules simplifies the overall task of managing the firewalls.

Change control. Every firewall software update and every change to policy must be authorized and recorded for auditing purposes. Central policy management tools have granular controls over who can make changes and enforces and logs those controls.

Audit and compliance. Compare policies to various compliance regimes such as PCI DSS (Payment Card Industry Data Security Standard) and generate reports for audits.

Watch this video interview I did with Nimmy Reichenberg, VP Marketing at AlgoSec, one of the vendors of firewall policy management solutions: https://vimeo.com/22021365

IS ANYONE SAFE? SPATE OF INCIDENTS RAISES SECURITY CONCERNS

JUNE 14, 2011

There is an unsettling tremor disturbing the cyber domain in recent weeks. The question is being asked: if RSA, CitiBank, Oak Ridge National Lab, Lockheed Martin, Google, and the IMF can be compromised and critical data stolen, is any organization secure? These organizations have survived thousands of attacks over the years and they have invested in multiple layers of defense. But they have fallen prey to what by now is a well-known methodology. The attacker customizes malware, spoofs a sending email address, often from Human Resources within the organization, and establishes a beach head on a key employee's computer. From there they access critical information and exfiltrate it to a command and control server.

I for one believe that security is possible. It just takes fore-thought, knowledge of adversaries and their methodologies, and the deployment of the right technologies.

The malicious outside adversary (or insider) will take steps to avoid detection. Malware—keylogger, rootkit, worm, or Trojan—is installed in subtle places. It's often encrypted, disguised in different file formats, such as images or Adobe files, assembled in separate steps, and made resilient by changing after each use. These techniques help criminals evade signature-based detection and stay on the network.

Once inside, many programs alter the registry keys that are checked during each start-up sequence, allowing the malicious software to be re-installed after a system has been remediated. This hard-to-defeat tactic enables re-infection and re-propagation, especially dangerous if an organization believes it has fully recovered.

Thus, thoroughly inspecting system configurations, file systems, and applications for suspicious behavior, unusual content, and the existence of malware is a critical step in fulfilling the cyber security strategic requirement of "recovering quickly from cyber incidents." Just as threats against digital assets—identities, intellectual property, account access information, and classified data—have risen to a new level, so too must investments in the ability to expose and eliminate hidden risks and threats. I interviewed Leo Cole at Guidance Software to learn about what they call "cyber forensics" and their ability to detect successful incursions and remediate them. https://vimeo.com/21562195

DDOS: COMING TO A NETWORK NEAR YOU

JUNE 15, 2011

It's more than a perfect storm, perhaps seeded by the heap of hurt piled on those that do not support WikiLeaks. It started last November when WikiLeaks released the infamous State Department cables. The first rumblings occurred when lone vigilante, The Jester, turned his Denial of Service (DoS) weapon, normally reserved for Jihadi recruiting sites, on the Wikileaks.org website and shut it down. (To this date Julian Assange claims it was a massive Distributed Denial of Service Attack, implying that government actors were involved. But no, it was just one guy.) It was then followed by reprisals against organizations like MasterCard, Visa, Swiss PostFinance Bank, and even the website of the Swedish Prosecutor's Office (aklagare.se), all deemed by the fearsome band of hackers dubbed Anonymous as being complicit in the world wide conspiracy to shut off WikiLeaks.

DDoS is not new. It was the subject of Joseph Menn's *Fatal System Error* where Russian hackers used Distributed Denial of Service (DDoS) to extort money from online gambling sites in Costa Rica seven years ago. On July 4, 2009, a newly created botnet was used to DDoS dozens of US and South Korean web sites. And just this past week the Anonymous splinter group, LulzSec, used DDoS to take down several online gaming-related sites.

Enter Top Layer, which has been in the DoS defense business for a decade but had focused its technology on IPS for the last several years. Acquired by Corero PLC (AIM: EPIC CORO) in February, we learn today that Top Layer/Corero is introducing a standalone DoS Defense System. Leveraging their existing platform that includes IPS and stateful firewall protections, they have added enhanced DoS defense features. A big part of the new defense is a reputation scoring algorithm that assigns good credits to source IP addresses if they are well behaved and revokes those credits if they misbehave. Thus, even a low and slow attack that intends to exhaust system resources by continuously loading a data intensive web page can be countered automatically.

One of the prevalent ways to counter DDoS is cloud-based scrubbing services. Prolexic, Verisign, and AT&T are in that business with specialized data scrubbing services. And Akamai, the largest Content Delivery Network (CDN), discovered that they were in the business, too. Most of the US government sites that succumbed to the July 4 attacks in 2009 were subsequently moved to Akamai's service.

But many organizations do not feel comfortable having a third party filter all their traffic and do not need the data distribution of a CDN. For them, a simple to deploy and manage DoS Defense system that they can put in front of their web, database, and DNS servers is ideal. Corero has brought just the right product to market at just the right time. Top Layer's customers can be encouraged by Corero's investment in the company and the introduction of cutting edge defensive systems.

DDoS is on the rise. As the storm clouds brew, Top Layer/Corero is in the same position as the building supply company in a coastal town. They provide the plywood to prevent the damage from the approaching hurricane.

IN PARTING SHOT, STEVE JOBS KILLS OFF INDUSTRY HE CREATED

AUGUST 26, 2011

It is not too hard to argue that Steve Jobs, by introducing the trifecta of productivity—personal computer, graphical interface, and the mouse—launched the desktop publishing industry and its components: printers and fax machines.

And now, with the release of Lion, the latest MacOS version, Jobs has crushed the fingers of the printer and fax industries as they scrabble to hold on to the edge of the abyss.

What is it about Lion that has the power to move markets, destroy businesses, and change the way commerce works? It's a seemingly insignificant feature built in to the way MacOS treats PDF documents.

I have an admittedly small business: only three employees. Five years ago, I grew frustrated with our dependence on computers that must operate without fail or we were dead in the water until they were repaired. So we began the move to the so-called cloud; Salesforce for CRM, Google and Yahoo! for email, and YouSendIt for large file transfers. And of course all of our communication with our clients and prospects is through email. We also moved our critical applications (office productivity) away from Microsoft to

OpenOffice, the free software developed by Sun and thankfully still supported by Oracle.

When was the last time you printed a letter on letterhead and put it in an envelope to mail? Email has done much to break our reliance on tree consuming printers with their tremendous revenue streams for the replacement cartridge industry.

But thanks to the requirement to sign documents, I was still tethered to two devices: the desktop printer for creating a signable copy of contracts, W-9 forms, and NDAs, and the fax machine for transmitting them.

But now I am free of even these last vestiges of Steve Jobs' original legacy. Lion has killed them.

I just open the PDF (the vast majority of contracts are in PDF), click the Pencil icon to bring up the Annotation Tool, and click the tiny squiggle of the Signature tool. Lion opens a view through my MacBook's camera. I write my signature on a piece of paper hold it up to the camera, and Lion digitizes it and inserts it in my document. I just save and email it back. No need to print-sign-fax. No need to head down to the hotel business center when I am on the road or search for a FedEx outlet in an unfamiliar town.

For those organizations that don't do email (most government services and schools), I just have them fax the document to my eFax service that digitizes it and sends it to me in an email. It works the other way as well. I email an attached document to eFax and they take care of the faxing.

I am finally free of printers and fax machines. And it may not be long before these two industries start to suffer from this one small innovation with dramatic repercussions.

It is a fitting cap on Steve Jobs' career to go out with one more burst of creative destruction.

DDOS DEFENSE: PREVENTING
BUSINESS DISRUPTION

SEPTEMBER 13, 2011

There was a time when you could cause a website to freeze up just by hitting enter repeatedly when your web browser was open to it. One of the techniques that became popular during the Iranian election protests was to use pagereload.com, a tool developed for click fraud, to continuously refresh a target site. If enough protesters could be induced to use the tool, the webserver would roll over and die. In 2007 the Estonian defenders realized that many of their websites were based on Content Management Systems that built every web page on the fly from a database. Their primary defense was to cache as much content as they could as static pages.

There are many tricks of the trade for executing an effective Denial of Service attack: from brute force floods of packets, to SYN floods, to GET floods—continuously requesting the same page. Identifying the most compute-intensive page to deliver is one trick of attackers. A site that has interactive data mining or an in-depth search function is particularly vulnerable.

I interviewed Mike Paquette, Chief Strategy Officer with

Corero, to learn more about these types of attacks and the technology required to fend them off.

Q: Tell us how Corero Network Security fits into the security landscape.

A: Corero Network Security is the new name for Top Layer Security. We changed our name just last week after the acquisition of Top Layer by Corero. Today CNS is the only company focused on the current and future of the network intrusion prevention solution as well as DDoS defense. You may recall Top Layer's technology was one of the earliest solutions proposed for DDoS defense back in the year 2000 when some of the earliest DDoS attacks took place. Today Corero has rolled up Top Layer's DDoS defense and intrusion prevention technology to provide technology solutions to enterprises worldwide.

Q: We've seen a number high profile DDoS attacks recently. What's going on with that?

A: We see this as the third wave of DDoS activity on the internet. The first was the one I mentioned in the year 2000. Then around 2004 and 2005 we saw a lot of criminal extortion under threat of DDoS. A lot of gambling sites and online betting sites were targeted at that point. Today we're seeing that the motivations for DDoS run the gamut from criminal extortion to personal or business unfair advantage to political or ideological motivations.

I use Google Alerts to track DDoS activity—I've done that for the past three years—and anecdotally I can tell you that the number of new instances of DDoS attacks has grown tremendously even in the last six months.

Q: We've even had state-motivated attacks against both Estonia and Georgia, along with Iran and several countries in the Middle East.

A: Absolutely. The internet has become both the voice of the people and another medium in which political activism can take place. If any organization today is taking a position or performing an action that might be controversial among their constituent community (or any other community), then if they don't expect a cyber response or DDoS attack, they're probably not thinking the situation through carefully enough.

Q: How have the attack technologies or methodologies changed?

A: In the early days we saw large-scale bandwidth consumption. Those DDoS attacks consisted of a large number of computers, usually organized into a bot-net, launching as much traffic as they could towards the intended victim. This caused overload of all kinds of network infra-structures, including switches, routers, and the internet service providers themselves.

Today we're seeing slightly more sophisticated attacks. Rather than just launching these big bandwidth consumption streams of random packets towards the victim, what we're seeing is that the bot-nets are making actual connections. They'll establish a network level connection to the victim, and then they'll initiate heavyweight transactions. They may have already profiled the victim website to find out which types of transactions consume the most back-end CPU cycles, and they'll make those requests repeatedly. Even though the attack may not be consuming all of the victim's bandwidth, it still has the desired effect of causing the denial of service condition.

Q: Typically, how many computers and people have to be engaged in that sort of computation-intensive attack?

A: The size of the bot-nets that we're seeing performing these attacks has shrunk. In the past, for these large volume attacks, it wasn't uncommon to see twenty or thirty thousand computers working in concert. Today one-tenth that number can be effective in causing denial of service.

Q: Can people who host those critical servers do anything to keep a computation-intensive page from being exposed?

A: That's very difficult to do. Suppose you ran a hardware

store, and you built a great website for your business with search and compare capability. Suppose one of your customers browses your website and wants to compare all the nuts and bolts you have in inventory. Your website then queries your database and pulls back all the hardware you carry. That transaction itself happens to be fairly heavyweight, because it makes an extensive query of the database, and that might take one second, whereas normal transactions take one hundredth of a second. You'd think nothing of it—a second is very quick—but if you get a bot-net of three or four thousand computers making connections to your web server and asking you for that same query over and over again, before you know it your database server is exhausted and can no longer satisfy those requests, and thus the bad guys have achieved their goal: Your good customers can no longer get their transactions through.

Q: Where does Corero step into this?

A: Corero steps in with technology that resides very close to where the servers are, so we call this server-side or on-premises protection against denial of service attacks. Our technology is able to inspect not only a given transaction, but the behavior of transactions over time from each potential attacker. It's very tricky because there's nothing wrong with each individual transaction. If that transaction came from a real customer wanting to see the nuts and bolts from your hardware store, you'd think nothing of it. But, in aggregate, an attacker can be identified based on the number of times they've made a particular request, or the number of times they make the same request over and over again in sequence.

The technology Corero is introducing tracks the behavior of all the possible attackers and watches what they do over time. It uses a technique that we call a demerit score-based credit scheme. As potential attackers perform transactions that are indicative of an attack, they get demerits and which take away from a credit score that is kept by Corero's DDoS defense system. If the activity continues, the attacker loses credits and is no longer able to send any transaction through the server, thus preserving the server's ability to satisfy real requests.

Q: So that's how you get around the problem with many solutions that use a strict reputation system, which may black-list IP addresses that are no longer bad.

A: That's correct. IP reputation-based approaches have some value, especially if they're timely and up-to-date. They can indicate that an IP is currently being used by a bad actor. But the technology I described works independent of reputa-tion. If someone is actively attacking in the way we talked about, even if we've never seen them in anyone's IP reputation database before, then we'll still be effective at mitigating the attack.

Q: What about the traditional SYN-floods and attacks which just try to exhaust the front server?

A: Someone who is worried about DDoS attacks does still need to consider that they could be a victim of these large-scale bandwidth consuming attacks. If that is a concern, then they do need to work with their internet service provider, and perhaps with a cloud-specialty anti-DDoS provider, because those organizations have infrastructures and massive amounts of internet bandwidth which can actually absorb gigantic attacks, filter out the majority of malicious traffic, and then send the good stuff through to the end user.

Q: Is there a particular client profile that should first look at Corero solutions before they explore more expensive in-the-cloud solutions?

A: I would think that any organization that has a high dependence on their ability to complete internet transactions for the preservation of their business or the organization's mission needs to consider us first. This includes organizations using e-commerce, transaction-based processing on the inter-net, and even online education, where the ability to deliver courses online is critical. Any organization with those types of dependencies should consider this technology.

Q: Certainly government organizations depend on that kind of presence.

A: That's correct. If politicians or governors need to communicate with their peers online, then that becomes business critical and nation-state critical.

Q: So Corero's got IPS, they've got DDoS defense, and they've actually got a specialty firewall. What's in the future for Corero?

A: Corero's strategy is about network security, so we'll continue to defend against network-based attacks. Corero has announced a strategy of buy-and-build to grow an expanded product set in network security solutions. Corero has adopted the Top Layer technology platform as the basis for an expanding future product set. I can't talk about specifics, but we'll be broadening a network security product portfolio.

UNCOVERING THE UNKNOWN THREAT VIA BEACONING DETECTION

SEPTEMBER 20, 2011

I recently sat down with Stephen Newman, Damballa's VP of Product Management, to get up to speed on their advances in beaconing detection. I have identified beaconing detection as the fastest growing segment of the IT security industry. While small, most of the vendors in the space are growing at 50-100% a year. The driver for this growth of course is the prevalence of malware within most networks; even those that already have deployed the dozens of other products needed for defense in depth (I count 80 different security product categories).

Beaconing is the communication between an infected host and a command and control server (C&C). It can take many forms. This paper from Lawrence Livermore describes what can be seen just by looking at network flow data.

More sophisticated beaconing can connect to a particular Twitter account for a link to the latest C&C server in case the original is taken down. Or malware can be programmed to phone home to a particular domain which can change on a pre-determined schedule.

By now you are aware of the danger from these botnets.

Attacks against RSA—the security division of EMC, Lock-heed, and the IMF are all characterized by these types of infections.

Damballa's Failsafe solution is a network appliance that connects to a span port and monitors all network traffic. The purpose, as Newman points out, is to discover the unknown: a Trojan or bot that has evaded detection and is sitting on some infected host. They also provide a slimmed-down version, Damballa CSPt, which relies mostly on DNS queries for ISPs that scales to 30 million subscribers for a single sensor in one case.

Damballa has uncovered some new methods of analyzing domain registrations and the reputation of domain-IP address couples to inform their devices of new malicious domains. This FirstAlert service is maintained in the cloud and relies on five years of history of domains and their reputations.

To get an education on beaconing and how detection can uncover those unknown infections, watch my interview with Stephen Newman. Since he claims that 100% of their prospects and clients have infections that Damballa discovers, it may be an interesting challenge to monitor your own networks for these digital spies that are siphoning off your information. https://vimeo.com/129326008

WHEN SHOULD YOU OUTSOURCE SECURITY?

SEPTEMBER 21, 2011

Managed security has evolved dramatically over the last ten years. The first round of vendors were really in the business of outsourced log management. Most of those were acquired by bigger players (Riptech by Symantec, Guardent by Verisign, Counterpane by BT). The new version of these Managed Security Service Providers add much more value by taking an active role in defending their clients' networks. I call this MSSP 2.0.

The decision to go with an MSSP is based on your answers to these questions:

1. Do you have 24/7/365 security staffing today? Do you plan on hiring?

2. Can you find, train, and retain Security Operations Center personnel?

3. Are you in the security business? Probably not if your business is retail, financial services, e-commerce, healthcare, state or local government.

4. Are you targeted by cyber criminals or nation-state actors?

The answers to these questions can lead you to calling on

an MSSP for continuous security operations by personnel who have seen everything.

The following is an interview with Solutionary Chief Security Strategist Don Gray.

http://vimeo.com/27059173

Q: Could you give us a quick introduction to Solutionary?

A: Solutionary is a managed security services provider that helps to protect our customers' infrastructure, services, devices, and endpoints, as well the information on them.

Q: Do you typically manage something the customer already has, or do you deploy your own devices as well?

A: We don't prescribe a certain set of hardware or vender technology. We're very open to using what the customer has in their infrastructure already, to maximize the investment that has already been made.

Q: How do you tie a variety of devices together into something you can make sense of?

A: We're very proud of ActiveGuard, our proprietary system for Solutionary. It takes all the information from those disparate sources, brings it together, normalizes it, and applies correlation and heuristic rules to that information.

Q: Then do you make that available to the customer?

A: Absolutely, we're completely transparent with our customers. As our customer you can see everything from the raw log line, to the events generated from that log line, to how they were queued up and correlated, to the incident that resulted. There's no smoke and mirrors—you get a full-depth view of what's going on inside the system.

Q: Do you have a regional focus? Are you limited to North America?

A: We're actually not. We operate primarily in North America, but we have a partnership with AsiaPac, and we also have a partner in Europe whom we provide services to.

Q: You have something called a SERT. Tell us about that.

A: SERT is our Security, Engineering, and Research Team. We feed back into the ActiveGuard platform the intelligence that we gather as we provide services to our customers, and I was very adamant about making sure that our team that does research and feeds it into ActiveGuard is multidisciplinary. Instead of having a set of separate researchers off to the side, we take individuals from our security consulting services, from our security operations center, and from our security engineering team, and then combine them into one team. As a result, I think we have a different focus than a lot of organizations from a research standpoint.

With our SERT, we've been able to understand how APT-type attacks are occurring and start to dissect them. We've been able to build some capabilities specifically to defend against these types of attacks. We've added malicious host identification and detection, so we maintain a proprietary malicious host list and subscribe to some well-known lists. If we see activity occurring from one of those hosts, we can flag it as potentially malicious, even if it doesn't trip a specific customer device.

We also do a lot of privileged user monitoring for our customers, so when our customers are working on SOX compliance, we're able to take that privileged user monitoring and integrate that with our analysis. If an APT-style attack happens, where an endpoint may be compromised, we're able to see if any privilege escalation may be happening from within that endpoint.

Finally, we've created an ability to understand if an exfiltration has occurred from a cloud perspective. When we take firewall log feeds from our customers we can look at the packet size of what's coming out of the firewall. Typically when we see these exfiltration activities, they're anomalous packet sizes.

That's an example in a nutshell of how having a multidisciplinary team, tying together our security consulting services, our security operations center, and our security engineering team, ultimately has a positive impact on our customers.

Q: It sounds like your SERT is outsourced cyber-defense.

A: It's not a separate service you buy or something you add on—it's part of our DNA as a service provider.

Q: Do you get involved when you see that a customer needs to deploy more technology? Do you get involved in those decisions?

A: We do have a security consulting arm geared towards helping customers understand what their security road-map should look like. We don't necessarily get involved in the actual implementation of devices—we typically have partners who do that—but we absolutely help with strategizing for the customer's security program.

Q: When your customers do move to a cloud for their data centers, private or public, do you help them do that securely as well?

A: I'm seeing a lot of security professionals being approached by businesses who say, "I want to do this cloud thing because it will save me a lot of money." The security professionals will reply, "It's saving you a lot of money because you aren't doing half the things you need to do for us to comply with our regulations and compliance frameworks." We're trying to address that gap. If organizations are moving to a cloud infrastructure with the service, we can help them monitor that securely.

Q: Do you deploy virtual sensors inside those clouds?

A: Absolutely, we do physical collector sensors, but we can do virtual collector sensors as well. In fact, we want to provide services to customers that are moving a portion of their infrastructure to the cloud and provide them with an integrated view, whether from the cloud or from their data center.

We're also working with partners. For example, we're working with Diebold to provide ATM monitoring, and we're actually using Diebold's cloud data center as a solution point for that. We're also partnering with SHI Intl., who are going to be delivering cloud services through a virtualized infrastructure. We think we've found a good combination of working with service providers who are able to offer a cloud framework or cloud service that has the security and compliance baked into it, and working with a customer who wants to move a piece of structure to the cloud. We may not be working with that service provider, but we certainly work with the customer.

Q: Does it cost a lot to add your security services into a cloud?

A: I don't know if it adds in a lot of cost, but it certainly adds in some cost. That's why we're working with service providers. If I'm working with the provider, I can offer shared cloud services. It's less expensive than if the customer just does it themselves.

Q: If there's one trend in IT that's bigger than cloud, it's mobile. What are you doing on the mobile side?

A: What we've decided to do is partner with McAfee. We think McAfee's Enterprise Mobile Management (EMM) solution is one of the better solutions out there. Mobile, to me, is at the point in its maturity where it absolutely makes sense to use a partner. Mobile is going to evolve very rapidly over the next year or two. Rather than trying to keep up with that, we let the partner do it.

Q: Do you do enrollment for all these devices as well?

A: One of the reasons we like the EMM (Enterprise Mobile Management) platform is that it allows the user to self-enroll. We think there's a lot of efficiency and ease-of-use to be gained there.

Q: Were you in the desktop management business before?

A: Yes, and it's the same model. McAfee touts that you'll have the same control over your mobile devices that you had over your desktops and laptops. There have been different models, all the way from the Cisco/CSA "command and control" model to much more open models. One of the things we found was an organization's culture was one of the biggest determinants of which endpoint security solution was going to work for them. I'm sure we'll see the same thing on the mobile side.

Q: We talked about Advanced Persistent Threat attacks earlier. Do those go after mobile devices as well?

A: Absolutely. These devices have the capability to store quite a bit of data that could be protected information. The EMM solution has the ability to force encryption on the devices and to make sure any storage cards are encrypted. Device loss is one of the biggest challenges that we face.

Q: How can you scale up to handle the needs of a customer with thousands of devices?

A: One of the reasons we've chosen to partner with McAfee is because the EMM platform has proven its scalability. It's capable of doing multiple thousands of devices and growing linearly. We have no worries from a technology standpoint. From a process and people standpoint, we have Fortune 50 customers and we bring on large installations all the time. Bringing on a large mobile customer doesn't bother us.

Q: What's the next step for Solutionary?

A: Everything we do has to make our core service—the ActiveGuard platform and our monitoring and alerting service—stronger. Everything we do, everything we add, and every feature we look at is geared towards making the platform stronger and giving our customers a better security result.

EVALUATING VENDOR CLOUD SECURITY STRATEGIES

OCTOBER 31, 2011

It is well documented that there is a difference between strategy and tactics, yet the two are often confused. As IT infrastructure is overwhelmed with the "move to the cloud," every vendor of security products is tasked with coming up with a cloud strategy. In my mind, tactics are based on "what do we have and how can it be virtualized?" whereas strategy is based on "what do customers need and how can we deliver it?" I have observed four approaches to cloud security strategy:

Sell more gear to support cloud initiatives. This is the approach being taken by the big network equipment vendors. They have fallen behind on the security front as their products are getting long in the tooth and they missed the rise in threats while ceding ground to upstarts. Let's call them C&J Big Iron, Inc. Just as their strategy throughout the Internet boom years was to sell more big routers and switches to ISPs and carriers, their current strategy is to be part of big cloud projects and continue to sell big iron to big projects. But do not be fooled by their cloud security strategy. They may have components of SaaS and virtualized software, but they have not figured out the big picture yet.

The second level of cloud strategy for security vendors is to **virtualize their software platforms** so that enterprises deploying virtualized environments can use the many CPUs and servers they have deployed without introducing the specialized hardware appliances that were the hallmark of network security for the last decade. Those vendors whose products ran on plain vanilla servers have been the first to make the switch. Many of them are also moving to a hybrid product offering whereby they provide a hosted management platform, usually within their own private cloud.

The third strategy is **Security as a Service**. This is a true cloud implementation and is best suited to consumer and SMB solutions, although there are cloud-based DDoS defense services that target the larger enterprise. The dozens of vulnerability scanning services that have sprung up in the wake of PCI DSS requirements for quarterly scans are the best example. Hosted web content filtering, VPN, and authentication are also coming into their own.

There is only one vendor I have identified which has jumped wholeheartedly into the cloud with a well-defined cloud strategy. Trend Micro started talking about their goal of securing cloud environments over three years ago and not only has stayed constantly on message but has executed on their strategy. The most important move was the acquisition of Identum, one of the first movers in identity-based encryption. Encryption of course is key to hosting data and processes in the cloud. But traditional PKI with its chains of trust and key management issues is already cumbersome to implement in traditional environments. Extending PKI to the cloud only exacerbates the issues. Identity-based encryption (IBE) is a simple concept that uses an identity record (an Active Directory entry or simply an email address) to generate and retrieve encryption keys. It is the basis of Trend's Secure Cloud offering. With it an enterprise can safely host their data and virtual servers in any cloud environment while retaining control of the keys. Regardless of the assurances of a cloud provider about their security, if your data is not encrypted it is not safe. With Secure Cloud you could architect a cloud service even on Amazon EC2 and rest easy that your data was secure.

Trend has also built on their traditional strength in server protection by acquiring Third Brigade and its Deep Security protection product, which can either reside on one VM on a host machine to protect all the other VMs, or in can be bundled with each VM to provide firewall, anti-malware, and host IPS.

The final requirement for Trend's cloud strategy is tight integration with the virtualization technologies and they have accomplished this with a partnership with VMWare and integration with Citrix XenServer and Microsoft Hyper-V.

The cloud is disruptive to the IT space, which is a good thing as increased flexibility, efficiency, and security are possible. All security vendors are developing cloud security product strategies. They will have to move fast to catch up with Trend Micro.

To hear Trend's founder describe their strategy, watch my interview with Eva Chen filmed earlier this month. (vimeo.com/30704108)

Full disclosure: I write position papers for many vendors of security products, including Trend Micro.

POST-APOCALYPTIC CYBER REALISM

NOVEMBER 1, 2011

Last week I had an opportunity to address a large conference in Cartagena, Columbia. Richard Clarke, co-author with Robert Knake of a book on Cyberwar, was gracious enough to provide a video introduction. I took advantage of having one cyberwar author introduce another to highlight the differences between Richard Clarke's book and my own. Put simply, Clarke wrote a prophetic book about the coming cybergeddon and successfully raised the issues around cyber conflict to the level of national attention they deserve. I, on the other hand, take the stance that some future scenario of power outages, collapse of infrastructure, and demise of the Internet is not required to incite action. There are plenty of recent examples of effective attacks against every industry and government sector to justify increased investment in defensive technology and revamping our approach to networking and computing in light of today's threat environment.

Being a prophet is a thankless task. Even Jonah, who should have been very self-satisfied at saving the entire city of Ninevah from destruction, was petulant because the promised fire and brimstone was thwarted by a repentant population.

Safely ensconced on a hill overlooking the city, one imagines he would rather have been in a position to say "I told you so," which is often the prerogative of the accurate futurist.

Look at these examples of successful cyber disasters and judge whether or not they justify a change in security stance. Ignore them at your peril.

Collateral damage from cyber conflict. While the debate rages over what constitutes cyberwar and even if cyberwar is possible, there is no denying that Georgia suffered network-based DDoS and defacement of key government outlets for communication while Russian tanks and fighter planes stormed across the border in South Ossetia. The conflict spilled over as Tulip Systems in Atlanta took over hosting for President Saakashvili's website, subjecting its hosting clients to a fire hose of 60,000 requests a second as the DDoS followed the site to the US.

Political activism leverages social media to incite cyber riots. Chaos on the streets of Tehran, Cairo, and yes, New York, have been supported by cyber instigators. Whether in support of Arab Spring, the Iranian opposition party, or hacker elites, thousands have been recruited to engage in Denial of Service attacks against those representing government, big business, media outlets, or anyone opposed to Wikileaks.

Insiders stealing data. In 2008 at the peak of the mortgage frenzy, Rene Rebollo was arrested for selling over 2 million mortgage applications to an accomplice who was re-selling identities to Countrywide competitors.

Backdoors created via software updates. Leading up to the 2004 Olympics in Athens, still unidentified actors managed to subvert the Ericsson switches at the local Vodafone central office. Through a series of benign software updates, they were able to turn on the "lawful intercept" function shipped with most telecom gear to eavesdrop on 104 officials of the IOC, athletes, and diplomats. The mysterious suicide of a Vodafone engineer still goes unexplained.

Hardware backdoors. Clarke identifies the risk of hardware backdoors that could turn over control of key telecom and network gear to nation-state actors. While there are no published reports of such incidents, there is also no effective process anywhere to ensure that such backdoors do not exist.

Insiders exploit business processes. As an auditor for PwC, my specialty was internal assessments. It usually took about three days to uncover weak links in the chain of trust at most large organizations. Jérôme Kervial demonstrated these weak links in 2008 when he amassed trading positions that exposed SocGen to over $50 billion in derivatives trading. Kerviel, who at one time worked in the back office—the IT department—knew how to subvert the accounting controls put in place to prevent someone at his level from exposing the company to too much risk. By the time SocGen unwound his positions, they suffered a $7 billion loss and had to announce it in January 2009, just when worldwide financial markets were least able to absorb another shock.

Internet routing vulnerabilities. The most dramatic demonstration of how backbone routers can cause network outages was when an engineer inadvertently re-routed all of YouTube to Pakistan. YouTube went down on January 24, 2008; as did all of Pakistan. On April 8, 2010, China inserted over 50,000 Internet routes they did not own into the Internet backbone. 15% of the Internet was party to a "man in the middle" attack for 18 minutes. And in January of 2011 Egypt dropped all of its networks from the Internet routing tables, effectively applying an Internet Kill Switch to the country in an attempt to quell the Arab Spring. (Thanks to the Renesis Blog for their excellent coverage of routing issues.)

Industrial and military cyber espionage. No need to list them all. David Cameron, UK Prime Minister, had this to say at today's London Cyber Conference. "Let us be frank. Every day we see attempts on an industrial scale to steal government secrets—information of interest to nation-states, not just commercial organizations".

Weapons-grade malware used for sabotage. Stuxnet. Need I say more?

Cyber attacks in support of military strikes. A New York Times report states that the Obama administration discussed using cyber attacks against Libyan radar systems in advance of NATO airstrikes. This recalls the Israeli use of Active Radar to somehow disable Syria's air defense radar prior to the invasion and destruction of Libya's nuclear reactor.

These are just ten examples that highlight the need for banks, nations, militaries, just about everyone, to re-examine their cyber defenses and, in addition to improving their processes, deploy new technologies to counter targeted attacks. There is no need to predict cybergeddon for these organizations. They have only to look at current events to realize that now is the time to act.

KASPERSKY AND CYBER TERRORISM

NOVEMBER 2, 2011

Of all the pronouncements coming out of the London Cyber Summit this week, the statements of Eugene Kaspersky are the most provocative. Rather than pile on and criticize him for uttering the words "cyber terrorism," it is worth taking a deep breath and considering what could give rise to his statements.

Kaspersky of course is the founder of anti-virus power-house Kaspersky Lab, responsible for some of the best research into malware and the cyber criminals who create it. It is safe to assume that he has pretty good insight into the world of cyber threats. He is rather flamboyant and has led a turbulent life; most recently rescuing his son from kidnappers in Russia. So yes, he may be prone to making controversial statements.

Sky News provides the following quotes:

"I don't want to speak about it. I don't even want to think about it," he said.

"But we are close, very close, to cyber terrorism. Perhaps already the criminals have sold their skills to the terrorists—and then...oh, God.

There is already cyber espionage, cyber crime, hack-tivisim; soon we will be facing cyber terrorism."

Before the semantic police jump all over this (Terrorism involves death and destruction! You can't do that over the Internet!), let's define our terms. What would we call it when terrorists engage in cyber attacks? I am going to assume Kaspersky thinks along the lines I do. Cyber terrorism would be cyber attacks carried out by terrorist organizations. Is that possible? Has it happened? Is it likely to happen soon?

First, is it possible for terrorist organizations to engage in cyber attacks? Of course. Denial of Service, defacements, doxing (publishing private information about public figures), extortion, cybercrime, even Stuxnet-like cyber sabotage, could all be carried out by terrorists as easily as by the current bad actors (organized crime, Anonymous, Lulzsec, etc.). I think the ease with which terrorists could engage in cyber attacks is what spurred Kaspersky to say what he did.

Have terrorists engaged in cyber attacks? In 2006 a popular e-commerce site received an email claiming to be from Islamic Jihad and demanding that they take offensive material, offered by one of their resellers, off of their site. When they elected to ignore the demands, their domain was subjected to a DDoS (Distributed Denial of Service) attack that took them down for several days. Forensics verified that the attacks originated in the Mid-East. I understand they reported the attacks to the FBI but never publicized the event, although it was clearly visible in up-time records kept by Netcraft.

This year the CommodoHacker, who claims to be a supporter of the Iranian regime, broke in to the Dutch Certifi-cate Authority DigiNotar and created signed certificates for at least 500 organizations including the CIA, MI6, Facebook, Microsoft, Skype, and Twitter. These fake certificates were used by Iran to spy on its own populace who use Google for email.

And of course trying to keep track of the hacking that

goes on in the Mid-East against Israel is an overwhelming task. But just because a hacker supports the same cause as terrorist organizations is a tenuous claim of cyber terrorism. At the same time, just follow the "Tango Down" posts of Th3J35t3r on Twitter to see all of the Jihadi recruitment sites that he has tasked himself with taking down. There is no question that terrorists use the Internet.

The final question of will terrorists engage in cyber attacks depends on their motivations more than their abilities, since the tools and capabilities are easily acquired. Will disrupting the Internet, major stock exchanges, banks, or government web sites be attractive to them? Since the costs and risks are so low you can see why Kaspersky is concerned.

THERE IS NO CYBER WAR THE SAME WAY THERE IS NO NUCLEAR WAR

NOVEMBER 2, 2011

One of the faculty at my school (King's College, London) recently published a paper that used Clausewitzian definitions of war to declaim that there has been no cyberwar, cyberwar is not happening now, and cyberwar is unlikely to occur in the future. Of course, it is easy to prove a point if you control the definitions and I will stipulate that the idea of two nations engaging in purely network- and computer-based attacks would result in nothing but fodder for cyber pundits and tech journalists.

But warfare has seen many more permutations throughout history than even Clausewitz may have been exposed to. How would Clausewitz have treated India's successful pacifist revolt? Would he have said you can't wage a war by fasting? What about asymmetric warfare, a topic that most academic institutions, including King's College, are focused on? Or psychological warfare? Clausewitz pre-dated the telegraph (invented six years after his death), let alone radio, television, and the Internet. Could Clausewitz have defined the 50-year protracted Cold War which entailed the largest arms buildup ever? Arms that were never used.

One could as easily argue that there has never been a nuclear war. While Japan was the victim of nuclear holocaust, it did not have nuclear weapons and was not in a position to retaliate. Japan had been so decimated by August of 1945 that Truman's war department had difficulty selecting targets worth flattening. Hiroshima and Nagasaki were effective political moves that helped Hirohito depose his military elite and surrender unconditionally. By Clausewitz's definition, it was not nuclear war.

In the ensuing 66 years there have been over 2,000 tests of nuclear weapons (2,053 up to 1998) and an expenditure on the part of the US, USSR/Russia, UK, France, Pakistan, India, North Korea, Israel, and Iran that is measured in trillions of dollars. These countries certainly believe that nuclear attacks are possible and that the only way to prevent them is to have a nuclear capability. Thus a demonstrable stability has been achieved. A conventional war between two nuclear-armed countries is unlikely because of the fear of escalation, resulting in a holocaust that neither country would survive.

So, while the likelihood of an all-out nuclear war is slim, there is a higher chance, thanks to rogue actors, of nuclear attacks that are not deterred by the threat of nuclear retaliation.

I make this somewhat facetious argument to illustrate a point. I have been tracking the IT security industry since 1995. Changes to the industry come in waves as new threats arise and technology is deployed to counter them. Since 2008 we have entered the era of state response to cyber threats. Arguing about the impossibility of cyberwar is a needless distraction. In a presentation I made to the National Police in Bogota, I walked the audience through the phases most countries have already experienced:

1. Widespread use of computers and the Internet.

2. A wake-up call. Note that the most rapidly advancing countries have had the rudest awakening. Think Estonia in 2007. The UK, Germany, and the US also had their initial

wake-up call in 2007 when they each experienced breaches of key email servers within their governments and militaries. There were earlier warning signs but they went unheeded. William Lynn, the just-retired Deputy Secretary of Defense, has claimed that the Pentagon's wake-up call was the USB-born malware that infected SIPRNet in 2008; though I imagine the breach of the Pentagon email servers in 2007 was actually what jolted the Pentagon awake.

3. Policy response. Governments move slowly and are only now beginning to see attempts to deal with the inherent vulnerability in critical infrastructure and government military networks. Eugene Kaspersky, speaking at the London Conference on Cyberspace this week, pointed out that he has been warning of the need for better security for the past eight years, as have many security professionals.

The epicenter of the security industry is moving from Silicon Valley, Atlanta, and Tel Aviv, to DC, London, Canberra, and Berlin. Government and military spending, policy, treaties, and legislation will become the drivers of this industry.

Debating the meaning of cyberwar bears little on the fact that governments are going to invest in cyber defenses, cyber intelligence, and yes, offensive cyber weapons. Call it what you will, IT security is undergoing a dramatic shift greater than any seen before. To ensure that this transition occurs logically and to the benefit of everyone it is tantamount that the policy makers engage the technologists. IT security experts understand what is possible and what can work. Their guidance must be sought in the formulation of policy, legislation and international cooperation or there will be years of thrashing, bad laws, disastrous breaches, and encroachments of digital freedoms.

MICROSOFT SOFTWARE ASSURANCE: INSURANCE? OR EXTORTION?

NOVEMBER 7, 2011

If you are like me, you hate being asked to purchase insurance against a product failing. I regularly refuse insurance coverage for computers and electronics. It always seems underhanded for the product manufacturer to make claims about the reliability of their products, yet ask you to pay extra for an "extended warranty." That said, hard drives, power supplies, and touch screens do break. I can see how in some cases purchasing hardware protection is justified. But software? That would be just too outrageous.

In 2005 Microsoft figured out how to tap into the revenue stream of extended warranties for software. Software Assurance is a clever protection racket. Large companies are asked to pay an annual fee, as much as 29% of the original licenses cost according to Forrester, to protect themselves against Microsoft releasing a new version of their software! That's right. If you own a license to Word, Excel, or Windows, Microsoft asks you to buy insurance against the possibility of them introducing a new major release.

This forces enterprises to calculate the risk of *not* paying for protection. If they knew a new version was coming out in less than two years it may be worth paying for Software Assurance. Or, if they knew they could stay on the current version for more than four or five years they could safely tell Microsoft to lump it, as many have.

This past August Microsoft began using security to induce more customers to opt for Software Assurance. Here are the steps they took to make this revenue enhancing strategy work.

Microsoft has been steadily investing in security. They acquired Whale Communications in 2006 and Sybari Antigen in 2005. Their product offerings now include:

Forefront Endpoint Protection

Forefront for Office Communications Server (formerly Antigen for Instant Messaging)

Forefront Online Protection for Exchange (formerly Exchange Hosted Filtering)

Forefront Protection 2010 for Exchange Server

Forefront Threat Management Gateway Web Protection Service

Forefront Protection 2010 for SharePoint Server

Microsoft sells access to their server line of products through something called Enterprise Client Access Licenses (eCAL). A customer purchases an eCAL bundle for every desktop user.

Microsoft bundles the Forefront Protection Suite in eCAL and then their sales teams push customers to adapt Forefront as their primary AV solution. Since customers have already purchased eCAL they are told that **Forefront is free!**

Forefront is not free, of course. There are additional server and access licenses to purchase to manage and deploy Forefront. And getting the level of immediate support needed for security issues is extremely expensive. And, if you read the fine print, you will discover that in order to get virus signature updates (a requirement for any AV product), you must have Software Assurance!

Microsoft is leveraging the immediacy and urgency of

security updates to force customers into paying for Software Assurance.

Microsoft licensing is the single largest IT expense for many organizations, often costing millions of dollars a year. Attempts to squeeze even more revenue out of their installed base, while great for stockholders, will fuel moves away from the Microsoft monoculture. General Motors is already close to switching to Google Apps. The perceived savings from standardizing on a single platform is coming back to haunt those organizations that fell for the Microsoft sales pitch.

FALLOUT FROM THE CHRISTMAS HACK OF STRATFOR

DECEMBER 28, 2011

Let this be the day that you change your password practices. On December 24, 2011, Anonymous, the group of hackers that includes anyone who chooses to adopt that label, announced that they had broken into the servers of the defense intelligence organization Stratfor. Despite Anonymous' belief in a vast military-industrial-government conspiracy, Stratfor is merely a think tank that researches and reports on global hot spots and events.

It is very important for everyone reading this to re-learn security 101. Anonymous has posted complete credit card records of those who subscribe to Stratfor's publications, and 28,517 email addresses and cracked passwords. Reading through those lists is very educational. Well-known security experts, executives at major networking companies, industry analysts, and government contractors have all had their passwords published on the text-file sharing site pastebin.com.

A cursory glance reveals the corporate email addresses and simple passwords from:

Cisco: 5 employees, including a high ranking executive who used a date for his password

Juniper: Only 1 employee.

Gartner: 4 industry analysts

IBM: 8 employees

Microsoft: 3 employees

Raytheon: 12 employees

SAIC: 15 employees

The passwords revealed are an abject lesson in password strengths. Do you really think adding a number to the end of a word makes it a better password?   optimus2, compaq23, Satellite1, kate29, magic78, chance10 were all easily cracked. Not to mention those that used: password, stratfor, chickens, bamboo, mentor, fishhead, trophy, chicago, or the lovely "kisses" or the beguiling "lovecakes."

What about non-words like "1qaz2wsx"?(Type it, you will see the easy to remember pattern on your keyboard.) Those do not work either.

What about number substitution for vowels?   Easy to crack, as the guy who used n0m3ncl8tur3 has discovered.

How about special characters? Slav85!, stratfor!, Cal!985, Godzilla!, Sith31!, redsox#1, 1q2W#E? All fail.

Lessons re-learned:

1. It is no longer even remotely OK to use simple pass-words. Even so-called "throw-away" accounts can lead to embarrassment for you or your organization. Do you really want your co-workers and the press to know that you used your birthday/pet's name/football team as your password? (I experienced this when Gawker was hacked in a similar event in 2010. Look it up to see my stupid password.)

2. Change the password to your email account on Google, Yahoo, or Hotmail today. Make it really strong.

3. NEVER reuse a password. Sorry but it has come to this. Yes, you will have to write them down or store them in a digital safe on your computer or phone. Only a truly deter-

mined hacker (or your spouse/boyfriend/teenage kid) will attempt to hack that.

4. Turn on two factor authentication with your email provider. Google and Yahoo provide a service that uses SMS messages to your phone to log into your account from a new computer. Use it.

5. Only do online banking with banks that provide strong two-factor authentication.

Now some tips for those that collect credit cards and account information on their Internet facing servers.

Lessons for website owners re-learned from Stratfor:

1. Use a password for your databases. Apparently Stratfor had no password protection for their SQL database.

2. Do not use the default password hash algorithm that comes with your CMS or Unix library. There are vast dictionaries of hashed passwords online. Once a hacker has stolen your password list they can look up any hash in these dictionaries or run simple tools to brute force them. Research and deploy salted hash algorithms. They make the job a lot more difficult for the hacker. Best practice: encrypt those passwords! And secure the keys.

3. Do a complete security review. Things have changed since you set up your Internet presence in 1995 or 2005.

The most painful lesson the Stratfor hack is about to demonstrate is the importance of email security. The Anonymous member who appears to be taking the lead in this attack against Stratfor has already posted to reddit.com that they will be recruiting volunteers to analyze the 3.3 million emails they stole from Stratfor. These emails have the potential for embarrassment and real harm that could equal the infamous State Department leak.

One last point. A quick scan of the 28,517 leaked email addresses reveals the conspicuous absence of any addresses belonging to .gov and .mil. Were there none, or does Anonymous have plans for those?

My only prediction for 2012: it is going to be a very interesting year.

Updates: More analysis of the leaked data provided by Mike Lennon at SecurityWeek, thanks to Identity Finder.

Dazzlepod has posted a search tool to determine if your own email address is in the leaked Stratfor database. You can also search by domain.

On December 29, Anonymous posted 859,311 email addresses, 68,063 credit card numbers, 50,618 addresses, and 50,569 phone numbers. Analysis posted here by IdentityFinder.

The latest list of leaked Stratfor emails does include .mil and .gov addresses.

January 3 update: Dazzlepod has added all 860,000 leaked accounts to their searchable database.

Steve Ragan at the Tech Herald has cracked and analyzed 10% of the passwords.

FIRST DOCUMENTED CASE OF CYBER ESPIONAGE?

JANUARY 11, 2012

There have been so many examples of cyber espionage that it is now the norm to just accept that it is rampant. MI5 in the UK, the German Chancellery, Titan Rain, GhostNet, the Pentagon email hack, Google Aurora—all are examples of cyber espionage, most on the part of China. But to date no evidence has been put forth other than claims from the injured parties.

Thanks to reporting from Anthony Freed of *InfoSecIsland*, we have learned over the past few days that a group of Indian hackers that align themselves with Anonymous (the catch-all movement for hackers these days) have breached several Indian government servers and uncovered gold. If taken at face value, their hacking has revealed:

1. The Indian government has source code for Symantec's AV software, albeit of 2006 vintage.

2. The Indian government is strong-arming cell phone manufacturers to provide backdoors into their handsets.

3. The Indian government is in possession of confidential internal communications from the US-China Economic and Security Review Commission (USCC).

And now in a new development we learn from Freed:

"Now YamaTough has provided potentially damning evidence that the Indian government is actively engaged in espionage efforts targeting not only the USCC, but potentially thousands of US government networks, ranging from those of federal agencies to systems used by state and municipal entities."

YamaTough is part of The Lords of Dharmaraja hacking group in India.

You can see the difference between these unfolding events and previous claims of cyber espionage. The exfiltration of terabytes of data on the US Joint Strike Fighter or last March's theft of "24,000 documents" has never been proved. They are just claims from admittedly credible sources. Thanks to a hacker group in India, InfosecIsland has source material that demonstrates widespread cyber espionage on the part of the Indian Government, which the hackers may publish.

This is a historically significant development for those of us who track cyber espionage.

IN CYBER, LOSERS IGNORE, SURVIVORS REACT, AND WINNERS PREDICT

FEBRUARY, 2012

Knowledge of the threatscape is one of the determining factors in an organization's ability to defend itself. There are three different approaches to cyber security. The first is to ignore the threat. Practically every outbreak of a worm or malicious virus has been preceded by warnings from the security community. The CodeRed worm targeted a vulnerability in Microsoft's web server software that had been known for months. A patch was even available. Yet, thousands of US Government and other web servers were successfully attacked in 2000. And the follow-on Nimda worm, which attacked the same vulnerability (and even a backdoor left behind by Code-Red), was even more successful at spreading and causing harm. TJX Company is the poster child for flying blind. Three years before they were infiltrated by hackers via an unprotected Wifi access point, Lowes suffered a similar attack targeting their credit card information. The recovery from the attack against TJX and the loss of over 90 million credit card records cost them more than $200 million.

Which leads us to the next level of preparedness: reaction.

Most organizations have begun to be able to react quickly to new threats. They institute patch and configuration management and they have organized Computer Emergency Response (CERT) teams. They pay attention to the news and begin to think about possible courses of action when they see new attack methodologies or even motivations arise. A vocal supporter of SOPA can expect DDoS attacks from Anonymous. A law enforcement agency can expect to be the next target of F**k FBI Friday (#FFF on Twitter). Very few law firms will be scrambling this week to review their security posture after the potentially devastating hack and subsequent leak of emails from Puckett Faraj. (Read The First Thing We Do is Hack All The Lawyers.)

Judging by the number of large enterprises that bring me in to speak to their boards and senior execs, there is still a problem at the top of many organizations with recognition of the rise of threats. Even though these organizations have their own security experts, they feel an outside expert can do a better job of justifying security investments and frankly, frightening their stakeholders into taking security seriously.

The very best organizations are taking measures to predict future threats to their data and operations. Their CERTs are evolving to what I call Cyber Defense Teams. They engage in active research on new threat actors, new methodologies, and new vulnerabilities exposed by the types of targets that are being selected by cyber criminals and state actors. Defense Departments and contractors are recognizing that their defenses are essentially porous to attack. Best practices at banks include concern for their major customers' data security. A bank that holds the assets of earth resource companies watches the rising threat against that sector and starts to build in the defenses to identify when their accounts are being monitored or attacked.

Every organization has a choice: They can become a victim of cyber attack and pay the cost of recovery, they can rely on quick reactions to changes in the threat space to ensure that they survive the next attack, or they can predict the next escalation in attacks and invest early in the defenses required to avoid ever becoming a victim.

FOR CLOUD SERVICES, SECURITY FIRST - GROWTH SECOND, IS THE WINNING STRATEGY

MARCH 20, 2012

My oft-repeated advice for technology vendors is that security sells. Given a choice between two vendors of similar products or services, an informed buyer will head for the vendor that can better protect his or her data. Large technology vendors forget this. Cisco, Juniper, Oracle, and Microsoft might have security initiatives and even good sales of security products. But security takes a back seat to functionality too often. Why are there no secure switches, secure apps for Windows, or secure databases? I like to think that the success of Apple's computers is based in large part on the higher perception of security around their products (although it is really a lack of threats that leads to this conclusion).

As more and more attacks on data stores hit the news it is becoming evident that security is going to be the primary concern of anyone moving their data off site, particularly to the cloud. I had an opportunity to interview the CEO of Egnyte, which has tackled the numerous security concerns that cloud storage introduces. Vineet Jain describes the enterprise focus they have at Egnyte. Central policy and administrative controls can tie in to Active Directory or LDAP.

Granular access controls down to the file level are possible. All data is encrypted in transmission and at rest.

As companies like Box and Dropbox take off, they are scrambling to build security features in after the fact. Often their security is encapsulated in a promise that their admins are constrained from viewing customer data. That of course is no security at all, since attackers target administrator accounts and are not likely to respect those constraints.

Cloud storage is one of the most rapidly growing services for small to large enterprises. I fear that these services are going to become rich targets of opportunity for attackers. Therefore, the strongest possible security measures are needed. Egnyte is taking the right approach: security first, growth second. https://vimeo.com/38864243

TEARING AWAY THE VEIL OF HYPE FROM PALO ALTO NETWORKS' IPO

APRIL 18, 2012

At long last the much-hyped Palo Alto Networks (PAN) has filed its S-1 in preparation for an IPO. Now that we have some visibility into PAN's real finances it is time to address some of their claims and perhaps throw cold water on the exuberance being expressed in some circles.

There is certainly cause for excitement whenever a new firewall vendor goes public. Network security is a booming space and the firewall is the core of the network security industry. That is why companies like SourceFire and F5 have announced their own firewalls. The opportunity for new vendors in the space is enhanced by the fact that two of the incumbents, Cisco and Juniper, have taken their eye off the ball.

PAN has claimed that the legacy stateful inspection firewall is dead; they even created a cheesy video depicting a funeral for the firewall held in their offices with founder Nir Zuk as the savior.

UPDATE: The funeral for the firewall video has been taken down. Instead, here is an interview I conducted with Nir

Zuk in 2009. (http://www.demosondemand.com/dod_security/events/rsa_sf_2009.asp)

Stateful inspection is a core functionality of firewalls introduced by Check Point Software over 15 years ago. It allows an inline gateway device to quickly determine, based on a set policy, if a particular connection is allowed or denied. Can someone in accounting connect to Facebook? Yes or no. Can a user in Russia connect to internal SCADA controls? Yes or no. The stateful part is that the decision to allow or block packets for the duration of the session is made only once. It was an innovation that changed the firewall market in a time when the first firewalls, based on proxying every session, were struggling to keep up with increased bandwidth and connection requirements.

As firewalls evolved and attacks became more sophisticated, it became necessary for additional protections: IPS, anti-malware, VPNs, and URL filtering. At first these were each provided by standalone products from specialized vendors. Nir Zuk created one such product, an IPS vendor OneSecure, after leaving Check Point Software. The trend today is to incorporate these capabilities in a single high power appliance such as those from Fortinet, SonicWall, and SourceFire.

But because inspecting 100% of traffic to implement these advanced capabilities is extremely stressful to the appliance, all of them still use stateful inspection to keep track of those connections that have been denied. That way the traffic from those connections does not need to be inspected, it is just dropped, while approved connections can still be filtered by the enhanced capability of these Unified Threat Management (UTM) devices, sometimes called Next Generation Firewalls (NGFW), a term coined by Palo Alto Networks.

But PAN really has abandoned stateful inspection, at a tremendous cost to their ability to establish connections fast enough to address the needs of large enterprises and carriers.

Bob Walder, Chief Research Officer, NSS Labs, Inc., had this to say about PAN's technology:

"Low connection rates due to application fingerprinting and single-pass integrated engine design may pose a problem for large enterprises that are considering deploying Palo Alto Networks firewalls as replacements for traditional firewalls. Protection is designed with default deployment in mind, including IPS. For those that wish to deploy as firewall only, protection may be weakened in certain areas compared to traditional firewall deployments, and the same low connection rates apply to the firewall even when IPS is disabled."

In other words, an enterprise deploying PAN's NGFW is getting full content inspection all the time with no ability to turn it off. That makes the device performance unacceptable as a drop-in replacement for Juniper, Cisco, Check Point, or Fortinet firewalls.

So how did PAN acquire the 6,500 customers they reveal in their S-1 filing? (Fortinet had 75,000 customers at their IPO and reports 125,000 customers today.) It's the application awareness feature. This is where PAN's R&D spending is going. All the other features made possible by their hardware acceleration and content inspection ability are supported by third parties who provide malware signatures and URL data-bases of malicious websites and categorization of websites by type. While anecdotal, the reports I get from enterprise IT professionals are that PAN is being deployed *behind* existing firewalls. If that is the general case, PAN is not the Next Generation Firewall, it is a standalone technology that provides visibility into application usage. Is that new? Not really. Flow monitoring technology has been available for over a decade from companies like Lancope and Arbor Networks that provides this visibility at a high level. Application finger-printing was invented by Sourcefire and is the basis of their RNA product.

While I will agree that application identification and the ability to enforce policies that control what applications can be used within the enterprise is important, I contend that application awareness is ultimately a feature that belongs in a UTM appliance or standalone device behind the firewall. Like other UTM features, it must be disabled for high connection rate environments such as large corporate gateways, data centers, and within carrier networks.

Now let's take a look at PAN's incredible growth rates. As the S-1 prominently declares, and this Forbes contributor is overly excited about, PAN grew revenue at the year-over-year rate of 109%. But looking at quarter-to-quarter growth a different story comes out.

Every technology vendor fights to level their sales within each quarter. Yet, because of the incentive plans for direct and channel sales forces they all experience an end-of-quarter spike. Some of them close more than half their sales in the last two weeks of the quarter. PAN points this out in their S-1 as a risk, and rightly so, because that end-of-quarter scramble to close deals (and ship product) can lead to misses that slip into the next quarter. But you will notice that PANs fiscal year is nicely staggered from the calendar year by one month. Its fiscal year ends July 31 and most importantly, the critical quarter that encompasses the last quarter of the calendar year ends January 31 of the next year. This is a valid strategy to address spikey quarters. Customers have long recognized that companies are most anxious to cut favorable deals at the end of a quarter and take advantage of that. The fourth quarter is the busiest for most tech vendors. By delaying the reporting quarter until January 31, PAN buys themselves time to protect their margins, relieve the last minute effort to ship between Christmas and New Year's, and gives their financial department breathing room to close the books in February instead of the first weeks of the new year.

So let's compare PAN's quarterly revenue for the last six reported quarters:

	Q1 2010	Q4 2010	Q1 2011	Q2 2011	Q3 2011	Q4 2011
Check Point	271.24	306.25	305.64	305.51	310	336.68
change		44.98%	44.42%	2.30%	0.55%	13.00%
Fortinet			85.6	95.2	101	104.4
change				12%	4.47%	11.53%
SourceFire	45.23	28.73	34.45	27.06	36.10	53.12
change		40.98%	17.56%	24.74%	42.34%	47.02%
Palo Alto Networks	20.16	35.09	31.16	44.22	57.13	56.68
		79.47%	11.59%	42.04%	29.41%	0.76%

SEE THAT? In the three months ending January 31, 2012, PAN's revenue is off from the previous quarter. The fourth quarter is usually the best quarter for technology vendors. There may be some extraordinary situation that accounts for this, but it is not evident in the S-1. Was there a general market downturn last year?

Look at the competition in the pure play security business. (Juniper and Cisco are predominantly switch and router vendors, so I left them out.) They all had respectable gains in revenue in Q4.

There is no denying that year-over-year PAN has been on a tear, almost doubling its revenue from Q4 2010 to Q4 2011. But the glaring fact is that PAN's revenue growth has completely stalled out in what was a great quarter for the industry.

Perhaps PAN has already begun to saturate the market for application aware security devices. In the enterprise firewall space it appears that Check Point, Juniper, Cisco, and Fortinet are not being displaced as frequently as PAN suggests.

OPERATION OLYMPIC GAMES, PROJECT X, AND THE ASSAULT ON THE IT SECURITY INDUSTRY

JUNE 4, 2012

Discussion is raging over the implications of Friday's revelation by David Sanger that the United States was responsible for Stuxnet. Sanger followed up with an Op-Ed on Sunday (Mutually Assured Cyberdestruction), and Paul Rosenzweig addressed the Title 10/50 legal implications of military versus espionage incursions. It will be months before policy analysts chime in with their thoughts on this new method of force projection in military affairs.

Also last week we learned of DARPA's Plan X, a $110 million project that will, among other things, seek to map the Internet and create a hardened operating system capable of launching attacks and withstanding retaliation.

As events snowball and there appears to be a unilateral buildup of offensive cyber capabilities by the United States, there are implications for the $40 billion IT security industry.

The 1,500 vendors of security products and thousands of security service providers have had a single-minded focus on defending against bad actors ever since the invention of networked computers. The bad actors have been hackers, cyber criminals, and nation-states that engage in cyber espionage. The entire industry is engaged in defending against these attacks and is geared towards researching the next attack methodology and preemptively countering it—regardless of the source of attack.

One of the industry's brightest and most prominent researchers, Mikko Hypponen of F-Secure, offered a public mea culpa last week for the failure of anti-virus vendors to detect and prevent advanced malware such as the recently discovered Flame. He also mentions Stuxnet, which we now learn was a *US attack* on Iran's uranium enrichment facilities.

"Flame was a failure for the anti-virus industry. We really should have been able to do better. But we didn't. We were out of our league, in our own game."

Hypponen is clear. While the AV industry is out of their league, it is still their responsibility to counter every threat regardless of its origins. My concern is that the world's IT industry will find themselves opposed to this new threat actor, the United States. If DARPA is developing new attack methodologies then the industry will develop new defenses in response.

Every secret weapon developed in the cyber domain remains secret only until first use. The target always sees the attack and often captures enough information to dissect the methodology, whether it involves malware or a network technique. Flame, Duqu, and Stuxnet were effective and secret for several years, but as Hypponen makes evident, the industry is ramping up quickly to address these types of attack.

The use of cyber weapons is going to pit the US military and intelligence community against the IT security industry. The repercussions are going to be complicated to sort out. President Obama recently issued an Executive Order making it illegal to sell filtering technology to Syria and Iran. This may be the first of many attempts to address a technological weakness with policy. It is a worst case scenario but not beyond imagination to foresee a future where laws are passed to restrict defensive technology in an effort to protect some cyber attack capability.

The fallout from last week's revelations of a new era in cyber force projection is going to have a wide range of effects. The impact on the security industry is one of them.

FLAME'S MD5 COLLISION IS THE MOST WORRISOME SECURITY DISCOVERY OF 2012

JUNE 14, 2012

In 2009, while I was researching *Surviving Cyberwar*, I attended the COSAC security conference outside of Dublin for the first time. During an open session I posed this question to the attendees: "Can you think of any cyber weapons we may see in the near future?" There were few responses during the open session, but that evening at dinner one of the attendees leaned towards me and said, "I have one for you, Microsoft update." What he was implying was that if an attacker could get between Microsoft's massive update service and an intended target, any machine could be compromised.

After the series of attacks against Certificate Authorities in 2011 that included Comodo, Diginotar, and StartSSL, I was perturbed to see a statement from the Comodo Hacker where he claimed to have completely reverse-engineered the Microsoft update service.

Last week we learned that the authors of Flame, the spyware that has infiltrated thousands of machines in Iran, were ahead of the Comodo Hacker. Flame uses an MD5 hash collision to create counterfeit Microsoft update certificates.

This is a frightening display of sophistication. One researcher claims that the expense of carrying out the collision could be as high as $200K. There is little doubt that Flame was created by a nation-state with considerable technical resources.

Microsoft has pushed out a software update (note that they could not just revoke certificates and replace them, they had to change their software) to address Flame and the authors of Flame have begun to erase it from infected machines. Microsoft's certificates now rely on the more secure SHA-1. They have effectively closed the door on Flame copycats of the future. But what about other certificates that are based on MD5?

Jeff Hudson, CEO of Venafi, tells me they have inspected the types of certificates deployed in Global 2000 organizations. Of the 450 companies they have scanned, 17% of all certificates are based on MD5. Flame has paved the way for future attacks against organizations that still rely on a technology that was proven vulnerable in 2008. I expect to see this type of attack within a year.

Hudson said:

"I often wonder why something so fundamental as knowing which certificates are active on the network, understanding their attributes, and managing the keys associated with the certificates is not a top priority. Especially when managing these instruments radically reduces the vulnerability. This isn't hypothetical, the compromise and threat has happened time and again."

At this point we have seen that Stuxnet, Duqu, and Flame have used false certificates to infiltrate a network. Flame is just the most sophisticated to date. Thanks to Microsoft's quick response the enterprise has dodged a cruise missile. Luckily, Flame was surgically targeted at Iran and not a weapon of mass cyber destruction or the carrier of a new widely deployed botnet.

Action must be taken today to discover and root out MD5 certificates from the enterprise. We are beyond the proof of concept stage. Certificate attacks will be with us as long as MD5 based certificates are used to authenticate critical systems.

THREE KEYS TO MANAGING FIREWALLS FOR BETTER SECURITY

JULY 23, 2012

My friend Alan Shimel has been attempting to put together a podcast debate between me and Roger Grimes, who penned a controversial piece at InfoWorld titled "Why You Don't Need a Firewall." I was looking forward to this debate because I wanted to slip in the line "ain't nuth'n dead until I say it is dead," but that is going to have to wait until another time.

This concept that firewalls do not provide value had its first incarnation in de-perimeterization as promulgated by the Jericho Forum. The general idea is that because network security is so hard, we should give up and focus on securing all the endpoints and the data that travels between them. But in reality, we have to defend four separate domains—network, endpoint, data, and applications. I am a great believer in de-coupling the management and defense of these four domains. I even coined my three laws of simple security to reflect this.

1. A secure network assumes the hosts are hostile
2. A secure host assumes the network is hostile
3. A secure application assumes the user is hostile

Networks need firewalls the way cars need brakes. Sure there are still auto accidents and we can postulate a future of autonomously piloted vehicles, but for now brakes are required on all vehicles.

To address the perceived issues with firewalls there are three suggestions I would make. Firewalls are policy driven. The administrator defines exact rules for what is and what is not allowed to pass. Like all control systems, the danger comes from misconfiguration, so the greatest enhancement to firewall security comes from reducing the risk of misconfiguration.

Standardize

In the early days of firewalls, it was common practice to put multiple firewalls from separate vendors inline to ensure that a vulnerability or misconfiguration in one would be caught and blocked by another. The trouble with this idea is that for every new management interface you introduce, you double the complexity of and cost of training, managing, auditing, and controlling. Best practice is to standardize on a single firewall platform for your entire infrastructure. This means that you have to choose a vendor with a range of products that meet your needs from your data center down to your remote offices.

Just as firewall management introduces complexity, so does having numerous inline security devices to perform other functions like malware detection, intrusion prevention (IPS), content URL inspection, access control, and application control. Consolidation is the biggest driver in the network security space today, as demonstrated by the rapid growth of multi-function firewalls variously called UTM or NGFW. Vendors like Fortinet, Check Point, Palo Alto Networks, Sonic-Wall (Dell), and WatchGuard have all profited tremendously from this trend and it explains why Cisco and Juniper, who are blind to the trend, have fallen off the cliff in network security.

Manage

Firewall infrastructures have matured over the last fifteen years. In the United States alone there are over 3,000 enterprises with over 200 firewalls they have to manage or outsource. As networks, applications, users, and devices proliferate, the firewall rule sets have grown in proportion. In the late '90s when I still did firewall audits, I would pore through firewall configurations that included only a couple of hundred rules. Today I talk to administrators who have over 20,000 rules in a single firewall! The need to manage firewall policies has given rise to an industry of separate management tools. They can audit a firewall, report on unused policies, and even simulate the effect of a change to the policies. They integrate with change control solutions like BMC Remedy and generate diagnostic reports that exceed the native capability of the firewall product.

Firewalls are an indispensable component of network security. Any report of their demise is premature. They are alive and well and growing dramatically in capability. Only through standardization, consolidation, and management will the enterprise be able to reduce complexity and cost while increasing security.

SPEAKING OF NEXT-GEN FIREWALLS

JULY 23, 2012

As near as I can tell, the salient feature of Palo Alto Networks' products that sets them apart is application awareness. Like most modern firewalls PAN has incorporated a slew of features, from malware blocking to content URL filtering. In my opinion, application awareness is just an extension of URL content filtering. You have to go deeper than just a URL for some web-based applications that use multiple ports and combine many components. Facebook is the example most often used. It embeds so many garbage functions (think Farmville and MafiaWars) that it poses a threat to office productivity. Most businesses are OK with employees checking Facebook and using it to keep up with their kids' activities but draw the line at online games. But should you change your firewall just to get this feature? Does your existing firewall already provide this and you were not aware of it?

A case in point is WatchGuard. This firewall vendor has a storied past with multiple lives first as a startup, then a publicly traded company, and now part of a private equity portfolio. But, like most innovative security companies, it is thriving. I believe that breadth of product choices is one of the key differentiators in the network security infrastructure space. A successful vendor will have the complete suite of UTM functionality in a product line that spans the needs of the remote office all the way to the headquarters and data center. Watch-Guard meets this requirement as demonstrated by the XTM 2 Series, which includes a wireless access point along with full UTM (yes, including application awareness). On the high end, WatchGuard has the XTM 2050 with multi-gig throughput.

I had a chance to talk with WatchGuard's Director of Security Strategy, Corey Nachreiner, about their research capabilities. We had a wide ranging discussion on APT, Stratfor, the Year of the Breach, and Anonymous. Well worth watching.

Research is what separates mere appliance vendors from full network security infrastructure players. Watch out for WatchGuard.

https://vimeo.com/45460772

IS PACKET CAPTURE CRITICAL?
HECK YES.

JULY 24, 2012

It has been 16 months since the world of cyber defense changed forever. 2011 has already been dubbed the Year of the Breach and in a year that included the Sony breach and DDoS, Anonymous, and Lulzsec attacks, and the Comodo Hacker, the successful breach of RSA—the security division of EMC—stands out as the most significant.

The RSA breach got the attention of every major enterprise around the world because 60,000 of them were contacted directly by RSA to warn them that the SecurID tokens they used had to be replaced. RSA's strong two-factor authentication solution had been targeted by foreign hackers (General Keith Alexander implies China in Congressional testimony), and the attack was successful. Subsequent attacks against primary members of the vaunted Defense Industrial Base (DIB), using compromised tokens, were evidently thwarted.

The biggest impact to the security industry was the realization, once again, that a determined hacker with the right resources can get into even the most secure environments. Firewalls, IDS, AV, VM, SEIM, NAC, and a cornucopia of other acronyms will do nothing to stop them. What other "keys to the kingdom" are at risk? The system the Federal Reserve uses for adjusting the money supply? The deal books on major M&A plans? The hallowed crop report from the Department of Agriculture?

The realization that attackers have the advantage and will stop at nothing to achieve their aims has led to the new security mantra, "if you can't stop them from getting in, at least detect them in the process and shut them down before they abscond with the goods."

How do you do this? Through packet capture and real time monitoring. Of course, just recording network traffic is not enough. You have to monitor the traffic for anomalies and threat indicators. One of the most glaring threat indicators is if an internal IP address is communicating with an IP address that has been identified as a Command and Control server for a botnet or belongs to an adversary. I call this beaconing detection.

It was through packet capture (from NetWitness) that EMC was able to quickly determine the severity of the RSA breach. The attackers had encrypted the exfiltrated data, but EMC had a copy of the code used which included the encryption keys. They were able to de-crypt the network traffic they had recorded, leading to sure knowledge of the severity of the breach.

Beaconing detection is a feature in the fastest growing security solutions in the market. I am tracking most of these vendors at 100% annual growth rates, a sure sign of a trend. Intelligent packet capture is a must-have technology in every cyber defense armament. If you don't have it you may well be a victim of a breach today and not even be aware.

SYMANTEC DOES NOT NEED BETTER OPERATIONS. IT NEEDS INNOVATION.

JULY 25, 2012

The news today that Symantec's board had ousted Enrique Salem sent its stock up 17%, a huge move for Symantec. Watch out as reality sets in. I have seen this played out over and over in the security space as grown-up management is brought in. They bring discipline, focus, and operational discipline. But because they do not understand the security space the company starts a slow decline into oblivion.

Admittedly, Symantec, under a previous CEO, pivoted away from being a pure play security company by acquiring Veritas for $10.5 billion in 2005. My prescription for innovation does not apply to the storage business.

This quote in the Bloomberg article on Salem's departure is classic:

"Brian Freed, an analyst at Wunderlich Securities Inc. in Memphis, Tennessee, who has a buy recommendation on the stock says, 'The combination of consistent execution and operational discipline is exactly the order Symantec needed.'"

Consistent execution and operational discipline is exactly what will kill Symantec. Or rather, relying on operational fixes alone will kill Symantec.

Bringing in Jack Welch-style management to a mature player in a mature market is usually a great idea. The company already dominates its market and any tweaks to operational efficiencies such as paring down the product catalog, rationalizing SKUs, normalizing points given to resellers and distributors, and optimizing sales, R&D, marketing, and the executive office, will lead to greater profitability and increased stock performance.

But the security industry is NOT mature. It is one of the few tech businesses that will NEVER mature. It is a completely different animal. The primary driver in the security industry is not the customers, as it is in every other industry. The primary driver is the threatscape, which evolves continuously. New threats and new threat actors drive innovators to create new products and services. Symantec took their eye off the ball when they acquired Veritas. 2005 was way too early for a software security vendor to attempt to mature into a tech holding company like IBM or HP. Sure, EMC managed to do it by going on an aggressive campaign of acquiring security vendors, starting with RSA, but they have succeeded by continuing to acquire the innovative vendors that are addressing the new threats. The NetWitness acquisition in 2011 is the perfect example of how RSA, now the security division of EMC, recognized and seized an opportunity.

The anti-virus industry is alive and well. There are almost one hundred vendors in the space, many of them thriving with over $100 million in revenue. The only reason that Symantec has for losing market share is the failure to recognize the opportunity in the space. White-listing, virtualization security, threat intelligence, beaconing detection, and APT mitigation are all fields that are growing rapidly.

THE NEW CEO OF SYMANTEC, Steve Bennett, should immediately prepare a sale or spin-out of the Veritas business. He should then pursue an aggressive acquisition spree of the

fastest growing security technology companies. Use that "consistent execution and operational discipline" to streamline the
on-boarding process. Only then can Symantec return to the
25% annual growth rates of the security industry as a whole.
If Mr. Bennett needs help identifying the best candidates for
acquisition, I have a list...

VULNERABILITY INTELLIGENCE VERSUS VULNERABILITY MANAGEMENT

JULY 26, 2012

Ten years ago I was one of those ivory-tower analysts who would issue warnings to enterprise clients to patch their servers whenever a new critical vulnerability in Microsoft was announced. Bear in mind that this was before Microsoft consolidated all of their patch announcements into one big blast on the second Tuesday of every month (patch Tuesday). Patching was an almost impossible task, as was made clear to me by CIOs who would tell me, "Do you realize what you are saying? We have 2,000 Windows servers in our environment. Patching even one of them means scheduling down time on a weekend, taking it offline for hours, installing a patch, fixing anything that breaks, and then bringing it online again. By the time we are done, there is another emergency patch to install!" I learned my lesson and you may have noticed that I do not warn people to patch, patch, patch every month.

Microsoft addressed their patch management issues with Systems Management Server (SMS), or the newer Windows Server Update Services (WSUS). The process is still remark-ably cumbersome. Microsoft's own advice for maintaining security patches is

- **Detect**. Use tools to scan your systems for missing security patches. The detection should be automated and will trigger the patch management process.
- **Assess**. If necessary updates are not installed, determine the severity of the issue(s) addressed by the patch and the mitigating factors that may influence your decision. By balancing the severity of the issue and mitigating factors, you can determine if the vulnerabilities are a threat to your current environment.
- **Acquire**. If the vulnerability is not addressed by the security measures already in place, download the patch for testing.
- **Test**. Install the patch on a test system to verify the ramifications of the update against your production configuration.
- **Deploy**. Deploy the patch to production computers. Make sure your applications are not affected. Employ your rollback or backup restore plan if needed.
- **Maintain**. Subscribe to notifications that alert you to vulnerabilities as they are reported. Begin the patch management process again.

They suggest using Microsoft Baseline Security Analyzer (MBSA) for vulnerability scanning, but of course there are many options from free to expensive. The trouble with using MBSA is that most organizations have many products that are not from Microsoft; Oracle, SAP, Adobe, and Cisco to name a few.

Despite the fact that every security framework from Cobit to ITIL to ISO calls for vulnerability scanning, and PCI DSS requires it, most organizations are still doing it on an ad-hoc basis, if at all. My friend Aviram Jenik at Beyond Security tells me that over half the enterprises his sales team approaches are unaware of the need for vulnerability management!

There is even the idea that you do not need to patch, you just need to protect vulnerable systems with IPS and firewalls. Nice idea, but in this day of sophisticated attacks you can be sure that hackers are already inside the network behind the firewall.

Secunia is a Copenhagen-based company that has pioneered the vulnerability intelligence space. If you watch my interview with its founder, Niels Henrik Rasmussen, you will learn that Secunia maintains and licenses a comprehensive vulnerability database of all (well, a lot of) products, not just Microsoft. Enterprises can license the vulnerability feed or use Secunia's own vulnerability scanner. They have even introduced a patch management tool.

For more of the product details watch this video of Morten Rinder Stengaard, Director of Product Management at Secunia.

https://vimeo.com/39470594

Hardening systems is one of the most important things you can do to counter targeted attacks, yet most organizations have yet to operationalize the process. I understand how hard —and expensive—it is. And it is easy for an analyst to wave the flag of "Patch now!" so forgive me for giving hard advice.

LET'S BE CLEAR ON ETHICAL HACKING

JULY 31, 2012

I see that Parmy Olson has allowed a couple of hackers to take over her blog today. Conrad Constantine and Dominique Karg work at AlienVault, the hybrid vulnerability management-threat intelligence company. Each of them has been in security for a while so it is hard to understand their rant against "ethical hackers." I am going to keep this short so you do not have to click through five pages.

Conrad and Dominique are using the popular interpretation of "hacker" as it appears in the press, "bad guys who break into computers" as opposed to the original "people who like to find out how things work." Then they attack the use of "ethical." Here is how the term "ethical hacker" came about.

First there were bad guy hackers. Then there were security professionals who would provide consulting services that were meant to mimic the effects and capabilities of the bad guy hackers. There are other names for what they do (security assessment, attack and penetration testing, red teaming), but "ethical hacking" stuck.

This diatribe is an insult to every security professional who does pen testing, including the thousands at PwC (me in the '90s), E&Y, Accenture, TrustWave, Deloitte, and inside major enterprises. Oh yes, we are ethical, and you cannot hire us to do something unethical. So, get your history right before trying to apply your own definitions to accepted terms.

IS YOUR IT POSTURE THAT OF A PROTECTOR, DETECTIVE, OR WARRIOR?

AUGUST 16, 2012

A new survey from CounterTack has gotten a lot of attention this week. The "Cyber-Readiness Reality Check" survey is a first-of-its-kind exploration and explanation of the state of cyber-readiness inside the enterprise. It reveals and corroborates the anecdotal evidence that many of us have been exposed to. We know that attacks against critical information are on the rise, we read about them every day. Last year's successful infiltration of RSA set the stage and the revelation in June by Paul Sanger, writing in the *New York Times*, that the US and Israel are evidently engaged in crafting advanced malware has shaken security practitioners to the core of their networks.

This survey of 100 IT execs with responsibility for security at companies with over $100 million in revenue reveals their perceptions about their own cyber-readiness posture and how it is not business as usual on the cyber battle front. I found it particularly interesting that 32% of security teams spend more than 50 hours per month studying malware permutations to identify attack characteristics. This re-enforces what I have been seeing develop over the last 18 months. Large enterprises, especially banks, are recruiting reverse engineers to look at attack code—an activity that used to be the sole purview of anti-virus vendors and independent researchers.

84% of respondents acknowledge they have some degree of vulnerability to Advanced Persistent Threats (APT). This is low in my experience. I would say that less than 1% of organizations have adequate defenses in place against APTs and those are of the most secure types: intelligence agencies and defense contractors with air-gapped secret networks. If organizations truly understood the sophistication of APT-style attacks, this survey response would be closer to 100%.

The two areas identified that pose the biggest challenge to combating APTs were disparate systems that don't talk to each other and the team's inability to gather relevant attack intelligence in real time (both over 60%). Integrating defensive technology to present one-pane-of-glass and automatic mitigation capability is an area that is going to see a lot of development resources over the next several years. Gathering real-time intelligence and presenting it in a way that helps defender's to respond is already an area of rapid development and is the fastest growing segment of the IT security market today. My research pegs it at a 100% annual growth rate.

This survey introduces the concept of personas—Protector, Detective, and Warrior—and asks respondents to rank what portion of their resources is dedicated to the activities of each persona. The result: 58 % Protector, 21 % Detective, and 21% Warrior. This supports the statements I have been hearing from leading IT security pros: that protection is no longer enough. No military commander would go into a mission without a plan that can continuously evolve to account for inevitable and constant change. Commanders put heavy emphasis on real-time intelligence and situational awareness so they know exactly what is happening, as it happens, enabling them to adjust and optimize their plans on the fly. Enterprise should follow suit. The attackers are going to breach your network to get what they want. The question is: how fast can you discover an intrusion, figure out what the attacker is after, stop the attack, clean up—and prepare for their return? After all, motivated attackers will be back. The survey supports this observation, in that 92 % of respondents agree that self-defense, in order to interrupt an in-progress attack, is a necessity. This is not to say that advanced protection capabilities are not important. The trouble is that IPS, firewalls, and anti-virus solutions focus on yesterday's threat-sonly observed threats are subject to signature creation or blocking. That won't necessarily thwart the attacks you face today. Look for advanced protection technology that proactively protects against zero day exploits or recognizes lateral movement within a network and blocks it.

This is the first survey that has posed questions about offensive measures by private enterprise. The results are startling but once again re-enforce what I have observed in my conversations with government and commercial IT security professionals. 21% of those surveyed responded that they were taking an offensive(Warrior) stance in their battle against attackers. And 54% believe they would be well served if they could strike back offensively. From my experience, this usually translates to incursions into attackers' command and control capabilities. If one quarter of enterprises are engaging in this type of activity, we have truly entered a new era of cyber defense that will entail the creation of new services and products to feed the demand: products that focus on identifying attack methodologies and thwarting them.

This survey is a snapshot during a time of rapid change as attackers invest in more and more sophisticated tools and methodologies and IT security vendors scramble to keep up. Enterprises have had to develop their own staff and tools to counter the onslaught. In order to counter these attacks they will be looking for ways to invest their finite resources. 80% of respondents believe that the enterprise could benefit from adopting a military-style approach learned from physical battlefields. If so, it means intelligence gathering, counter intelligence operations, measured in-kind response, and escalation will become part of everyday security operations. It's a chilling but accurate picture.

In addition to having a hand in reviewing the survey questions before they went out, I had a chance to interview CounterTack's CEO, Neal Creighton, at the RSA Conference 2012. Watch the video to get an idea of how CounterTack addresses targeted attacks.

https://vimeo.com/39385272

WHY THERE COULD BE COLLATERAL DAMAGE FROM AN ISRAELI FIRST STRIKE ON IRAN

AUGUST 18, 2012

Blogger Richard Silverstein claims to have received a document that outlines an Israeli first strike against Iran. The plan seems fairly comprehensive. As this story develops I am sure there will much discussion. My concern is with two parts of the plan that could induce collateral damage from the rest of the world. One is cyber, the other is fiber.

First cyber. From Silverstein's translation of the document:

"The Israeli attack will open with a coordinated strike, including an unprecedented cyber-attack, which will totally paralyze the Iranian regime and its ability to know what is happening within its borders. The internet, telephones, radio and television, communications satellites, and fiber optic cables leading to and from critical installations—including underground missile bases at Khorramabad and Isfahan—will be taken out of action."

The chances are pretty high that the teams involved in creating Stuxnet and Flame, and maybe Duqu and Gauss, would be in a position to architect such an attack against Iran's infrastructure. Along with severing fiber entry points, Iran's communication could be shut down. But what happens to the Internet when such an attack is launched? Will the weaponized malware work perfectly and not escape to the rest of the world? This document pretty much describes all-out war with Iran. In such a gamble, do the planners even care about minor disruptions to power grids in the rest of the world? Or does that not carry much weight in the balance? This specter of an Israel-Iran war, whoever starts it, has become a looming threat for IT and communication systems everywhere.

The document goes on with this:

"The electrical grid throughout Iran will be paralyzed and transformer stations will absorb severe damage from carbon fiber munitions, which are finer than a human hair, causing electrical short circuits whose repair requires their complete removal. This would be a Sisyphean task in light of cluster munitions which would be dropped, some time-delayed and some remote-activated through the use of a satellite signal."

Carbon whiskers unleashed to disable transformers??? Oh yes. I remember my very first boss, Curt Vail, who had introduced computer structural analysis at Boeing, relating the story of Boeing engineers who were developing carbon whiskers, amazingly strong and stiff materials. Somehow just a few grams got released into the atmosphere and shorted out transformers throughout the Pacific Northwest. I do not like the idea of kilograms of this stuff escaping the target area and even reaching the upper atmosphere. It could be decades before power grids could be free of this menace.

Here are two credible threats to global systems: a massive cyber attack that could spread to the rest of world and interfere with SCADA systems everywhere and carbon whiskers that could short out power transmission systems. Defenses against both should be put in place as quickly as possible.

IS AN INTERNATIONAL CYBER REGULATORY AGENCY NEEDED?

AUGUST 22, 2012

I happened to attend Kaspersky Labs' Cyber Conference 2012: IT Security in the Age of Cyber Warfare in Cancun, the same conference that resulted in this feature piece on its CEO, Eugene Kaspersky. I moderated a panel that included representation of two sides of an ongoing battle of the minds between those at the ITU who favor an international treaty on cyberspace under the auspices of the United Nations, and the Council of Europe who argue that the Budapest Convention is already in place and should serve as the model.

I talked to Kaspersky on this topic. His reasoning is simple: the cyber domain is just like the real world, and in the real world we have treaties and oversight agencies to monitor adherence to them. It works for nuclear weapons, biological and chemical, so why not cyber? Kaspersky suggests the equivalent of the International Atomic Energy Agency. The IAEA has 154 member states and seeks to regulate the peaceful use of atomic energy. It was established in 1957 by a separate treaty outside the UN. It employs 2,300 people around the world.

While Kaspersky acknowledges that it is much easier to

create cyber weapons than it is to construct a bomb, he believes that the existence of a treaty will at least establish that a signatory is breaking international law if they engage in cyber attacks.

I can imagine that the concept of such a treaty and regulatory body will not gain much traction in the military academies and think tanks around the world. Why restrict a nation's options in war fighting—especially when cyber weapons are inexpensive compared to fighter jets, tanks, and aircraft carriers?

On top of the reluctance of military strategists, there are potentially insurmountable issues around definitions. What is a cyber weapon, for instance? Kaspersky limits his definition of cyberwar to the use of cyber weapons to cause physical damage. To date, only Stuxnet fits that definition. But cyber weapons can be deployed to disrupt command and control without physical destruction. They can also be used to garner situational awareness, i.e., espionage, as apparently Duqu and Flame are purposed. How would an international body treat open source tools that are already freely available and widely deployed, such as Metasploit for exploiting vulnerabilities, or LOIC, used for denial of service attacks, or the thousands of pieces of malware already used for nefarious purposes?

This debate is going to rage for quite a while. There will be no short-term resolution and we will see an escalating arms race and cyber weapons incorporated in most arsenals long before we see any international agreement to restrict cyber arms.

THERE IS NO NEED FOR A CYBERSECURITY EXECUTIVE ORDER

SEPTEMBER 8, 2012

Since the collapse of the Congressional attempt to pass the Cybersecurity Act of 2012, there has been mounting pressure for the Obama Administration to "do something," that something being the imposition of a regulatory regime to protect critical infrastructure. But the Cybersecurity Act of 2012 failed because it was fatally flawed.

On Friday, Federal News Radio reported that they had obtained a copy of a proposed Executive Order that would attempt, through executive fiat—as Steve Bucci at the Heritage Foundation terms it—to impose most of the measures called for by Senators Lieberman and Collins.

Bucci raises an important point:

[Regulation] is exactly the wrong approach for dealing with a fast-moving and incredibly dynamic field like cybersecurity. Give hackers—whether working for themselves or for another nation-state—a static standard, and they will waltz around it and have their way with the target entity.

Congress has gone through several dozen cybersecurity bills in the last three years, not to mention the failed attempt to pass a data breach law which dates back to 2005. Even as they revise and re-write, there have been dramatic changes in the defensive posture of our critical infrastructure providers. Effective changes.

Let's look at the proposed Executive Order as revealed by *Federal News Radio*. There are ten sections of the draft. Most of them call for nebulous voluntary information sharing or requirements that DHS create frameworks within three months. I can just see the scramble that will occur, and the watered-down frameworks that will result, after multiple extensions to the due date are granted.

THREAT-BASED cybersecurity is the fastest growing sector in the IT security industry. The rapid uptake represented by 100% annual growth rates indicated that without a single regulation or Executive Order, the problem is being addressed. Forcing utility operators, banks, and earth resources companies to comply with frameworks based on outmoded asset and vulnerability methodologies will distract them from implementing threat-based defenses. The draft Executive Order, if issued, will do much more harm than good.

AN OPEN LETTER TO SENATOR ROCKEFELLER

SEPTEMBER 19, 2012

Senator John D. Rockefeller
Chairman Senate Committee on Commerce, Science, and
Transportation
Washington, DC

Dear Senator Rockefeller:

I am in receipt of your letter dated September 19, 2012, that expresses your disappointment in not being able to pass the Cybersecurity Act of 2012. You voiced your confusion over what you claim are views expressed by various business lobbying efforts to kill the bill. I hope my answers to your eight questions below will help.

You addressed your question to the CEOs of the 500 largest businesses in the United States. While I do not represent any of them, I have worked with most of them over the last 15 years to develop what you term "cybersecurity best practices" and responses to the continuous onslaught they have been fending off. Perhaps I can give voice to their perspective that will clarify matters.

Your questions:

1. Has your company adopted a set of best practices to address its own cybersecurity needs?

Yes we have. We have a large IT security staff overseen by a Chief Information Security Officer who works to identify and implement best practices.

2. If so, how were these cybersecurity practices developed?

These best practices were developed in the crucible of day-to-day operations and in response to the hostile environment that would make most computers, data, and communications unworkable if they were not in place.

3. Were they developed by the company solely, or were they developed outside the company? If developed outside the company, please list the institutions, associations, or entity that developed them.

We have studied and borrowed from the best practices of many organizations. Our outside auditors (PwC, Deloitte, E&Y) have required that we adopt best practices and regularly check to ensure that we continue to do so. We participate in many organizations to ensure we learn from and contribute to the body of knowledge. These include SANS, ISACA, ISC(2), ISO, OWASP, and the Cloud Security Alliance. We rely on the IT security industry, comprised of over 3,000 product vendors and service providers, to provide us with the defensive tools to manage the ever evolving threat.

4. When were the cybersecurity practices developed? How frequently have they been updated? Does your company's board of directors or audit committee keep abreast of developments regarding the development and implementation of these practices?

We created the office of the Chief Information Security Officer beginning in 1995 with the appointment of Steve Katz at Citi Corp, the very first CISO. By 2003 just about every business had appointed a person to oversee best practices and implementation of security defenses. This is a step we are still waiting for the federal government to take. Our board and audit committee get regular updates on our security posture, the cyber threats we face, and the investments that are needed to ensure that we stay in business.

5. Has the federal government played any role, whether advisory or otherwise, in the development of these cybersecurity practices?

Not directly, but the work of NIST to establish standards of security has been very helpful. The federal government has also served to distract our IT security teams as numerous bills have required an onerous documentation and reporting regime to comply with Sarbanes Oxley and HIPAA, while failing to pass legislation that addresses the morass of state breach disclosure laws we have to comply with.

6. What are your concerns, if any, with a voluntary program that enables the federal government and the private sector to develop, in coordination, best cybersecurity practices for companies to adopt as they so choose, as outlined in the Cybersecurity Act of 2012?

We are in a constant battle against malware, cybercrime, and nation-state espionage. Creating a new department to engage in such an exercise would be expensive and distract us from our current efforts to find, hire, and retain the skilled security people we need as the threat rises, the methodologies of the attackers gain in sophistication, and the targets of their attacks expand to all of our intellectual property.

We have engaged in such a voluntary program already, Infragard. While we appreciate the connection to the FBI this has provided, the sharing of information with the government has been mostly one way. We also already engage with the Information Sharing and Analysis Center for our industry segment. Some of the 16 ISACs are having more impact than others, the Financial Services ISAC, in particular, is proving to be very effective. Why is an Act required at all, when we already share threat intelligence and best practices?

A key component of our cybersecurity best practices is the extension of trust through IT security controls and audits to our key vendors, suppliers, and partners. We require them to comply with our best practices. Is the federal government able to comply with our requirements for strong authentication, file encryption, vulnerability and patch management, and privileged user controls? Would a government agency that received our information be able to ensure its security?

We are also not comfortable with violating our own privacy agreements with our customers to share information with the federal government. Also, what information about our operations will be "shared" by our telecom provider or bank? What oversight regime will ensure the confidentiality of the information and prevent its misuse?

7. What are your concerns, if any, with the federal government conducting risk assessments, in coordination with private sector, to best understand where our nation's cyber vulnerabilities are, as outlined in the Cybersecurity Act of 2012?

Our primary concern is that so called "risk assessments" are a very old methodology that rely on asset identification and classification. IT assets in particular are fluid and even identifying them is a Sisyphean task. The idea of a federal risk assessment of the private sector is daunting, especially when the federal government has not been able to perform such an assessment of its own risks.

The best way to understand the problems with risk based approaches is via metaphor. Does the President receive a daily briefing that walks through all of the assets and vulnerabilities of every US facility in the world? Or is he presented with a breakdown of the threat from various nations and non-nation actors? The latter is what is termed threat-based security methodology and is what most business are in the process of evolving to today. The Cybersecurity Act of 2012 is an example of how legislation, especially in high technology, cannot keep up with current thinking and methodologies.

8. What are your concerns, if any, with the federal government determining, in coordination with the private sector, the

country's most critical cyber infrastructure, as outlined in the Cybersecurity Act of 2012?

Our concern is that another year of pondering vulnerability will not get us any closer to a more resilient and defensible cyber infrastructure. We already know that water, power, and communications are critical. The Cybersecurity Act of 2012 does absolutely nothing to reduce vulnerability, encourage best practices, or delay the moment when criticality will be demonstrated by a cyber attack that shuts them down.

Senator, I would suggest that, like in many matters involving science and technology,t the scientists and technologists should be brought into future deliberations on cyber legislation. Fiascoes like the failed SOPA act can be easily avoided if the right conversations are held with the right stake holders. The technologists that make the Internet operate and the security experts that are battling to defend it need to be brought to the table in order to form better policy.

Respectfully,
Richard Stiennon
The Senior Fellow
The International Cybersecurity Dialogue

SECURITY INTELLIGENCE ENTERS MAINSTREAM

NOVEMBER 17, 2012

If you spend any time with the top banks and defense contractors you will have noticed a dramatic change in their approach to defending their networks from intrusions. Traditional security operations of vulnerability management, configuration management, and policy exceptions are being beefed up dramatically. New teams are being formed to counter the onslaught of highly targeted and sophisticated attacks.

MY FIRST INKLING that something was changing was the job postings for malware researchers at banks. That was two years ago. Today, most cutting-edge IT security departments have several malware researchers. Why? Because malware is being written just for them and their anti-virus products will never have signatures for these custom attacks.

In addition to dissecting malware, these new teams are engaged in security intelligence gathering. This involves studying the methodologies, tools, and delivery methods used by their adversaries. Even the acknowledgement that they have adversaries is new. This collected intelligence, called *key indicators*, is correlated so that separate attack campaigns can be identified. If a particular threat actor is after something, they will not stop just because their first attempt was thwarted. They modify their tools, switch which employee they are targeting, change the domain they attack from, and up their game.

A few of the major security vendors have recognized this trend and are starting to incorporate security intelligence into their products. FireEye deserves recognition for being one of the first. While their advanced malware protection, essentially an in-line sandbox that executes suspect code, was a first, they did not start to gain momentum until they introduced beaconing detection. Beaconing detection is the act of identifying the communication between an internal compromised host and its command and control server.

Trend Micro has been relatively quiet about the development of their Custom Defense product line. Their advanced sandbox technology, Deep Discovery, is available as an out-of-band gateway device (Deep Discovery Inspector) to scan all incoming traffic and a standalone server (Deep Discovery Analyzer) to accept suspicious executables from email gateways and other sources. Unlike FireEye, Deep Discovery can host multiple, custom versions of operating systems and application configurations.

It extracts actionable intelligence from malware and informs the other components of Custom Defense. Hostile IP addresses and URLs can thus be blocked. Custom Defense is integrated with Trend Micro's Smart Protection Network (SPN), thus leveraging and contributing to intelligence from millions of sources. Leveraging a large install base is going to be one of the requirements for intelligence tools.

The security platform vendors are demonstrating their quick reaction times to changing market requirements. Two of them have introduced security intelligence components in recent weeks.

Sourcefire announced their Advanced Malware Protection

capability this past week which leverages what they call their collective security intelligence cloud. They use millions of fingerprints (hashes) of files to provide real-time inspection of executables at the gateway. They also have the unique ability to perform retroactive protection. If an unknown piece of code snuck past the defenses but is now known, they can identify it on the hosts. Sourcefire also provides real-time feeds of known malicious hosts and command and control servers so beaconing can be blocked.

Fortinet, the largest security platform vendor, introduced several security intelligence features in its just-announced FortiOS 5.0., including beaconing detection and in-line malware analysis.

Incorporating security intelligence is the latest trend in security products. So far they are making it easier to operationalize advanced defenses against targeted attacks. The next step will be to introduce the classification of events into campaigns, and beyond that associate the campaigns with known threat actors.

PACE OF US CYBER-PREPAREDNESS ACCELERATING

NOVEMBER 26, 2012

Three recent moves by the Pentagon, State Department, and White House indicate that the pace of preparation for engaging in offensive cyber attacks is increasing. The first was the speech given by Leon Panetta, Secretary of Defense, on October 12 where he used the term "cyber Pearl Harbor." Of course to anyone who follows these developments the term is not at all new, as Jason Healey of the Atlantic Council pointed out at the recent FedCyber conference in DC, credit for being first goes to Winn Schwartau who warned of an "Electronic Pearl Harbor waiting to happen" in testimony to Congress in 1991. Winn was amazingly far sighted considering that the Internet was in its infancy in 1991. Regardless of the hyperbole, when the former head of the CIA, who most probably has intimate knowledge of the development of Stuxnet and the potential harm that could be caused by attacks against critical infrastructure talks about cataclysmic risks, it may be well to pay attention. From the full text of Panetta's speech:

"As director of CIA and now secretary of defense, I have understood that cyber threats are every bit as real as more

well-known threats like terrorism, nuclear weapons prolifera-
tion, and the turmoil in the Middle East."

Less covered by the media swere Harold Koh's comments
on September 18 where he laid out the US strategy for
international cyber policy creation. He addresses such questions as whether a state is permitted to respond to a computer
network attack by exercising a right of national self-defense
and whether attacks must adhere to the principle of propor-
tionality. Koh's statement is a major milestone and well worth
reading.

And then on Wednesday, November 14, Ellen Nakashima
at the *Washington Post* reported that a secret Presidential Policy
Directive (PPD 20) had been signed that grants the Department of Defense the legal basis it needed to engage in offensive network attacks to protect itself. It may come as a surprise
to many that the US Military did not have the legal standing
to do so. It meant that even when they had identified the
source of attacks against their systems, they were powerless to
do anything short of taking military action. Now, presumably,
the Defense Department can take down command and
control servers for hostile botnets and do a little counter
hacking of assailants.

There is one more player that I expect to chime in with its
own announcements soon: the Department of Homeland
Security. Pay attention to the next speech given by Secretary
Janet Napolitano.

PPD 21: EXTREME RISK MANAGEMENT GONE BAD

FEBRUARY 14, 2013

On Tuesday, February 12, 2013, President Obama issued Presidential Policy Directive 21: Critical Infrastructure Security and Resilience. PPD 21 represents my worst nightmare: the misguided mantra of management consultants writ large. How large? The entire Federal juggernaut is to be roped into a tangle of coordination, data exchange, R&D, and risk management to address ephemeral threats to critical infrastructure. It even stretches around the world to include governments that may host critical facilities and assets of the United States.

Information security (cybersecurity) is just one component of PPD 21 which addresses "all hazards that could have a debilitating impact on national security, economic stability, public health and safety, or any combination thereof." This means one policy directive has to encompass natural disasters like earthquakes, super storms, coronal mass ejections, and climate change, in addition to threats from terrorists and cyber assailants. Only one framework could possibly address so many things: risk management.

But risk management does not work in unpredictable environments. Risk management is the framework that most banks, hedge funds and trading desks use when addressing financial risks like those present in the real estate, commodities, or derivatives markets. We know how well that worked. Management consultants and bureaucrats love risk management. It foists responsibility away from individuals and onto a process.

Before dissecting PPD 21, let me say that it is sufficiently laced with protections for privacy and civil liberties that I am not concerned at all that the White House is using the pre-text of infrastructure protection to extend the surveillance state. I leave it up to the heroes at the Electronic Frontier Foundation and the ACLU to pounce on any erosion to our rights that PPD 21 may engender.

The first three steps to rolling out a risk management program are to

1. Identify all critical assets
2. Identify their vulnerabilities.
3. Prioritize them based on risk.

PPD 21 is a plan to accomplish these three impossible tasks to

"address the security and resilience of critical infrastructure in an integrated, holistic manner to reflect this infrastructure's interconnectedness and interdependency."

The Directive proposes no new regulations but calls on each Sector Specific Agency (SSA) to use the existing legal structure within their purview, creating a de facto new regulatory regime targeting critical infrastructure. A predictable outcome will be that critical infrastructure providers will continue to spend more on attorney fees than firewalls in the next four years.

Much of the responsibility for coordination falls on the shoulders of the Secretary of Homeland Security.

"Effective implementation of this directive requires a national unity of effort pursuant to strategic guidance from the Secretary of Homeland Security".

The first of the roles set for the Secretary of Homeland Security is right out of the risk management play book:

"Identify and prioritize critical infrastructure, considering physical and cyber threats, vulnerabilities, and consequences."

And responsibility 7 is of particular interest:

"Coordinate with and utilize the expertise of SSAs and other appropriate Federal departments and agencies to map geospatially, image, analyze, and sort critical infrastructure by employing commercial satellite and airborne systems, as well as existing capabilities within other departments and agencies."

At first glance mapping all critical infrastructure with reconnaissance satellite imagery seems logical and innocuous. After all, how could you possibly manage risk to critical infrastructure without knowing where it is and having a neat prioritization with accompanying infographics? Security professionals should be getting cold sweats about now. Of course, threat actors do their own research of open source documents such as this map of all undersea cables, or this map of 2.5 million miles of oil and gas pipelines, or this map of the National Highway System, or these aeronautical charts of airports, or this map of commercial nuclear reactors. But threat actors have to do their own prioritization of criticality and vulnerability. How will an uber-map of critical infrastructure be kept out of the hands of the very threat actors that are targeting these systems? PPD 21 will, in effect, create yet another critical information asset that will end up at the top of the list of critical vulnerable assets. But why worry? This mandate was in HSPD7 in 2013 (word for word) and there have been no repercussions since.

THE DIRECTIVE GOES on to spell out in very broad terms the responsibilities of the Departments of State, Justice (FBI), Interior, Commerce, the 16 member groups of the Intelligence Community, the Government Services Administration, the Nuclear Regulatory Commission, and the FCC.

These "federal departments and agencies shall provide timely information to the Secretary of Homeland Security and the national critical infrastructure centers necessary to support cross-sector analysis and inform the situational awareness capability for critical infrastructure."

There are two national critical infrastructure centers to be established by DHS, one for physical and one for "virtual" (cyber). Centralized information collection and dissemination is a natural requirement for risk management. It is akin to the economic data collection and analysis that command economies resort to in place of free markets.

These two centers will somehow, "Provide a situational awareness capability that includes integrated, actionable information about emerging trends, imminent threats, and the status of incidents that may impact critical infrastructure…"

Just how the two national critical infrastructure centers are to operate is one of the first things that the Secretary of Homeland Security is assigned on this timeline.

By June 12: "develop a description of the functional relationships within DHS and across the Federal Government related to critical infrastructure security and resilience. It should include the roles and functions of the two national critical infrastructure centers and a discussion of the analysis and integration function." This report will serve as a roadmap for critical infrastructure operators to navigate the morass of government agencies they will have to interact with.

By July 12: "shall conduct an analysis of the existing public-private partnership model and recommend options for improving the effectiveness of the partnership in both the physical and cyber space." I will anxiously await the result of this analysis.

By August 11: "convene a team of experts to identify baseline data and systems requirements to enable the efficient exchange of information and intelligence relevant to strengthening the security and resilience of critical infrastructure." A daunting task considering the years it takes for the IETF to create a new data exchange format.

By October 10: "demonstrate a near real-time situational awareness capability for critical infrastructure that includes threat streams and all-hazards information as well as vulnerabilities; provides the status of critical infrastructure and potential cascading effects; supports decision making; and disseminates critical information that may be needed to save or sustain lives, mitigate damage, or reduce further degradation of a critical infrastructure capability throughout an incident." I hope "demonstrate" means provide a proof of concept for a very small segment of critical infrastructure. Even that would be an extraordinary task to accomplish in 240 days.

Also by October 10: Update the National Infrastructure Protection Plan to "include the identification of a risk management framework to be used to strengthen the security and resilience of critical infrastructure; the methods to be used to prioritize critical infrastructure; the protocols to be used to synchronize communication and actions within the Federal Government; and a metrics and analysis process to be used to measure the Nation's ability to manage and reduce risks to critical infrastructure."

And finally by February 12, 2015: Create a National Critical Infrastructure Security and Resilience R&D Plan that takes into account the evolving threat landscape, annual metrics, and other relevant information to identify priorities and guide R&D requirements and investments.

PPD 21 revokes Homeland Security Presidential Directive 7 (HSPD7) published in 2003 by the Bush Administration. Frankly, PPD 21 resets the clock ten years later and gives the Secretary of Homeland Security an additional eight months to comply with its mandates.

PPD 21 makes previous unfunded mandates seem simple by comparison. Its breath and scope is a giant overlay on top of the existing system of Federal agencies that, if executed as directed, will turn what was a of collection of connected puddles of government regulatory bodies into a single giant quagmire. It is a top-down solution that expresses the frustration of good intentions to "do something." Even if all the hurdles of implementing an overarching risk management framework were overcome, there would still be the errant tree branch or targeted malware that could shut down the power grid.

READ THE MANDIANT APT1 REPORT. NOW.

FEBRUARY 19, 2013

If you are responsible for the IT security of your organization, drop everything you are doing and read Mandiant's just-published report APT1: Exposing *One* of China's Cyber Espionage Units. You will find the implications astounding and chilling.

Immediately after reading the report, grab the appendix of Key Indicators (KI) and Indicators of Compromise (IOC) and parse the last six weeks of network traffic you have captured. Uh-oh, have you not have been recording network traffic? Fix that. Today. Download and install Wireshark or another packet capture tool right now. Then, call Solera Networks or RSA NetWitness and get some real tools. Better yet, install Solera's free tool while you are waiting for the call back. Begin to parse that network traffic looking for signs that you too are compromised by Unit 61398 of the People's Liberation Army.

Next, look at every Windows machine on your network. Start with yours. Mandiant provides a free tool, Redline, that can quickly check for the Indicators of Compromise.

GO. Stop reading.

If you are on the policy, compliance, or risk management side of the house, please continue reading. You have a lot of soul searching to do in the coming weeks. You must reevaluate your role and responsibility in light of a clear and present danger:

A secret, resourced organization full of mainland Chinese speakers with direct access to Shanghai-based telecommunications infrastructure is engaged in a multi-year, enterprise scale computer espionage campaign right outside of Unit 61398's gates, performing tasks similar to Unit 61398's known mission.

There are hundreds of organizations within governments, financial, technology, and energy sectors that already know about this. By the end of the week there will be at least a million thanks to Mandiant's audacious but considered report. Resources, in terms of consultants, vendors, and people, are going to be in high demand. Act fast.

BARRACUDA INTRODUCES NETWORK VIRTUALIZATION PLATFORM: EON

MAY 8, 2013

Barracuda has surprised the security industry by introducing a network virtualization platform. The surprise is that a company that is best known for single function appliances such as anti-spam and email gateways has leapfrogged the normal product development path with a ground-up innovation that could allow it to branch out of the security business. Somewhat reminiscent of the Crossbeam platform, the eon virtualized network platform overcomes the proprietary nature of Crossbeam's offering that led it to eventually become a load balanced high-end platform for Check Point firewalls.

Built on a carrier-grade ATCA chassis, Barracuda's eon is a general purpose platform for running network intensive applications. Sure, security is the most likely early use of the platform, but it is not hard to see that routing, content delivery, load balancing, and packet capture and inspection could all be assisted by eon.

One way to explain away the surprise is to look at the brains behind eon: John Peterson. In addition to experience gained at Cisco, 3Com, Juniper, Fortinet, Websense and

Netscreen, Peterson is listed as co-inventor on a 2006 patent titled

System and Method for Implementing a Virtualized Security Platform.

You can get a feel for the potential in the eon platform by watching this interview I conducted with John Peterson at this year's RSA Conference.

Richard Stiennon interviews John Peterson, VP & General Manager, Barracuda Networks: https://vimeo.com/65338051

SHOULD WE ABANDON DIGITAL CERTIFICATES, OR LEARN TO USE THEM EFFECTIVELY?

MAY 14, 2013

A frightening trend is observable in the advance of targeted attacks. That is the realization on the part of attackers of the value of credentials, be they username/password pairs, strong authentication tokens, or digital certificates.

It is ironic that digital certificates, the basis of the most carefully thought out security paradigm of today, are the most highly sought after, and effectively targeted, digital assets of the day.

Public Key Infrastructure has been criticized for its OCD level of security. It was designed to be perfect. Every possible hole was plugged, trust models were devised of such complexity and rigor that no one could conceive of problems with the system itself. But perfection was PKI's undoing. It was too expensive, too cumbersome. In the late '90s hundreds of meetings, conferences, and symposia were convened for what should have been a logical system of e-checks that would allow banks to accept digitally signed checks for all sorts of financial transactions. It failed not because it was not well designed but because it was too well designed. The physical security system required to allow a bank to issue digital certificates, maintain certificate revocation lists, and accept other banks' digitally signed checks was estimated to cost $2 million. eCheck was abandoned in favor of ACH, a mechanical reproduction of the physical check-clearing process then in common use. And the Check 21 Act allowed truncation and storage of digital images of physical checks. Digital cash, a further extension of the power of digital certificates to change the world with Chaumsian math, was completely displaced with PayPal, a simplistic plug-in to existing banking infrastructure.

PKI relied on a trust model that was pyramidal in structure. For each industry, an uber Certificate Authority would sign the signing certificates of the CAs below it in the pyramid. Each CA in the cascade would have bullet proof security built into it with Hardware Security Modules, dual or triple authorization for issuing certs, and safe rooms constructed to hold the servers which would be protected by air gaps from the Internet.

The first unresolvable problem was who to trust to maintain the top level CA? The US Treasury, the US Post Office, and multiple specialized organizations were proposed. Other than some country CAs for issuing passports, few came about.

Companies like Entrust, RSA, and Verisign, as well as dozens of fly=by-night organizations sold the systems for creating CAs and issuing certs. One such certificate issuer, Thawte, was located in Mark Shuttleworth's parents' garage in South Africa. He sold to Verisign for $575 million in 1999.

BUT WE NEEDED certificates for SSL to work. Taher Elgamal and the team at Netscape did an end-run on the SET protocol, a proposed method of securing credit card transactions. They created a relatively simple model of server certificates and unique certificates in every browser. "Secure" transactions were immediately implemented and e-commerce took off. Dozens of vendors sold server certificates for SSL.

But where was the uber CA? There isn't one. The browser

is tasked with determining the validity of any server certificate for SSL. It contains a list of authorized signing certs and does a quick and simple check. Other than with EV (Extended Validation) certs, most browsers do not check for revoked certificates. The trust model is critically broken. Read Netcraft's recent article on how certificate revocation is broken.

SSL is bad enough, but the real culprit for bastardizing digital certificates is Microsoft. In the mistaken belief that they were adding security to their enterprise systems, MSFT built PKI into everything and started to give away the MSFT Certificate Server, often bundling it with other systems to further its penetration into the enterprise. Any and all organizations became issuers of certs—certs issued and maintained on Windows Servers with no physical security, no inherent protections at all.

So, we created the perfect security solution that relied on perfect trust models. We then deployed certificates everywhere with a flawed trust model.

Let's look at some of the results.

March 26th, 2011: the 21-year-old Comodo Hacker breaks into InstantSSL.it, a reseller for Comodo, one of the dozens of commercial CAs. This guy is good; at face value, one of the smartest hackers out there, or so he would have us believe. And he is apparently Iranian, or at least has an affinity for the Iranian regime.

September 5, 2011: the Diginotar breach leveraged to sign certs for Microsoft, Google, Yahoo, CIA, etc. Iran then executes a man-in-the-browser attack to spy on its citizens, at least 300,000 of them. Diginotar, which provided many of the certs for the Dutch government, is no more.

Let me backtrack a moment and tell you a story. In 2009 I attended the COSAC residential conference in Naas, just outside Dublin. During one session I was given three minutes to propose a question. I was researching my book on cyberwar so I asked the audience of 60 what a cyber weapon would look like. No one wanted to suggest anything during the open session, but that night at dinner a gentleman from Switzerland leaned over and whispered, "I have one for you, Microsoft update." Brilliant. Everyone trusts signed code from Microsoft. Someone who compromised that system would be able to target any Windows machine with a valid Microsoft license.

Just last year it was discovered that Flame, an extremely sophisticated piece of spyware, spoofs a Microsoft update, exploiting an expensive MD5 hash collision using a new attack method. Researchers estimate the collision would have cost $200k on Amazon's EC2 to calculate.

One more example from last September: Adobe build server breach led to compromised certs. We may never learn who these sophisticated attackers were targeting.

What does this mean?

The most sophisticated attackers have recognized the importance of digital certs and are targeting the root of trust, the CAs. Malware such as Stuxnet and Flame are being signed, to bypass system security checks.

This means that the explosion of the use of certs within the organization has introduced a vulnerability, one that needs to be managed, starting with discovery.

Device certs have to be protected on the device and the signing CA for them has to have Fort Knox quality security.

Certificates and PKI are not broken, the original perfect security models still work, and they just have to be taken seriously.

FIVE CRITICAL USES OF NETFLOW DATA FOR SECURITY

MAY 15, 2013

Flow data is already generated by most network devices. There has always been sufficient justification to collect and look at flow data if only to get a picture of what your network is being used for. Now, as attacks become more and more common, using flow data for security is easy to do and often much less expensive to deploy. Read this whitepaper for a detailed discussion of NetFlow and security.

In a recent interview with Amrit Williams, the CTO of Lancope, he highlighted many of the uses of flow analytics for security. These capabilities go far beyond the traditional use of flow data for application performance monitoring, visualization, and trouble shooting.

Application discovery

There has been a recent surge in interest in application discovery, thanks mainly to the explosion of cloud-based apps. Learning what your users are doing on your network and enforcing an acceptable use policy are the drivers behind the inclusion of application control into such UTM devices as Palo Alto Networks, Fortinet, and WatchGuard. NetFlow analysis is a way to get there quickly without swapping out your gateway security products.

Anomalous network behavior

With NetFlow it is possible to profile "normal" network traffic and alert network administrators when something changes. A Swedish startup called Unomaly has a taken this anomaly detection to a very granular level for network and system trouble shooting.

Identification of compromised hosts

When Mandiant released the history-making APT1 Report, many researchers put in efforts to build the Key Indicators of Compromise into their tools. Lancope pushed this data out to their customers within 24 hours. One customer discovered that they had indeed been compromised by the Comment Crew, the Chinese team identified in the Report. Continuous updates of new IP addresses associated with botnets and the subsequent identification of compromised hosts is one of the most valuable capabilities any organization can acquire.

Insiders engaged in nefarious actions

Amrit points out that Lancope has built in network, application, and user context to their NetFlow analytics. This makes it possible to identify anomalous user behavior. If an employee or contractor is downloading large amounts of data to his laptop, or using network scanning tools, or hacking in general, NetFlow can be used to catch and identify them.

Policy enforcement

Even access attempts that violate policies can be identified using NetFlow. This could be as simple as visiting inappropriate websites from work or as dangerous as repeated login attempts to a database server.

NetFlow has come a long way from its early days of network monitoring and profiling. Parsers for SNMP, Syslog, and firewall logs have extended the correlation capabilities and transformed NetFlow analysis into an indispensable security tool.

GRASPING THE PROBLEM WITH PRIVILEGED ACCOUNTS

MAY 16, 2013

I alluded earlier this week [Should We Abandon Digital Certificates?] to the issue of attackers targeting credentials, the keys that open the gates to an organization's data assets. Many in the security industry tend to focus on authentication strength and user directories, but Udi Mokady, CEO of CyberArk, informs me that in many larger organizations there are three to four times as many privileged accounts as there are users. A privileged account is how administrators log into servers, switches, firewalls, routers, database servers, and the many applications they must manage. Many of these systems are not within a Windows domain and by default allow simple username/password pairs to log in. In the worst case default passwords are never revoked; often username "admin" and a blank password.

Over the years organizations have learned to disable the default passwords, but often the default is replaced with a single login that is shared by anyone who needs to get on a machine. Others have graduated to separate credentials for each administrator but then do not manage them, so when an employee or contractor leaves, their credentials are never erased. Still another issue is with machines that must talk to each other and the code is hardwired with usernames/passwords that are hard to change. In one of the most egregious cases, Microsoft, even after 15 years, still allows an attacker who has admin rights on one machine to log into any other machine on the network just by using stored hashes of credentials! (See the website devoted to pass-the-hash exploits here.)

CyberArk is one of a handful of solutions that address these issues of Privileged Account Security. Every privileged user must log into a proxy that then enforces authorizations and tracks every login. Strong two-factor authentication can be implemented once at the CyberArk proxy and immediately the Jérôme Kerviel issue is removed. Kervial is infamous for covering his trail at Société Générale by logging in to the trading desk back office using another employee's username and password. He caused the bank to lose over $7 billion. Centrally managed privileged accounts should be deployed at every organization with extensive infrastructure.

MANY COMPLIANCE REGIMES call for privileged account management but it is surprising how thinly penetrated these solutions are in the market.

Watch my interview with Udi Mokady to learn more about CyberArk. https://vimeo.com/61477667

And then watch this interview with John Worrall, CMO of CyberArk, for a higher-level discussion of the problems organizations face in protecting themselves from targeted attacks and insider abuse.

https://vimeo.com/61479929

TAMING THE FIREWALL

MAY 20, 2013

Despite the oft-repeated claims that changes to computing infrastructure are leading to the demise of the perimeter, in fact what has happened is that firewalls have continued to be deployed everywhere. Many large organizations still back-haul most of their network traffic to headquarters where they can apply firewall policies and URL filtering, but most organizations have evolved to a distributed architecture where enforcement points, UTM devices such as Fortinet, Palo Alto networks, SonicWall, and WatchGuard, are deployed at the gateway of every remote office around the world.

On top of the explosion in devices and vendors that provide them, there is an explosion in the number of rules present in each firewall, which in turn has led to the rise of Firewall Policy Management solutions. Get an update on how these solutions are addressing the fractal perimeter of today by watching this interview with the CEO and CTO of Tufin Technologies.

https://vimeo.com/91016821

APPLYING INTELLIGENCE TO BIG DATA FOR SECURITY

MAY 21, 2013

Much has been said about Big Data and security.

The theme of RSA Conference 2013 was Security in Knowledge and many vendors were talking about Big Data and security. This gives rise to a lot of confusion in the security industry. What is Big Data in terms of security?

Certainly there is a lot of data associated with security. Much of that Big Data is stored as events in huge repositories of logs. Even more Big Data can be captured on the network and parsed into events and records of network activity. But is this Big Data in the sense that Walmart uses Big Data? Or the way Amazon or Netflix figures out what you like? Or the way Facebook magically feeds you ads based on things your friends are posting on your wall? Or the way you *wish* your credit card company would take note that you purchased a flight overseas and does *not* call you with fraud alerts when you appear in a different country?

No, security Big Data is about matching security intelligence with the right collected data.

Security intelligence is comprised of knowledge of threat actors, the tools they use, the IP addresses they use, and even who they are targeting. Security intelligence can even *reduce* the amount of data that has to be captured, stored and managed. After all, if ten groups are attacking you on any given day, do you really get any value out of collecting alerts from millions of devices, thousands of users, and hundreds of applications if only a few of them are part of the attack? I would suggest that the data itself is of zero value. The value comes from the security intelligence that can winnow out the attacks from the data. See how Anton Chuvakin of Gartner thinks about Big Data security in his post about security exploration versus responding to alerts.

As Rob Sadowski, Director of Marketing at RSA, Security Division of EMC, points out in this video, this activity is changing the way security teams operate. Instrumentation and data collection are still critical, but applying filters derived from intelligence is the path to achieving better security. https://vimeo.com/65905603

INFORMATION SHARING CRITICAL TO CYBER DEFENSE

MAY 22, 2013

I kicked off a conversation with Dan Holden, Director of ASERT at Arbor Networks, by asking him about the Mandiant APT1 Report that was generating a lot of buzz at this year's RSA Conference. Dan emphasized the benefit to the community of security researchers that resulted; especially the second part of the APT1 Report that enumerated the IP addresses and key indicators of compromise that Mandiant had collected. Within hours of publication, open source and commercial products had incorporated that data into their tools.

If you think about it, information sharing, especially when it comes to IP address reputation, has become a critical, and sometimes differentiating feature, of many security products, from URL content filtering products like those of Websense, Blue Coat, and Fortinet, to IPS products like those of HP, Sourcefire, and IBM . Even host security solutions like Source-fire's AMP and Trend Micro have elements that collect information, analyze, and categorize it in the cloud and then push out that intelligence to their entire customer base.

Information sharing is an effective way to get ahead of the

bad guys. It increases their expense by making them shift their ground. They cannot target many organizations from the same compromised server because the first one detects it and the rest block subsequent attacks.

This information sharing is easiest to accomplish when the information is IP reputation. Even sharing hashes of malware and traces of files left behind by attackers are being shared. Higher-level intelligence such as that provided by iSIGHT Partners, Mandiant, and specialized cyber security firms are not as easily shared but their customers benefit from subscribing to that information. Critical infrastructure industry sectors share within themselves: the Information Sharing and Analysis Centers (ISACs). Red Sky Alliance is a private information sharing forum that is growing rapidly and I expect more of these are cropping up.

Having sensors deployed widely is the competitive differentiator for security vendors. Those with the largest install bases have the most information and have invested the most in quickly analyzing and pushing out intelligence to their customers. As Dan points out, Arbor Networks has those sensors imbedded in the majority of ISPs in the world, which has positioned them well for defending against Distributed Denial of Service Attacks (DDoS). Even Dan's presence at Arbor indicates that they are taking research into attack methodologies further and starting to concentrate on targeted attacks beyond just DDoS.

Richard Stiennon interviews Dan Holden, Director of ASERT at Arbor Networks: https://vimeo.com/91989565

SILICON VALLEY IS NOT AT FRONT LINE OF GLOBAL CYBERWAR

JUNE 5, 2013

I have been an IT security industry analyst for 13 years. For much of that time the epicenter of the business was indeed in the San Francisco Bay Area. Industry giants like Cisco, Juniper, McAfee, Symantec, and Fortinet are based there. In 2008, out of 1,200 security vendors worldwide, 237 were based in Silicon Valley. Even Israeli firm Check Point Software moved their headquarters to Silicon Valley prior to their IPO. Check Point's move back to Israel is one reason they are no longer dominating the firewall space, giving ground to Fortinet and Palo Alto Networks.

The biggest driver in the security industry is the evolving threat space. As long as the threats were hackers and cyber criminals, Silicon Valley was where the action was. As that threat has shifted to nation-state cyber espionage, the center of gravity of IT security has shifted to Washington, DC. Here is where the security giants of the future are thriving. NetWitness, acquired by EMC, Mandiant of APT1 Report fame, Sourcefire, iSIGHT Partners, and hundreds of security consulting companies call the area home. On a smaller scale, London, Ottawa, Tel Aviv, and Canberra are experiencing their own growth of vibrant cyber businesses.

Yesterday an Associated Press report that seeks to gain local relevance by tying the Obama-Xi summit to cyber security issues mistakenly portrayed Silicon Valley as the front line of global cyberwar. The Bay Area is still home to hundreds of great security companies that continue to supply the nuts and bolts of effective security, but fighting highly sophisticated targeted attacks from professional adversaries is now the realm of innovative companies based on the other coast.

There is a conference on cybersecurity almost every day in Washington, DC. I have not seen a single conference in the Bay Area that uses the word cyber in its title. The traditional IT security industry practitioners scorn anyone who even utters the word cyber. This semantic myopia has contributed to Silicon Valley falling behind. Luckily, vendors follow the money. Look for them to establish first sales offices and then engineering offices in DC. As the preponderance of development moves to Washington, so will the headquarters. Either that or the new security vendors will be acquiring the old.

NSA SURVEILLANCE THREATENS US COMPETITIVENESS

JUNE 7, 2013

The vast foreign and domestic spying by the NSA revealed this week threatens the global competitiveness of US
tech companies.

We are told we live in a digital world and the future is
bright for tech startups, as costs of launching new products
and services plummet and global markets open up to the
smallest vendor. Yet, there is a worldwide perception that any
data that is stored or even routed through the United States is
sucked into cavernous NSA data centers for analysis and cata-
loging. That perception was solidified in 2006 when former
AT&T technician Mark Klein blew the whistle on the fiber
tap that AT&T had provided to the NSA in some of its data
centers. Those perceptions have had real consequences for US
tech firms seeking to offer global services. Email archiving
services such as Proofpoint could not sell to even Canadian
customers without building local infrastructure. Even establishing separate data centers in Canada and Europe is not
enough to assure customers that their data would forever stay
out of the grasp of US intelligence services.

One of the fastest-growing segments of the tech industry

is cloud services, with Salesforce.com one of the leading examples. Box.net and other cloud storage solutions are burgeoning. Cloud infrastructure providers like Amazon, Microsoft, and Rackspace are investing billions to serve markets that should be global but will be barred from most countries thanks to the complete abandonment of trust caused by NSA/FBI spying.

Since 2006, every time I present outside the US the same question has been asked: "Is the US reading our email?" Answers that allude to 'protections from abuse' and 'oversight' now seem specious. From this week forward a universal suspicion has transformed into acknowledged fact. Yes, US government agencies are reading email, tracking phone calls, and monitoring all communications.

Brian Honan, Board Member of the UK & Ireland Chapter of the Cloud Security Alliance, provided this opinion:

The revelations about the PRISM program could have major implications for US companies doing business within the European Union. Under the EU Data Protection directive it is illegal for European companies to export the personal data of EU citizens to countries outside of the EU and the European Economic Area. Exceptions to this are for certain countries that have similar privacy legislation in place to that of the EU or where the strong contracts protecting the privacy of that data are in place. The US in not one of the approved countries but has put in place the EU Safe Harbor program which US companies can sign up to and agree to apply EU privacy protections to private data. Many of the companies allegedly involved in PRISM are part of the Safe Harbor program. The fact the US government is potentially accessing that data could place the European organizations in breach of EU Data Protection regulations.

The news will also heighten concerns many European organizations, especially EU government ones, will have in selecting a US Cloud Provider for their services.

Gabriel Yoran, Managing Director and Founder of German security company Steganos, added:

The European Union traditionally favors strong privacy regulations. However, this policy has been under attack recently, being seen as a competitive disadvantage in the cloud services space. This could dramatically change now in the light of the recent Verizon findings. Privacy software maker Steganos traditionally stresses it being headquartered in Berlin and therefore subject to the even stricter German data protection law (one of the strictest in the world). According to a February survey, 64% of Steganos customers said it was important or very important to them that Steganos is a Germany-based company.

Trust is the very foundation of all commerce. Once lost it is almost impossible to regain. This week's revelations that the NSA has blanket data harvesting arrangements with Verizon, AT&T, Sprint-Nextel, Google, Microsoft, Apple, Skype, Yahoo, Facebook, and even credit card processors, will have immediate repercussions. Non-US customers of any US business will immediately evaluate their exposure to these new risks and look for alternatives. European, Canadian, and Australian tech companies will profit from this. Competitors in those regions will offer alternatives that will also draw US customers away from the compromised US services.

While the FBI and NSA leverage the dramatic intelligence opportunities of a digital world, their Orwellian actions are crushing opportunity for tech giants and startups in the United States.

Reuters has a report about European reactions. Relevant quote:

"The US government must provide clarity regarding these monstrous allegations of total monitoring of various telecommunications and Internet services," said Peter Schaar, German data protection and freedom of information commissioner.

And this from the Wall Street Journal, Credibility Crunch for Tech Companies Over Prism. With a quote:

German Justice Minister Sabine Leutheusser-Schnarrenberger told daily newspaper *Die Welt* that "German citizens don't want their data to automatically end up with American authorities. It's good and necessary for the US to rethink its anti-terror legislation."

Trevor Pott, a Canadian, writes in the UK Register: NSA Prism: Why I'm boycotting US cloud tech—and you should too.

I'm rapidly moving from being "uncomfortable hosting my data in a US-controlled cloud" to "feeling ethically bound to vote with my wallet in order to send a message."

CRISIS OF CONFIDENCE COULD SPUR FLIGHT FROM US TECH

JUNE 14, 2013

The dream is over. The era of US tech dominance in everything from servers to routers to the cloud is facing a crisis of confidence that could have far-reaching impact. Trust is the basis of all commerce and the rapid realization that companies such as AT&T, Sprint, Google , Yahoo , Microsoft , and Apple are actively assisting the NSA in their unrelenting quest to know everything could be the beginning of the end for US dominance in technology.

This is not new. The ITU has been working for years to wrest control of the Internet away from US domination. Since the reports that first arose in 2005 that the NSA was spying on data communication and even gathering phone records, Europeans have distrusted US carriers and worked to prevent their data from crossing US networks. This has forced cloud providers like Amazon to build and segregate data centers in multiple regions around the world.

But the news that is circulating today via Bloomberg is that the NSA appetite for intelligence goes far beyond network traffic. When dealing with foundational trust, perception is everything, regardless of the true extent to which the US leverages its relationship with US tech companies. Bloomberg reports:

Microsoft, the world's largest software company, provides intelligence agencies with information about bugs in its popular software before it publicly releases a fix, according to two people familiar with the process. That information can be used to protect government computers and to access the computers of terrorists or military foes.

Even more chilling to those who do not share the US' interest in protecting the US at all costs:

Makers of hardware and software, banks, Internet security providers, satellite telecommunications companies, and many other companies also participate in the government programs. In some cases, the information gathered may be used not just to defend the nation but to help infiltrate computers of its adversaries.

Even before these direct accusations, the leaks provided by Edward Snowden, the fugitive whistle-blower, were creating loud reactions from Europe. My friends in Australia are reporting similar reactions that have not yet made their way into public statements.

Rickard Falkvinge, the founder of Sweden's Pirate Party, is direct, if a bit hysterical:

In short, practically every single service you have ever been using that has operated under the "trust us" principle has fed your private data directly to STASI-equivalent security agencies.

These are reactions published before today's Bloomberg report. In the coming weeks *every* government agency and every major corporation around the world will be evaluating its exposure to US spying. They will have to evaluate their trust relationships with US tech giants like Amazon, Microsoft, Google, Cisco, Oracle, and IBM. After determining that they are indeed at risk of at the very least being in violation of Safe Harbor provisions and local data privacy regulations, they will have to consider alternatives.

There will be startups that offer alternatives to these vendors with particular attention paid to those in each country that can be trusted to abide by local regulations. While open source projects have their own issues, they have the advantage that they are not completely controlled by US companies with secret relationships with the NSA.

Ericsson, Siemens, Alcatel-Lucent, Nokia, and, in the supreme irony, Huawei and ZTE are going to have distinct advantages when competing against US telecom equipment vendors.

DuckDuckGo, the alternative to the Google search engine, is already seeing a surge in usage.

The US tech industry is in danger of being sidelined by this loss of trust. Stated guarantees and even refutations of allegations of cooperating with the NSA are not going to help. It is too late. Trust has been compromised.

WE ALL HAVE SECRETS

JUNE 27, 2013

Here is a chilling thought regarding the wholesale surveillance that much of the world has only recently discovered they are subject to: What happens to the legal underpinnings of commerce—trust and the expectation of confidentiality in communication?

It is natural to think you have no secrets to hide if you are not engaged in illegal activity and have no intention of ever communicating with terrorists. Perhaps elected officials who call or email hookers, or congressional staffers who talk to their brokers have cause for concern if a future political regime engages in a witch hunt.

BUT WHAT ABOUT the vast majority of us? Why should the fact that the NSA has the ability to see all of our email, phone calls, and online activity be of any concern?

Have you ever signed a Non-Disclosure Agreement (NDA)? Have you ever entered into a confidentiality agreement? If you are employed by a large company you probably have. If you are dself-employed, as I am, you have probably signed many agreements to maintain the confidentiality of your clients' information. I have signed agreements that stipulate that the very information that a client has engaged me is not to be disclosed, usually during the due diligence phase of an acquisition. Many NDAs have escape clauses that acknowledge court orders, but I doubt blanket court orders are what most parties have in mind.

Knowing that you have not maintained the confidentiality of your employer/client may well put you in breach of all those contracts you have signed. "Oh piffle, Stiennon. You are grasping at straws." Maybe. The NSA is, after all, led by principled people who are just doing their job protecting the nation from terrorists. They have no motivation to snoop on the communication between an attorney and her client, a defense contractor and its lobbyist, a bank executive and his board, a journalist and his source. There is no Anthony Comstock sifting through your mail for lewd content. For "United States persons" the NSA or FBI need a warrant and probable cause. Maybe.

What about communication with non-United States persons, like every client or employer overseas? Do you work for Chrysler-Fiat? T-Mobile? There is even some indication that taking steps to honor your confidentiality agreements, by encrypting your communication, may expose you to more scrutiny and longer retention of your encrypted data after it has been captured.

Next time you promise to keep something confidential, think what that means. Are you really able to fulfill that promise?

NSA SURVEILLANCE EXTENDS THE THREAT HIERARCHY

JULY 29, 2013

I have used the Threat Hierarchy, first portrayed by my prede-
cessors at Gartner, for a dozen years to launch my narrative on
what drives the IT security industry. As I explain at least twice
a week to eager investors who want to develop a security portfolio, IT security is different than any other technology sector.
There is no maturation. There will not be three or four big
players who dominate the space as there are in PCs, databases, ERP, or CAD/CAM. Because there is an outside
driving force: threat actors.

It was only in 2008 that I realized the threat hierarchy was
actually a predictor of future trends. In 2001 I would argue
that cybercrime was not really a threat: it did not exist in a big
way, there was no Lex Luther skimming pennies off of every
transaction on the Internet. Obviously that changed pretty
dramatically within a couple of years. It was that realization
that led me to research what used to be called Information
Warfare, now cyberwar.

Cybercrime and then cyberwar (or nation-state prepara-
tions for cyberwar and certainly nation-state cyber espionage)
have had transformative impacts on the IT security industry.

National cyber strategies abound and spending is on the rise, along with amazing companies like iSight Partners, Mandiant, ThreatGRID, and CrowdStrike, all fighting targeted attacks.

What's next? All of the threats in this old chart have been realized and the IT security industry is morphing to address them. What could possibly be higher on the list than US-China-Russia-Iran's use of cyber attacks to project force?

There is only one actor that could pose a greater threat to our digital lives than a foreign agency.

The NSA.

On June 5, the veil was torn away from the massive all-encompassing surveillance state that has been constructed since 9/11 and the Patriot Act. An insatiable fetish to "collect everything" has led to a new reality: nothing is secure.

Why bother worrying about China stealing industrial secrets when everything already resides in vast oceans of data that the NSA has collected? Phone records, phone conversations, Google searches, social media interactions, and email are all compromised. Every security control, audit regime, risk management policy, and compliance requirement is broken. Sarbanes-Oxley requires officers of publicly traded companies to attest to these controls in the form of COBIT and ITIL. HIPAA imposes fines for unauthorized access to health records. GLB requires privacy of communication of financial data. Every CISO in the world has to revise their assessment of their own posture in light of these revelations.

The IT security industry is poised at the brink of a cathartic transformation. It *will* respond to this new threat actor. How? By developing the technology to securely communicate, store data, and thwart the surveillance state. All of the building blocks already exist. Savvy communicators, like some hackers, criminals, drug lords, spies, and terrorists are already effectively evading the surveillance state. Security cognoscenti already encrypt key communications. Hundreds of tools exist for secure communications. They are just ridiculously cumbersome. Even the simplest measures, like using proxies to mask browsing and search activity, are painful to use. Throughput and response time decrease dramatically if you are hopping through a proxy server in another country over encrypted links. And encrypting data introduces the very messy problem of managing and protecting encryption keys–keys that have to be extraordinarily strong because the adversary, the NSA, has more computing power than anyone else.

Trust is a very fragile thing. Once broken it takes 100 times the effort to reestablish. The clock cannot be turned back. Even if the NSA and its cousins in practically every technologically advanced state around the world were to be reined in, it is too late.

The new revolution in security affairs will be kicked off by a move to encrypt everything all the time. But, as one writer fears, encryption is nothing without protections for encryption keys. Keeping keys safe means that authentication, continuous monitoring, defenses against APTs, gateways, and endpoint security will have to become a part of every architecture. This is no more than what has been required from day one. But now there is a threat actor whose actions have justified taking extraordinary measures to secure our communications and data.

Just as the threat from hackers can be thanked for the eventual improvement in Windows security and cyber criminals can be thanked for better bank security measures, the NSA should be thanked for creating what will be the dominant driver in the security industry: the surveillance state.

But the NSA will not sit still as defenses are deployed to counter their data harvesting. Watch as Congress moves to classify encryption and other means of avoiding spying as "cyber weapons." The argument will be made that only criminals and terrorists use these tools. We've seen it before, and there are already bills in motion. This is where the battle will be fought. We must stand our ground.

IT SECURITY INDUSTRY TO EXPAND TENFOLD

AUGUST 14, 2013

Governments around the world have commandeered the Internet, as Bruce Schneier so succinctly points out in The Atlantic. How is that going to impact the IT security industry? This $60 billion industry researches, develops, and sells firewalls, anti-malware, authentication, encryption, and 80 other categories of products. With each advance in the threat level represented by hackers, cyber criminals, and cyber spies there has been a new batch of vendors who come on the scene to counter threats that bypass previous technologies and spending has increased.

Spending on IT security is poised to grow tenfold in ten years. Every organization from the largest oil and gas refiner to the smallest bank has underspent on security. Classic risk management methodologies call for trade-offs in security. Unlikely events, Black Swans, are not accounted for. This protect-against-the-known philosophy is what led to most defense contractors and even the Department of Defense being completely vulnerable to sophisticated targeted attacks from foreign spy agencies. The recent rapid growth of technology vendors to ward off cyber attacks is a blip compared to what is coming.

Even the most sophisticated Chinese cyber spies do not appear to be well funded. They use shelf ware and their teams work regular hours. The NSA on the other hand is shockingly replete with funds. The US Intelligence Community budget of $70 billion is twice the size of the Australian military budget. The NSA has donated $160 million to its sister agency, GCHQ in the UK, for intelligence gathering. The investment in creating Total Information Awareness over the last decade has stunned the industry.

There will be a response to this threat against all communications. That response will be hundreds of new IT security vendors cropping up all over the world. Thanks to a dramatic increase in distrust of US companies, this boom in technology will not be centered on Silicon Valley. Just as the draconian anti-encryption measures of the '90s drove development offshore, major cloud providers will have to push their engineering and research into countries that are more open and considerate of privacy and transparency.

As engineers do, great minds around the world are today figuring out the technology to route around surveillance. The market is there. Funding will be readily available. It will be the ultimate irony if a tech giant like Huawei becomes a trusted provider of infrastructure because there is less chance that its executives are secretly working with the NSA.

What is needed to re-establish trustable communications? Roger Grimes sums up the difficulty, although his conclusion, to not use the Internet, is defeatist. Look to these technologies to experience a boom:

Encryption: Encryption predates the Internet, and yes, code making and breaking was what the NSA was created for, but encryption technology is in the hands of private enterprise and is the easiest part of the solution.

Certificate Management: The reason most people and most enterprises do not use encryption, other than SSL for web access and WPA for Wifi, is that key and certificate management is cumbersome. That is already changing with companies like Entrust and Venafi rolling out certificate discovery and management tools. Even SSH has introduced key management for its secure remote access tool.

Authentication: Having encryption and good certificate management is useless against a sophisticated attacker unless measures are taken to protect those keys. One of the primary measures is two-factor authentication. Attackers know to target credential repositories like Active Directory. Keys should be well protected. Signing certificates should be air-gapped and access to them should require at least two-party authentication, like in a missile silo.

All the rest. Protecting keys, certificates, and the infrastructure to contain them involves everything the IT security industry has provided to date. Firewalls, IPS, anti-malware, vulnerability management, patching, etc., account for $60 billion in spending today.

The hard part. The scariest part of the surveillance state is that it has tapped the backbone of the Internet. Every connection from every computer and smart phone can be logged. Even encrypted packets have to have clear text headers to be routed over the Internet. The surveillance state can garner amazing amounts of intelligence from collecting this meta data. A journalist and his source, or an attorney and her client, or a CFO and an acquisition candidate, or a Congressperson and his or her lobbyist are all subject to linkage analysis.

There are several systems today that seek to obfuscate Internet communications, but they are becoming increasingly suspect as even Tor was recently compromised in a major bust. Making multiple encrypted hops to avoid tracking is expensive in terms of latency and download times. New protocols and technology will need to be developed and new infrastructure rolled out.

What does this mean for the growth of the IT security

industry? It means a tenfold increase in spending and a doubling in the number of products and services.

Look at the numbers. The very best IT organizations report spending 6-8% of their budget on security. That is going to have to double in the short term to counter the threat of the surveillance state, just to account for the deployment and management of encryption everywhere. Telecom costs will rise dramatically to pay for the new infrastructure to obfuscate traffic. Those are the thought-leading enterprises. All the rest have to play catch up. Gartner sizes the entire IT spend at $3.3 trillion and security infrastructure spending at $60 billion in 2012 with an 8.4% growth rate. In order to counter the surveillance state that growth rate will need to quadruple to 24%. Extrapolated to ten years, IT security spending will be $639 billion by 2023—a tenfold increase.

Growth rates of this magnitude are going to change the IT landscape, not just security. The ramifications are well worth contemplating.

Investors. Now would be a very good time to make strategic investments in IT security companies, as many private equity companies are beginning to recognize. Even poorly managed companies can thrive in a fast growth environment.

Policy makers. Politicians, think tanks, and NGOs have to become well educated in the implications of a surveillance state and the technologies being developed to counter the new reality. Voting for legislation to make the use of countervailing technology illegal may fly in the face of popular sentiment.

Universities. This type of growth will have far reaching impacts on the job market for college graduates. Computer science departments will have to teach secure software development practices and graduate security specialists. Reach out to large technology vendors for research grants to develop secure communications and networking infrastructure.

Businesses. The surveillance state is going to have a

dramatic impact on your operating costs as you rush to re-comply with your audit regimes.

Security vendors. Revise your product road maps today to account for a dramatic increase in demand for surveillance proof technology. Cybercrime, cyber espionage, and even cyberwar are no longer the next big thing.

Security practitioners. Learn what end-to-end security and zero-trust means. Look at your architectures to see what investment it will take to get to these end states.

Consumers. Pay attention to the new spate of vendors that will rise to replace the Lavabits and SecureCircles. They may be off-shore. In the meantime start using proxies for web browsing and and switch to the two factor authentication offered by the major web services.

Google, Yahoo!, Facebook, and Twitter. It's up to you to fix a problem we now know you were complicit in creating. Push back on the legal and legislative side while at the same time put your best minds to work on the problem of regaining the trust of your users.

NSA. Under the veil of secrecy and a compliant legisla-ture and judiciary you have profited tremendously from an intelligence bubble. That bubble will burst. Ten years from now you will *not* have access to all communications of all people. Make plans for winding down the surveillance state. You have already done untold damage to the country you are striving to protect. If you continue the current path you will bankrupt us.

NSA SET TO APPROVE TPM FOR GOVERNMENT USE

SEPTEMBER 10, 2013

Speaking at the Trusted Computing Conference in Orlando Monday afternoon, Debora Plunkett, Director of Information Assurance for the NSA, announced that she is preparing to sign an Information Assurance Advisory that permits the purchase of Trusted Computing components for National Security Systems. This is great news for the small community that is the Trusted Computing Group and the vendors who have worked for over a decade to provide technology for hardware based cryptography, key repositories, self-encrypting drives, and device authentication.

It has been a long road for the TCG. Tackling some of the most difficult challenges in security, an open standard for hardware-supported security, TPM 2.0, has been meticulously cranked out. Yet, even though the NSA has been one of the strongest supporters of the standards process, it has been remiss in actually approving, let alone recommending or even requiring, the use of TPM for government systems. Plunkett's announcement leapfrogs the approval step to go directly to recommending TPM for use in National Security Systems.

The TCG and the vendors who support TPM are deservedly elated. An official approval of TPM for some of the most stringent security environments should help to raise awareness and drive adaption.

WILL ATTESTATIONS SOLVE THE VENDOR TRUST PROBLEM?

OCTOBER 22, 2013

I have written and presented on the great harm that has come from the NSA's pervasive surveillance programs. How are vendors of network and security products going to re-establish trust with their customers?

Those companies that specifically provide surveillance evading technology have been hardest hit. There is no option for them if they are based in the US. Yesterday Y Combinator startup CryptoSeal shut down its consumer offering stating:

With immediate effect as of this notice, CryptoSeal Privacy, our consumer VPN service, is terminated. All cryptographic keys used in the operation of the service have been zero-filled, and while no logs were produced (by design) during operation of the service, all records created incidental to the operation of the service have been deleted to the best of our ability.

Essentially, the service was created and operated under a certain understanding of current US law, and that understanding may not currently be valid.

Law-abiding owners of Lavabit and Silent Circle have had

to take the same measure: ritual seppuku of their private email services to avoid betraying their users. (Note that Silent Circle is alive and well and still provides a secure messaging platform.)

But what about the manufacturers of network gear? As distrust in US vendors grows what can they do to assure their international customers that they are not deploying NSA-compromised devices in their networks?

One step would be to publish a strongly worded statement that they are not working with the NSA or any intelligence agencies. Perhaps the following:

We can confirm that we have never received any instructions or requests from any Government or their agencies to change our positions, policies, procedures, hardware, software, or employment practices or anything else, other than suggestions to improve our end-to-end cyber security capability. We can confirm that we have never been asked to provide access to our technology, or provide any data or information on any citizen or organization to any Government, or their agencies.

That statement comes from Huawei, the much-maligned Chinese vendor of routers and switches. While such a claim may induce Gertrudian doubts, it is important to remember that commercial entities have more to lose from making false claims than say politicians or generals. Huawei has set a high bar for attestation, one that US networking companies will be challenged to meet, especially if they are indeed working with the NSA, even to the extent of providing vulnerability information before it is public knowledge. Some vulnerabilities, after all, are backdoors regardless of the lack of intent on the part of the manufacturer.

Attestations of freedom from surveillance are a good thing and every vendor who can honestly make them should. But are they enough? Of course not. In the cyber domain, as opposed to that of statecraft, the mantra should be **do not trust *and* verify**.

Thanks to the rise of cyber defense tools that look specifically for indicators of compromise, it is now possible to effectively protect against backdoored hardware. Continuous packet capture and analysis would immediately alert on any Command and Control communication to a router or server within an organization. Any discovery of a backdoor in any equipment would spell the end of that manufacturer's prospects. Security architectures must be built around the no-trust model. Gear from multiple vendors must be deployed in watch-the-watcher mode.

Jurisdiction plays a role, too. A suitably paranoid approach would assume that a manufacturer based in a particular country has been compromised by that country's intelligence agencies. But most vendors have indicated a willingness to comply with each country's laws and regulations in order to do business there. Remember Yahoo! and Google's weak arguments for complying with Chinese persecution of "dissidents?" Would a network gear vendor comply with local requirements to provide backdoors to local intelligence agencies?

Here is an interesting thought experiment. If you are a US person or company, would you feel more comfortable deploying gear from a Chinese company that has attested that it has received no requests from any government, or a US vendor who has not made that attestation? Think about it.

TRUSTED COMPUTING MUST REPUDIATE THE NSA (UPDATED)

NOVEMBER 16, 2013

Update December 21, 2013: Developments this week support the notion that the NSA is seeking to compromise security systems, especially crypto systems. First, this report from Reuters claims that RSA, the security division of EMC, accepted a $10 million payment to make the flawed random number generator, DUAL_EC_DRBG, its default in its BSAFE encryption suite. Documents from Edward Snowden had earlier revealed that the NSA had influenced the NIST process to get this "backdoor" approved as a standard. To RSA's credit, they did issue a warning to customers to stop using the suspect code on September 19.

Second, Trevor Perrin posted a request to remove the co-chair, Kevin Igoe, of an influential crypto working group within the IETF, because it appeared that he was adversely impacting the security of proposed systems. Kevin Igoe is an NSA employee.

Read this comment from Dan Goodin at Ars Technica and see how it relates to the argument that the Trusted Computing Group should repudiate the NSA:

In a post-Snowden world, there's new legitimacy to criti-

cism about NSA involvement, particularly when employees of
the agency are the ones actively shepherding untested
proposals.

Trust is fragile and the decade-long effort on the part of
the NSA to compromise all security models has destroyed
trust. From its inception, the coalition of industry giants who
have backed the concept of hardware-based security,
the Trusted Computing Group (TCG), has been at odds with
the "information should be free" crowd. The problem these
giants (Microsoft, Intel, AMD, IBM, HP) faced a decade ago
was software and media piracy. As the biggest backer,
Microsoft was the most suspect. In recent weeks that suspicion
of Microsoft has exploded into bald-faced claims from the
German BSI that the Trusted Platform Module, the hardware
component of Trusted Computing, is an NSA backdoor. And
who knows what further releases of the Snowden files will
unveil about the NSA's involvement with the Trusted
Computing Group?

The NSA jumped on the Trusted Computing bandwagon
early. In recent years they have sponsored the Trusted
Computing Conference in Orlando, often shrouded in spooki-
ness as Ellen Mesmer, the intrepid industry reporter, relates.
This year the NSA begged off sponsoring the event claiming
budget sequester, despite its $10 billion budget. The remaining
sponsors and organizers could only muster about 60 attendees.
Speakers from Microsoft, Wave, Infineon, and other hardcore
crypto security experts only alluded to the elephant in the
room, usually to deride the poor state of journalism and laugh
off the unsupported claims of the German government.
Denial is a common symptom in reaction to tsunami shifts in
markets and global politics. Those who have devoted their
careers to parenting super secure architectures are overly
confident in their own children. They neglect the perfidy of
unconstrained government forces such as an intelligence
community whose budget is twice the size of that of
Australia's Ministry of Defense.

. . .

THE TRUSTED COMPUTING standard is open and good. It offers a solution to all of the issues that plague the Internet today. Device attestation, strong crypto with unbreakable key storage, identity, code signing, Trusted Network Connections, even secure end-to-end communication are all made possible by a little silicon wafer shipped with most business computers. The day is coming when over a billion computers will be equipped with TPMs. Yet, the actual number of TPMs that are utilized is miniscule.

The reasons for the failure of Trusted Computing will be familiar to many in the security industry. Products do not sell unless they solve a real problem, and security products do not sell unless they address a real and present danger. The community of Trusted Computing advocates, which includes the manufacturers of TPMs, Microsoft, and the Information Assurance Directorate of the NSA, are frustrated that their perfect security models do not catch on. There has been no market driver to incorporate TPMs into security architectures. Until now.

In an ironic twist, the other side of the NSA, the Signals Intelligence Directorate, has inadvertently created the market driver that could propel Trusted Computing forward. In its blind pursuit of its mission, the NSA has embarked on a massive surveillance program to "collect everything." The NSA has compromised all security. All communication is targeted. It has used its legal muscle to force vendors to give up the keys to the kingdom. It has corrupted security models that rely on trust: trust of Certificate Authorities, trust of vendors, trust of encryption protocols. The NSA has done irreparable harm to trust.

The Trusted Computing Group, in order to realize its own mission of moving the world towards a hardware root of trust for security, must completely repudiate the NSA. It must formally cut the ties that bind it to the NSA with a public statement of repudiation. Current and former members of the NSA must be barred from participation at all levels including working committees, the board, and from a presence at the Trusted Computing Conference. The members of the Trusted Computing Group must seek to re-establish trust by demonstrating the absence of complicity in the NSA's surveillance programs. The manufacturers of TPMs must demonstrate that there are no backdoors in their products.

Only after repudiating the NSA can the Trusted Computing Group begin to participate in the tenfold boom in IT security spending that has begun. New products and services can be deployed that completely prevent communications from being consumed by the NSA. Trusted Computing will immunize the Internet from a pathogen that is killing trust.

SNOWDEN CALLS FOR TERMINATION OF UNWARRANTED SURVEILLANCE

JANUARY 23, 2014

This post excerpted from securitycurrent.com.

In a live chat hosted by The Courage Foundation, Edward Snowden called on the US to stop the mass collection of telephone records by the NSA, authorized under section 215 of the Patriot Act.

The Courage Foundation is a trust, audited by accountants Derek Rothera & Company in the UK, for the purpose of providing legal defense and campaign aid to journalistic sources. It is overseen by an unremunerated committee of trustees. Edward Snowden is its first recipient.

In response to Twitter user @Valio_ch's question: Do you think that the Watchdog Report by Privacy & Civil Liberties Oversight Board will have any impact at all? Snowden responded:

I don't see how Congress could ignore it, as it makes it clear there is no reason at all to maintain the 215 program. Let me quote from the official report:

"Cessation of the program would eliminate the privacy and civil liberties concerns associated with bulk collection without unduly hampering the government's efforts, while ensuring that any governmental requests for telephone calling records are tailored to the needs of specific investigations."

Snowden also denied in no uncertain terms the report from Reuters that cited "government sources" that he had used social engineering to steal co-workers credentials to get access to NSA documents.

With all due respect to Mark Hosenball, the Reuters report that put this out there was simply wrong. I never stole any passwords, nor did I trick an army of co-workers.

In a lengthy response to one question on legitimate spying by the NSA, Snowden said, "Not all spying is bad..." but he concluded, "When we're sophisticated enough to be able to break into any device in the world we want to (up to and including Angela Merkel's phone, if reports are to be believed), there's no excuse to waste our time collecting the call records of grandmothers in Missouri."

WILL THE LEADER OF THE FREE WORLD ADDRESS THAT WORLD?

JANUARY 28, 2014

This column first appeared in securitycurrent.com.

I know it seems archaic to refer to the President of the United States as the "leader of the free world," especially after 14 years of apparent decline in standing of the United States. Let's face it, trumped up charges of weapons of mass destruction and grueling never-ending wars in Afghanistan and Iraq have eroded that title considerably.

We often forget the promise and bright future that the Internet portended when it first came about. While the Cold War ended abruptly and unexpectedly in 1991, it was just in time for the unleashing of the communication revolution and force for community building worldwide that was the Internet.

I was an automotive engineer working in Detroit and found myself participating in design communities around the world. When I was called on to spend a couple of weeks in Munich working at BMW's engineering center, my international connections led to meetings with fellow engineers pushing the envelope of the then-burgeoning field of solid modeling in mechanical design. The realization that the

Internet was a revolution led me to start an ISP and never look back. After 25 years, the Internet has exceeded even the early pioneers' expectations in transforming commerce, communications, production, and yes, governments and sovereignty.

Amongst the two billion people who engage in social media, communication, and commerce, there is rarely any thought about what national interests the other person represents. Yes, there is deep curiosity about different cultures, perspectives, and what the weather is like on the other side of the globe. But national boundaries have truly been eroded. The Internet is all about personal connections, not national divisions.

All this talk about spying on other countries and national security is divisive and flies in the face of a new reality that is easily discernible if you have a short chat with anyone in their 20s. Or tune into reddit for even a few minutes. Globalization and a new world order, if not quite what George Bush Senior envisioned, have happened.

Will President Obama recognize that reality in his State of the Union Address tonight? Will he speak to assuring the American people that their right to privacy is unassailable while painting the targets of surveillance as non-US persons? A term that permeates the legal discourse within the NSA, Congress, and secret courts.

It strikes citizens of the new world as offensive that US persons somehow have more rights than their friends overseas or even north of the 49th parallel.

The draft report out of the European Parliament's Committee on Civil Liberties, Justice and Home Affairs on NSA surveillance makes European sentiment all too clear. The 52-page report cites 46 historical documents for the justification of its findings.

It: "Points specifically to US NSA intelligence programs allowing for the mass surveillance of EU citizens through direct access to the central servers of leading US internet companies (PRISM program), the analysis of content and meta data (Xkeyscore program), the circumvention of online encryption (BULLRUN), access to computer and telephone networks and access to location data, as well as to systems of the UK intelligence agency GCHQ such as its upstream surveillance activity (Temporaprogram) and decryption program (Edgehill)."

Data privacy is a concern that transcends national borders. Privacy rights in a connected world cannot be determined unilaterally by the country with apparently the most egregious collection activity.

The early speculation is that President Obama's address will be political and domestic. It will be a call to arms for the executive branch as a soon-to-be lame duck president chooses to go it alone and enact by decree the measures he sees fit. Will that do anything to assuage the trepidation these non-US persons feel when confronted with surveillance over reach?

Until 1913, State of the Union Addresses were made in written form to the two houses of Congress. Wilson began the tradition of the oral address. The idea of the State of the Union is wholly American. It is, after all, ensconced in the Constitution. Yet, as communications evolved and the SOTU became more and more of a public event, the addresses reached further around the world. Coolidge's 1923 address was the first to be broadcast on the radio. And Truman's 1947 address was the first to be televised.

FDR's most famous address was the Four Freedoms speech given at the beginning of his unprecedented third term, January 6, 1940. He used the moment to express the need to support the defenders in wartime Europe. He defined the four freedoms the West was fighting for: freedom of speech, freedom of worship, freedom from want, and freedom from fear.

Today, it will be possible for over two billion people to

listen live to President Obama's address. The world's attention is focused on the US as it struggles to be the leader of the free world. Will that leader take the bold step to declare that all peoples should share in *freedom from surveillance?*

YOU MAD, BRO? YOU WILL BE, AFTER WATCHING THESE JACOB APPLEBAUM VIDEOS

FEBRUARY 19, 2014

This post originally appeared on securitycurrent.com.

The reactions to the depth and scope of the NSA's surveillance apparatus have varied from ho-hum, "that's their job," to OMG "it's the end of the world as we know it!" Somewhere in the middle is the slow-boil rage that is going to transform the IT industry.

If you are of the ho-hum mindset that is perplexed at the outrage, even looking down at those that are so naive in their surprise at NSA surveillance, you should watch these videos of Jacob Applebaum.

Applebaum is a security researcher best known for his involvement with the anonymizing Tor network, but also famous for breaking Apple's FileVault encryption system. He came under the spotlight for his advocacy of Wikileaks, which reportedly led to his Twitter account being subpoenaed by the US Justice Department in 2010. Applebaum has been subject to numerous detentions at US borders, every traveler's nightmare expectation. He believes that he is under constant surveillance and that his apartment in Berlin, where he resides now, was subjected to a black-bag job.

With that as background, watch this presentation at the recent Chaos Computing Conference in Germany. Applebaum itemizes some of the more spooky capabilities of the NSA that appeared in a seminal article in *Der Spiegel* the same day. It was an article that he helped write, as he is one of the few technical people who has had access to the trove of Snowden documents.

[Note: Contains Classified Material]

Watch it to the end. Your lack of surprise will begin to turn to shock.

Next, watch this meeting that occurred at the Whitney Museum of Art in April 2012, well before the Snowden June 6 revelation of the NSA's secret collection of meta data from Verizon. Jake Applebaum interviews Bill Binney, one of the ThinThread whistleblowers. ThinThread was a data capture and analysis project of the NSA that was abandoned post 9/11 in favor of Trailblazer.

Binney's presentation skills are no match for Applebaum's, but pay particular attention to the clips they show of Congressional testimony. Remember, this is prior to Snowden.

And finally, continuing our reverse chronological order, watch Applebaum soon after he moved to Berlin last summer. Note the foreshadowing of things to come.

You mad, bro? You should be.

WHAT WILL A RUSSIA-UKRAINE CYBERWAR LOOK LIKE?

MARCH 4, 2014

The following post appeared in securitycurrent.com on Monday, March 3. I have added updates to reflect recent events.

This playbook has already been written. Peaceful street protests. Government crackdown. Russian agitation on behalf of "Russian speakers." And finally, Russian tanks and war planes settling the matter. Of course I am talking about Georgia in 2008, and even some similarities to Estonia in 2007.

We have come full circle in one sense. Remember the Orange Revolution in Ukraine and the popular uprising that led to new elections? One of the overlooked repercussions of those events in 2004-5 was the creation of the Nashi in March 2005, a government-sponsored youth movement in Russia, reminiscent of Nazi Germany's Brown Shirts. The Nashi, under pro-Putin Vasily Yakemenko, were created as a defense against future youth-led protest in Mother Russia.

Numbering some 120,000 aged 17-25, it is no surprise that the Nashi were implicated in the network attacks and web defacements associated with the so-called cyberwar in Estonia and attacks against Estonia's ambassador to Russia. I say so-called because there was no war. No tanks. No fighter jets. No troops crossing the borders.

The Georgian cyberwar did involve tanks, troops, and fighter jets, along with web defacements, massive DDoS attacks, and cutting of Internet access into Georgia. There was also an eerily similar coincidence with the Olympics. You may recall the 2008 Summer Olympics in Beijing with Putin and George W. Bush sitting in the stands together while Putin's playbook played out.

If Putin sticks to his playbook, here is what can be expected about the time the shooting starts in Crimea:

The "information war" that is playing out now (propaganda) will escalate to web defacement and DDoS attacks against government websites, new sites, and prominent businesses in Ukraine. The purpose will be to silence Ukraine's side of the story during the chaos.

Of the six fiber links into Ukraine, half connect to Russia. These will be cut off as they were in 2008 against Georgia.

Five and a half years since Georgia, we can expect a little more sophistication in the arsenal that Russia can bring to bear. These could include targeted attacks against telecom and power grids using malware, routing, and DDoS. There is probably no need to attack the oil and gas pipelines because Russia already controls those. Putin can simply shut off the flow, just as trains carrying supplies to Estonia were stopped at the border in 2007.

One major escalation that suggests itself is true cyber warfare: targeting intelligence, surveillance, and reconnaissance (ISR) capabilities of Ukraine's military and any country that provides such services to Ukraine. Cyber attacks against Ukraine's defensive missile guidance and targeting radar systems should not come as a surprise.

If cyberwar breaks out in the Russian-Ukraine conflict, be prepared for collateral effects including: network routing issues, network congestion, inaccessibility of Ukrainian news sites, and hacktivist attacks on Western news outlets and businesses that support Ukraine.

These reports indicate that communications in the Crimea may already be under attack.

Update March 4: According to a Renysis Blog post from February 26, Ukraine has very resilient Internet connectivity not likely to be disrupted by a single event.

According to Reuters this morning, Valentyn Nalivaichenko, the head of Ukraine's SBU security service, told a news briefing, "I confirm that an IP-telephonic attack is under way on mobile phones of members of Ukrainian parliament for the second day in row."

And this report from Georgetown Security Studies Review covered early signs of interruption of communications in Crimea on March 2.

STEM STINKS FOR CYBERSECURITY

MARCH 23, 2014

I am getting fed up with the clamor on the part of policy makers for more degrees in Science, Technology, Engineering, and Math (STEM) as the path to success in the United States, especially in cybersecurity. The numbers don't add up, and the problem of not having enough cybersecurity workers will not be solved in the short term by ramping up four year degree programs in cybersecurity.

I obtained one of those vaunted STEM degrees from the University of Michigan in 1982; a degree in aerospace engineering just when the Space Transportation System (the Shuttle) was in its final production phase and most rocket, jet, and airliner programs were on life support.

But I got lucky. In my last years at U of M, Professor Bill Anderson, a specialist in structures, began teaching graduate level courses in Finite Element Analysis (FEA). He used a new software program called MSC/NASTRAN in each of three semesters. I took every course and became adept at modeling structures and performing stress simulations for optimal design. As graduation approached, I responded to a three line ad in the Ann Arbor News looking for aerospace engineering grads with MSC/NASTRAN proficiency. I started my job at Hoover Universal, designing car seat structures and mechanisms, at the beginning of a revolution in automotive design.

By the time I was 25 years old I was owner of an engineering contracting company with 22 employees, and I went back to the University of Michigan to address the engineering staff. My thesis: Teach Tools! The response was vehement. Professors stood to denounce me. "This is a research institution! If you want to learn tools, go to VoTech!"

Fine. But wait. What VoTech? In state after state, the university systems have displaced vocational education. Other than Cass Tech and the facilities of Focus Hope, vocational education is practically dead in Michigan. When my son entered Michigan Tech, I was horrified to hear the newly appointed Dean of Engineering declare that his goal was to make Michigan Tech the number two research university in the state! The best engineers I ever worked with (or for) came from Michigan Tech. I hate to contemplate the future when this school churns out more theoretical and fewer hands-on engineers.

This past October I addressed the first Wisconsin Cyber-Security Summit at Marquette University. I reminisced about learning welding at Madison Area Technical College (MATC). I took every welding shop class they had and went on to become a welder at Bay Shipbuilding in Sturgeon Bay, Wisconsin. To this day I swell with pride when I see the Edwin H. Gott, the 1,000-foot ore carrier I built, steaming down the Detroit River. After my luncheon keynote I was informed by several people that MATC is now called Madison College, disowning the "technical" aspect. Thankfully, they still offer a one year diploma program in welding.

Yes, we still need degreed engineers, scientists, and mathematicians. But those degrees and the people who earn them are the promise of the future, not the present.

What we need in every state is a vibrant VoTech education

system while simultaneously working to remove the onus from not having a four year degree.

I was inspired by the plan of action offered by Josh Kemp, a blacksmith turned programmer, who taught himself the skills to become a junior developer and land a $70,000 salary in only seven months.

When I first made my own rapid twelve month transition from engineering to networking in 1993, I began to work with IT directors and senior management. I was surprised by how many did not have college degrees. They all had a similar story. They were COBOL programmers that entered the work force when mainframes were beginning to change the business world. They all related how they could not afford to turn down lucrative jobs as programmers to attend school. Cybersecurity represents another such turning point. Getting the skills and getting to work quickly should trump degrees.

Mike Rowe of Dirty Jobs fame has a lot to say about four year degrees and debt. He founded the mikeroweWORKS Foundation to address these problems.

Here is my prescription for creating a cybersecurity VoTech, extracted from a proposal I helped put together for the State of Michigan.

"In addition to working with the various certificate organizations, we will work with security vendors to teach and award certifications in major security tools. This is the fastest road to creating a work force that will have immediate marketability."

The top cybersecurity professionals I have worked with take one of two paths: hacking or security operations. The hacking route involves researching malware, reverse engineering, and coding. Typically these security researchers are self-taught, but there are opportunities to start at the bottom with the new breed of security intelligence vendors that are cropping up.

The other path, operational security, begins with learning tools and applying them on the job. This is the path that will generate the quickest results. Just becoming proficient in configuring and maintaining a single tool can lead to marketability in cybersecurity. Hiring managers I talk to are interested in finding people that can be productive on day one. If a candidate has experience with one of the tools in use at a company, they can jump right in.

Examples of certifications available:

Cisco Certified Network Associate Security (CCNA Security). Cisco has excelled at pushing their programs to the high school and community college level. Getting Cisco certified is one of the best ways to learn networking.

Fortinet Certified Network Security Associate. With close to a million devices deployed, having a Fortinet certification is a good market move.

Check Point Certified Security Administrator. I was in the very first class of Check Point Certified people because it was developed at Netrex, where I worked.

Palo Alto Networks Accredited Configuration Engineer. If you want to get in on the cutting edge of Next Gen firewalls, PAN is a great place to start. You can even get started with their free online learning.

Certified McAfee Security Specialist. McAfee (now Intel Security) has many certifications available in each of their products, which are widely deployed in some of the largest companies in the world.

Symantec Certified Specialist. Symantec has one of the broadest portfolios of security products. Getting certified could open doors at many companies.

RSA, the security division of EMC, has great training resources for those interested in learning advanced threat defense techniques. The NetWitness training in particular would make someone immediately employable. Most organizations I talk to are setting aside budget now for hiring active defense teams.

IBM recently announced the addition of nine schools to its Academic Initiative which already includes 200 universities and colleges. IBM assists in providing curriculum material, and most importantly, suggests which IBM tools to use in the courses.

The resources are already available to construct a course of education that could lead to lucrative employment in cybersecurity without a four year degree and for considerably less money. Those looking to address the shortfall in trained cybersecurity professionals should look to these resources for their programs. States that have systematically evolved their education systems away from VoTech have an opportunity to reverse that trend with online education supplemented with lab work using existing industry tools.

HOW SYMANTEC CAN PULL OUT OF A TAIL SPIN

MARCH 25, 2014

It should come as no surprise to anyone that the strategy of Symantec's recently fired CEO, Steve Bennett, to cut costs and improve operations, has failed miserably. As I wrote when Symantec's board replaced then-CEO Enrique Salem with Bennett, in the IT security industry innovation far outweighs the usual business practices of accounting, inventory control, and workforce "optimization." At the time I warned:

Watch out as reality sets in. I have seen this played out over and over in the security space as grown-up management is brought in. They bring discipline, focus, and operational discipline. But because they do not understand the security space the company starts a slow decline into oblivion.

A financial analyst made the comment: "The combination of consistent execution and operational discipline is exactly the order Symantec needed."

To which I responded:

Consistent execution and operational discipline is exactly what will kill Symantec. Or rather, relying on operational fixes alone will kill Symantec.

Most security product companies (there are over 2,000 of

them) are focused on one or two products that provide some differentiated value to the market. But large companies face a growth and competition wall. Symantec in particular demonstrated the model of innovation by acquisition, based on the valid concept that it is easier to identify a market-winning product than it is to invent one.

Large vendors with tens of thousands of customers globally can thrive by acquiring product vendors that their existing customers will purchase. Customers have lots of reasons to do so. In their own drive towards operational efficiency they seek to reduce the number of vendors they have to deal with: fewer contracts, fewer license agreements, and often, lower prices.

In some rare cases the vendor can even consolidate the administration of multiple products into one management console, which means lower costs for operations—and might even lead to better overall security.

Symantec cannot afford to continue to shuffle through the typical A-list of contenders for chief executives of publicly traded companies. It is time for drastic measures. Here are two things the next CEO must do:

1. **Divest.** Symantec should reverse the merger with Veritas that cost $13.5 billion in 2004. Security is not like other market segments. The space is constantly evolving because it has a driver that only Aerospace and Defense shares: threat actors. Being one-half data center software company and one-half desktop anti-virus company makes no sense at all. Split off the data center business and let the two halves thrive.

2. **Acquire.** The IT security industry experienced a tremendous disruption with the publishing of Mandiant's APT1 report in 2013. Startups and fast-moving established companies have been rushing to address the need to shorten the time from successful incursion to cleanup. It is an acknowledgement that anti-virus is powerless to stop attacks and products have to be deployed that detect the breach,

analyze it, and manage the remediation. Which vendors should Symantec acquire? Well, I have a list…

To choose its next leader, my advice to Symantec's board is look for an industry insider. Only someone that has lived and breathed the daily battle against rising threats can understand what is needed. There will be acquisition, integration, and sales challenges. Judging by Symantec's falling revenue and rising profits, I would say the operational efficiencies have all been put in place. The new CEO can focus on making the hard strategic decisions needed to save the company.

WHY NETWORK SECURITY VENDORS SHOULD STAY AWAY FROM ENDPOINT SECURITY, AND VICE-VERSA

APRIL 7, 2014

There would be many more successful security companies if their founders and leaders had a better understanding of the IT security space.

One fallacy that will not die is the idea that to grow, a vendor must be a full stack solution. There is no question that every organization needs to deploy layered security. Solutions are needed for data security, user identity and access management, endpoint security, server security, network security, and most recently, cloud and mobile device security. No matter how enthusiastic Wall Street may become, there will *never* be a single vendor that dominates in the complete stack.

Let's go back to basics. At the simplest level of security, commandments are these rules:

1. A secure network assumes the host is hostile.
2 .A secure host assumes the network is hostile.
3. A secure application assumes the user is hostile.

These rules are very powerful when applied to product strategies. Any proposed product that binds any two of host, network, and application, will be a market failure. Sadly, the messaging around coupling can be very compelling.

Thus, when FireEye acquired Mandiant, there was wide acceptance of the idea that somehow FireEye needed an endpoint product to complete its solution; so much so that Pal Alto Networks just burned $200 million in acquiring Israeli endpoint security solution Cyvera.

Symantec is a case in point. Symantec has acquired over 75 security vendors over the years. Many of them are network security. Remember the Symantec firewalls acquired with Axent? Today, Symantec has 121 products in its catalog. Only web gateway security is a network product. Despite billions spent on trying to get into the network security space, Symantec failed. Actually, Symantec succeeded at becoming a dominant endpoint security vendor with forays into certificates and endpoint encryption.

McAfee also has attempted to have a firewall solution, first with Gauntlet, which it spun off to Secure Computing, and then re-acquired along with Secure Computing. Most recently, probably thanks to Gartner's market-confusing ramblings about Next Gen Firewalls, McAfee acquired StoneSoft. McAfee's acquisition of Intruvert and successful market penetration of its IPS solution is the best example of an endpoint security vendor being successful in the network security space. However, when Intel acquired McAfee there was no mention of the large network security business McAfee had built by acquisition. Perhaps Intel did not want to highlight to the broad base of partners that use Intel processors in their network devices that they had entered the space?

Sophos, an anti-virus vendor, has just acquired its second UTM vendor, Cyberoam. What does that say about the success of its first acquisition in the space, Astaro? (See Sophos + Astaro: Good companies, bad deal). Perhaps Sophos is actually attempting to pivot away from endpoint security and become a network security vendor. That would be a good strategy as traditional anti-virus becomes less and less effective at countering the latest malware.

Check Point Software has had its own less-than-stellar attempts to get into endpoint security, first with the acquisition of consumer desktop firewall vendor ZoneAlarm, and then with the acquisition of Pointsec, a full disk encryption vendor. Its market share in endpoint is small and probably does not justify the investment it made in those acquisitions.

None of these companies have experienced any benefit from having end-point and network solutions. There is no synergy and the most successful acquisitions come when the acquirer keeps the two businesses separate.

The reason network and endpoint security solutions do not mix are plentiful:

1. Buying centers. Endpoint security is managed by a different team within the enterprise than is security. That means different sales cycles, different sales teams, separate contracts, and most importantly, different skill sets. There is a broad gap between the Microsoft Windows experts responsible for laptop and desktop configuration and the wizards that maintain switches, routers, and firewalls.

2. Brand perception. Let's face it, anti-virus products are a pain to work with. Every end user has had frustrating slowdowns, system crashes, and false positives from their endpoint AV. Those users include the network administrators. The last thing they want is a product from the same vendor on their network where slowdowns and crashes are damaging to productivity. Ever wonder why Microsoft never introduced a router and every attempt at introducing a network firewall has failed completely?

3. Best of breed. Every organization needs the best firewall and the best endpoint protection for their environment. They will always make those decisions independently.

A full stack security strategy is one of consolidation. But the security industry does not consolidate. Unlike every other segment of the IT industry, security has an outside driver: threat actors. Cybercriminals and nation-states force each security vendor to innovate or die. It is hard enough to stay ahead of the curve in one space. Attempting to do it in two spaces is futile.

WHERE ARE THE US TECH HEROES?

APRIL 7, 2014

It has been three months since the world learned that the NSA's Signals Intelligence Directorate, through its Tailored Access Operations (TAO), has been deploying backdoors in Cisco, Juniper, Huawei, Dell, and several hard drive manufacturers' gear.

The response from them so far? Weak protestations that they knew nothing of this. What they don't get is that this response is inadequate. Don't Cisco and Juniper understand that their flagship products, their routers and firewalls, have been demonstrated to be insecure?

Don't they understand that this is an existential threat to their business? And conversely, that fixing these issues with their products would be a differentiator that could protect their market share?

On December 30, I called for vendors to offer a substantive response, including:

- Develop tools to detect when their systems have been compromised and make these available to their customers.

- Conduct a comprehensive review of their architectures with an eye towards a much more sophisticated attacker than ever before. All security is a compromise. But too often compromises justified by underestimating an attacker's resources eventually succumb.

- Assign a Red Team to break its own products.

- Use network-fuzzing tools to discover previously unknown vulnerabilities.

- Evaluate how hardware roots of trust that store keys to authenticate software and updates can be incorporated in product designs.

- Look at architectures that use separate monitoring devices in front of and behind their products to detect when they have been compromised.

With no response from Cisco, Juniper, or Huawei to date (at least publicly), every customer of these vendors should be planning their own response.

Perhaps the most comprehensive approach will be the result of a fundamental shift in trust. Knowing that persistent malware is being deployed to network gear, even possibly at the point of manufacture if the latest revelations of NSA attacks against Huawei are believed, means that network gear cannot be trusted.

While inspections of installed routers and firewalls from these vendors is required to establish that an organization is free of BANANAGLEE, ZESTYLEAK, and JETPLOW persistent backdoors, that will not be enough.

Monitoring of routers and firewalls is now required. The best way to do this is put network-sniffing appliances on the outside of the network to look for command and control communications with the NSA. Network gear should be re-imaged and updated. Any communication from the firewalls and routers should be detected and blocked to prevent FEEDTROUGH from reinstalling the persistent TAO (Tailored Access Operations) malware.

Network vendors are going to have to dramatically revamp their architectures. The descriptions in the ANT Catalog indicate that BIOS attacks are part of the NSA's approach. In the near future, cryptographically secure assurance modules will have to be deployed so that customers can be confident that the OS kernel has not been compromised in their primary networking gear.

These are trying times for the IT security industry. As much as vendors don't like to talk about it, networking gear is not capable of fulfilling the basic expectations of resilience to attack. All organizations are going to have to spend more to ensure their own security. The vendors with the most effective fixes will win.

20 CYBER POLICY EXPERTS TO FOLLOW ON TWITTER

APRIL 7, 2014

The emerging field of cyber policy is attracting government, academic, and technology experts. Here is a list of cyber policy experts from around the world who are well worth following on Twitter. You can follow them individually or read their posts on this Twitter list we have created. Please tweet suggested additions to the list to @securitycurrent.

David Betz is Senior Lecturer of War Studies, King's College London and co-author of Cyberspace and the State with Tim Stevens. Follow @Betz451

Myriam Dunn Cavelty is a Lecturer, Master of Strategic Security Management for the Austrian Federal Security Academy. Follow @CyberMyri

Ron Deibert is the Director of the Citizen Lab, Munk School of Global Affairs, University of Toronto. He is the author of Black Code: Inside the Battle for Cyberspace. Follow @RonDeibert

Bill Hagestad (@Red-DragonRising) is a consultant, speaker and expert on Chinese cyber warfare. He is author of 21st Century Chinese Cyberwarfare and Chinese Information Warfare Doctrine Development 1994 - 2014, among others. Lieutenant Colonel (ret) US Marine Corps. Follow @RedDragon1949

Jason Healey is the Director, Cyber Statecraft Initiative at the Atlantic Council. He is also the editor behind A Fierce Domain: Conflict in Cyberspace 1986 to 2012. Follow @Jason_Healey

Toomas Hendrik Ilves is the president of Estonia. Follow his tweets at @IlvesToomas

James A. Lewis is the Director and Senior Fellow Strategic Technologies Program at the Center for Strategic and International Studies in Washington, DC. Follow @james_a_lewis

Sean Lawson is a professor in the Department of Communication at the University of Utah. He Tweets about cyberwar, ICTs & security, and military theory. He is the author of Nonlinear Science and Warfare: Chaos, complexity and the US military in the information age and a Forbes contributor. Follow @seanlawson

Stefano Mele is an attorney in the Intelligence & Security Legal Department of Carnelutti Law Firm in Milan, Italy. He writes frequently on cyber policy issues. Follow @MeleStefano

Patrick C. Miller is an Advisor on Critical Infrastructure Security and Compliance. He is Managing Principal at The Anfield Group and Founder, Director, and President Emeritus of EnergySec. Follow @PatrickCMiller

Lynette Nusbacher is an expert on horizon scanning and strategy. She was part of the team that created two of the UK's National Security Strategies and set up Britain's National Security Council. She is principal at Nusbacher Associates. Follow @Nusbacher

Dan Philpott is a solution architect at Natoma Technologies and curator of FISMApedia. Follow @danphilpott

Tom Quillin is the Director of Cybersecurity Technology & Initiatives at Intel Corporation. Follow @tomquillin

Thomas Rid is Professor of Security Studies at King's

College London and author of Cyberwar Will Not Take Place. Follow him @RidT.

Rafal Rohozinski is CEO of SecDev Group and Senior Fellow at the International Institute for Strategic Studies. Follow @rohozinski

Adam Segal is the Maurice R. Greenberg Senior Fellow China Studies at Council on Foreign Relations. He is the author of Advantage: How American Innovation Can Overcome the Asian Challenge. Follow @adschina

Peter W. Singer is the Director of the Center for 21st Century Security and Intelligence at the Brookings Institute. He is the author of Wired for War and Cybersecurity and Cyberwar: What Everyone Needs to Know. Follow @peterwsinger

Tim Stevens is a Research Associate in the War Studies department at Kings College London. He is co-author of Cyberspace and the State with David Betz. Follow @tcstvns

Tiffany Strauchs Rad is an independent researcher and Adjunct Professor at the University of Southern Maine. Follow @TiffanyRad

Dave Weinstein is a Senior Cybersecurity Consultant for Deloitte. He was a Strategic Planner for US Cyber Command. Follow @djweinstein23

There are many more experts on cyber strategy, policy, and national security to follow. I update the list continuously at @cyberwar.

WAS THE HEARTBLEED BUG DISCLOSED RESPONSIBLY?

APRIL 16, 2014

Responsible disclosure is a burning issue in the world of software and security. If a security flaw is discovered by a researcher (sometimes called a hacker), what are the responsible actions the discoverer should take? There was a time when many security flaws were just published willy-nilly to a mail list or website. Researchers sought the fame and glory of being the first to uncover a serious flaw in Microsoft, Adobe, or a network firewall.

Over time, a set of behaviors became the norm:
1. Notify the software provider
2. Wait a reasonable amount of time
3. Disclose

Vendors have encouraged this behavior by publicizing the names or identities of the researchers who report a security bug, and even pay bounties for responsibly disclosed bugs.

Bad guys like cyber criminals and certain intelligence agencies do not disclose at all. They exploit. A so-called zero-day vulnerability is too valuable to them.

. . .

OPEN SOURCE SOFTWARE projects have a continuous process for reporting and fixing bugs. The disjointed communities of developers, like that of OpenSSL, work continuously to address flaws.

Was the potentially devastating Heartbleed bug disclosed properly? You decide.

An abridged timeline of events is:

- Friday, March 21 (or before): Neel Mehta of Google Security discovers Heartbleed vulnerability.

- Monday, March 31 (or before): Cloudflare patches for the bug

- Wednesday, April 2: Finnish IT security testing firm Codenomicon separately discovers the same bug.

- Monday, April 7 ~13:13 - Most of the world finds out about the issue through heartbleed.com.

There was quite a bit of back and forth within the open source community in the short two weeks from discovery to public disclosure. See the complete timeline put together by Fairfax Media.

My take is yes, considering the severity and the complications, Google and Codenomicon could not have done much better.

GOING BACK TO (CYBER) SCHOOL

MAY 3, 2014

Academia is acquiring an interest in cyber education on many fronts. Not likely to crank out cyber warriors at anywhere close to the rate needed to meet current demand, they are nonetheless anxious to participate in a real trend.

De Montfort University's Cyber Security Centre in Leicester, England, offers undergrad, graduate, and PhD degrees in cybersecurity and forensics. Tim Watson, its first director, has recently moved on to the University of Warwick to lead the Cyber Security Centre at WMG, University of Warwick. WMG offers degree programs at the Masters level.

In early April, Israel's Tel Aviv University announced the formation of new center for Cyber Interdisciplinary research in cooperation with the National Cyber Bureau and led by Major Gen. (Ret.) Professor Isaac Ben-Israel.

And now the most hallowed of military academies, West Point, has announced plans for a cyber school. The Chairman of the Army Cyber Institute will be retired Lt. Gen. Rhett Hernandez, the first chief of Army Cyber Command. The Director of the Army Cyber Institute, Col. Greg Conti, said that they would be bringing on 74 staff over three years. According to military news site C4ISRNet:

The institution, which aims to take on national policy questions and develop a bench of top-tier experts for the Pentagon, will be defining how cyber warfare is waged, to steer and inform the direction of the Army.

This is an interesting development, considering that the US Cyber Command was formed well before there was any sort of cyber discipline within the Pentagon. Of course the military has had extensive experience warding off attacks, or succumbing to attacks, as was the case with the Agent.btz worm that traversed SIPRNet to infect a good portion of defense networks. But senior leadership within the military has not been exposed to cyber history, cyber policy, or cyberwar fighting disciplines.

Most military academies and centers of thought leadership are justifiably accused of teaching how to fight the last war. This is evident even today when a large proportion of teaching and academic research goes into counter-insurgency (COIN). Cyber is different than traditional war fighting in that on any given day there are thousands of low-level battles being fought. The military is exposed to those. For once it is possible to foresee the future of war fighting that will surely involve the use of network attacks, embedded backdoors, autonomous weaponized software, attacks on satellite communications and ISR platforms, and exploitations of the many vulnerabilities in weapons platforms.

SANDBOX VENDORS IGNORE MICROSOFT LICENSE AGREEMENTS

MAY 20, 2014

An examination of Microsoft's Customer License Agreement (CLA) for embedded systems indicates that there is no provision for a vendor to ship appliances with multiple virtual instances of Windows, or its popular Office productivity suite. In fact, shipping Windows in a virtualized environment is expressly prohibited.

From the CLA:

(2b3) Company may distribute more than one Product (or copies of the same Product) on the same Embedded System, but only if all configurations of the Embedded System containing such Products (individually or in combination) comply with the terms of this Agreement and ATs.

And from a document of those "ATs" titled ADDITIONAL TERMS FOR RUNTIMES FOR OEM EMBEDDED DESKTOP OPERATING SYSTEMS PRODUCTS:

(12) Virtualization

Company may not install this Product in any virtual (or otherwise emulated) hardware system. Unless otherwise provided in these ATs and except for use of the VHD Boot feature in Windows 7 Ultimate for Embedded Systems and Windows Embedded 8 Pro, Company's license excludes rights 1) to use any virtual machine software that is part of the Product, or 2) to create or use files in the VHD file format supported by this Product.

As attackers have become more sophisticated they have concentrated on creating malware that avoids detection by endpoint anti-virus, leaving the enterprise exposed.

Sandboxing technology involves executing an attacker's payload in a virtual (or sometimes emulated) instance, usually Windows because it is the most highly targeted, and examining its actions for malicious intent.

Once advanced malware is detected it can be quarantined. In addition, key indicators are extracted from the malware such as file names and the IP addresses it attempts to call back to. These Key Indicators of Compromise are then used in security analytics solutions to detect activity by the attackers elsewhere on the network.

FireEye, the advanced malware protection vendor that was the first to market with a virtual sandbox using up to ten instances of Windows XP, appears at least initially to have neglected to resolve the licensing issues with Microsoft before going to market. FireEye's Web MPS 7.1.0 Operators Guide even pushes licensing responsibility on to its customers, stating in part:

THIRD PARTY SOFTWARE IS (IN ADDITION TO THE TERMS AND CONDITIONS OF THIS AGREEMENT, SUBJECT TO AND GOVERNED BY (AND LICENSEE AGREES TO AND WILL INDEMNIFY FIREEYE FOR NONCOMPLIANCE WITH) THE RESPECTIVE LICENSES FOR SUCH THIRD PARTY SOFTWARE.

A FireEye document titled "The FireEye Difference" lists the software installed on FireEye guest images. In addition to Windows, the list includes Microsoft Word, Excel, and PowerPoint; products that Microsoft also limits the distribution of in embedded systems. When asked, FireEye chose not to provide comment on this issue.

Other vendors are selling sandbox appliances that host multiple instances of Windows and other Microsoft applications.

Palo Alto Network's sandbox, WildFire, is a high-end hardware appliance. According to its documentation, Wild-Fire contains Windows XP and the full Microsoft Office suite. An update announcement from Palo Alto Networks states:

Expanded Sandbox Operating Systems—Microsoft Windows 7 32/bit has been added to the WildFire environment. When a file is analyzed by WildFire, it will be run in *both* Windows XP and Windows 7. On a WF-500 WildFire appliance, you will need to select an image that will contain Windows XP or Windows 7 as well as a combination of other applications, such as different versions of Adobe Reader, and MS Office.

Other vendors such as Trend Micro, which ships a sandbox called Deep Discovery Inspector, encountered the Microsoft licensing issue early on and designed their product in such a way that the end user installs their own licensing for Microsoft products, often the standard corporate image. Trend Micro reports that only in the last three months have they been able to help Microsoft create a new licensing regime that recognizes the need for running desktop software in a virtualized sandbox.

Fortinet, a vendor of primarily gateway security appliances, told securitycurrent that they delayed the introduction of their FortiSandbox product when they noticed (and Microsoft confirmed) this issue with Microsoft's CLA. They eventually resolved the issue for Microsoft Windows and launched the FortiSandbox product in February.

Check Point Software's datasheet for its Threat Emulation Private Cloud Appliances also lists Microsoft Office products Word, Excel and PowerPoint. Check Point too has worked with Microsoft to ensure that they are authorized to ship Windows in their sandbox products.

New entrant in the sandbox segment Cyphort reports that they ensured that they had a CLA from Microsoft that allowed them to embed licensed products before they went to market this March. Each product ships with a card that lists the Windows licenses on the appliance.

The licensing agreements Fortinet and Trend Micro reached with Microsoft will likely become the template for the other vendors once they address this issue. However, there apparently is still no agreement that permits the distribution of virtualized embedded instances of products other than Windows (e.g., Office suite or products). One work-around is for sandbox vendors to ship the free readers for Office and Adobe products.

It appears that FireEye and Palo Alto Networks have taken short cuts in getting their virtual Windows-based appliances to market.

This is most likely an issue that will be resolved in due course after Microsoft adjusts to a market reality they did not foresee: that security vendors would need to host multiple versions of their desktop operating systems inside Linux-based appliances. Specifically, these vendors will need to reach a similar agreement with Microsoft. And even then, Microsoft Office will have to be removed from these sandboxes unless yet another CLA amendment can be agreed upon. But in the meantime these vendors are most likely in violation of their existing license agreement with Microsoft.

SECURITY INDUSTRY FIGHTS SURVEILLANCE STATE WITH WORDS

MAY 26, 2014

Full disclosure per Forbes policy: All of the vendors mentioned in this post have been my clients for strategic advisory services during the last ten years.

On May 13, Cisco's General Counsel Mark Chandler reacted strongly to further news of NSA exploiting Cisco gear, sparked in part by the publication of Glenn Greenwald's book on Snowden and the leaked documents.

Chandler protested that the US government is causing damage to the tech industry. Along with the publishing of No Place to Hide: Edward Snowden, the NSA, and the US Surveillance State, Greenwald posted supporting documents that had not been previously disclosed.

One of the new documents (p. 149 of *No Place to Hide*) depicted the interdiction lab at the NSA's Tailored Access Operations (TAO) with three operatives, faces averted, unpacking a box with conspicuous Cisco branding on the side.

The bellicose document goes on:

Such operations involving **supply-chain interdiction** are some of the most productive operations of

TAO, because they pre-position access points into hard target networks around the world.

In his reaction to these documents, Chandler speaks strongly:

The tension between security and freedom has become one the most pressing issues of our day. Societies wracked by terror cannot be truly free, but an overreaching government can also undermine freedom.

And then he goes on to claim:

When we learn of a security vulnerability, we respond by validating it, informing our customers, and fixing it. We react the same when we find that a customer's security has been impacted by external forces, regardless of what country or form of government or how that security breach occurred.

John Chambers, CEO of Cisco, has lodged a formal protest with President Obama over the NSA's interdiction and compromising of US tech gear. His letter, published by re/code, repeats Mr. Chandler's claim: "...when we learn of a security vulnerability, we respond by validating it, informing our customers, and fixing it as soon as possible."

Both the General Counsel's statement and the CEO's letter to the President make valid points. But where are the responses that are within Cisco's power and fulfill the statements above? For that matter, Dell, HP, Juniper, and several hard drive manufacturers have also been implicated in the TAO ANT Catalog published by *Der Spiegel* last December.

On December 29, 2013, these vendors did indeed learn of vulnerabilities in their products, vulnerabilities that the NSA claims cannot be removed even with a complete wiping and updating of firmware.

What has been done to "validate" the existence of the code-named malware such as BANANAGLEE in Cisco PIX and Juniper firewalls? Or ZESTYLEEK, malware crafted by the NSA's Cryptanalysis and Exploitation Services (CES) for Juniper?

Has there been any communication between these compromised vendors and their customers? Were any procedures recommended for determining if their gear had NSA backdoors? Have any such infected devices been located?

From the pictures, the TAO interdiction lab is not set up for large scale operations, so it may be difficult and up to customers to identify compromised machines. Greenwald provides a document that may lend a clue to finding them (p. 145 of *No Place to Hide*).

In the document titled CLOSE ACCESS SIGADS, September 10, 2010, the HIGHLANDS mission is identified as "collection from implants." Implant is the NSA's term for backdoors. The embassies of Brazil in Washington DC and New York City are identified with the HIGHLANDS mission, as are those of EU/UN, France, Greece, India, and Japan. It is highly likely that these embassies are customers of either Cisco or Juniper, or Dell or HP.

What have these vendors done to fix the problem, as John Chambers claims are the normal practice?

Strongly worded protests can put elected officials on notice, especially coming from those with successful lobbying teams. But words of protest fall short of allaying distrust of customers worldwide. Actions are needed to back those words.

The full scope of the NSA's activities can be terrifying to contemplate for a technology vendor, but a technological response is possible. It will be important for the entrenched vendors to act before smaller or foreign vendors take the lead in producing surveillance-proofed solutions.

Pressure from the big vendors with a voice in DC can be applied to limit the surveillance state from continuing to spend taxpayer dollars to counter the defenses devised to protect privacy and security. But action must be taken immediately to reassure customers.

IS GENERAL ALEXANDER WORTH $30K A DAY?

JULY 1, 2014

Congressman Alan Grayson made waves last week when he sent letters to the Securities Industry and Financial Markets Association(SIFMA), the Consumer Bankers Association, and the Financial Services Roundtable assailing former head of the NSA, Keith Alexander. In each letter, Grayson cited a Bloomberg article that revealed that Alexander's new consulting firm was commanding hefty fees of anywhere from $600k to $1 million per month.

Grayson reminded these organizations that General Alexander was in possession of classified material and that he should not be selling that information:

Disclosing or misusing classified information for profit is, as Mr. Alexander well knows, a felony. I question how Mr. Alexander can provide any of the services he is offering unless he discloses or misuses classified information, including extremely sensitive sources and methods. Without the classified information that he acquired in his former position, he literally would have nothing to offer you.

Those are strong words coming from a Congressman. They also indicate a lack of understanding of the IT security mindset. All consultants share valuable information every day on the job without revealing sources or clients. It is part of the job. I have worked closely with General Alexander's predecessor and have seen him provide tremendous value to his clients without even hinting at classified information.

Are the astronomical fees that Bloomberg reports worth it? If Alexander actually moved the needle at these financial services organizations and got them to understand the level of threat they face, then yes, a million dollars is well worth it.

Could they get those same services for less? Yes, but whoever delivered the message would not carry the same weight of conviction as the man who led the building of the surveillance state, an endeavor that took advantage of an intelligence windfall that other nations and organizations are quickly recognizing and exploiting.

IS THERE A SECOND NSA LEAKER?

JULY 3, 2014

This morning a partial analysis of the NSA's **XKEYSCORE** code was published in Germany. Jacob Applebaum, an evangelist for Tor, was one of the authors.

The report details specific rules written for one of the NSA's data collection tools, **XKEYSCORE**, which collects the IP addresses of Tor bridges and users of the Tor network.

Tor is an anonymizing service used by many human rights activists and dissidents around the world to access the Internet and escape persecution from their governments, like China. It is also reportedly highly targeted by the NSA.

One of the amazing offshoots of today's story is that first Cory Doctorow speculated that the revealed source code came from a second leaker, not Snowden:

Another expert said that s/he believed that this leak may come from a second source, not Edward Snowden, as s/he had not seen this in the original Snowden docs; and had seen other revelations that also appeared independent of the Snowden materials. If that's true, it's big news, as Snowden was the first person to ever leak docs from the NSA. The existence of a potential second source means that Snowden may have inspired some of his former colleagues to take a long, hard look at the agency's cavalier attitude to the law and decency.

This was quickly backed up by a statement from Bruce Schneier, who has worked directly with Glenn Greenwald to help analyze the Snowden trove, specifically in relation to the subverting of encryption algorithms.

Schneier posted on his site:

And, since Cory said it, I do not believe that this came from the Snowden documents. I also don't believe the TAO catalog came from the Snowden documents. I think there's a second leaker out there.

In other words, Schneier apparently is confirming that he had not seen the TAO ANT Catalog in the Snowden collection, which he keeps on a separate laptop that he has never connected to the Internet.

A second NSA leak spells big trouble for the surveillance state.

HOW PIVOTS ARE CREATING THE NEW CROP OF FAST GROWING IT SECURITY VENDORS

AUGUST 20, 2014

In decades past, the trajectory of new enterprise security vendors was easy to project. There was the early development phase, which after 12-18 months would transition to beta customer acquisition, which invariably included Bank of America and Morgan Stanley, which appear to buy one of everything. Then would come the launch and a 2-3 year period of customer growth. After a total of five years, market momentum would either push the vendor to an IPO or a high valuation acquisition by a bigger player.

Along the way there would be variations on this model. Sometimes it would be a marriage of equals to create a more complete offering, sometimes it would be an early acquisition for the people or the technology. Sometimes it would be a pivot to an adjacent space.

As the IT security industry continues to grow at an overall pace of 24% year over year, we are beginning to see something new. Established vendors, sometimes already public, apply their successful products in other spaces to the security problem. Or, they pivot from an OEM model to a direct sales model.

There are three vendors worth noting that are executing on such pivots.

Mocana has an entrenched business selling software libraries to developers for encryption and containerization for mobile device apps. They have built a successful business selling to device manufacturers and are already embedded in many of the devices sold by other vendors. Now they are embarking on an enterprise strategy. Atlas by Mocana is an end-to-end security solution for mobile devices. Client software connects to the Atlas appliance at the enterprise edge. It is not another MDM (Mobile Device Management) solution. It is a way to secure access to corporate apps remotely.

CSG Invotas is a division of the 3,700-employee CSG International, a company that has worked with large organizations, mostly telecom providers, to automate problem resolution. The Invotas division has correctly determined that the next big thing in IT security is automated response to targeted attacks. The software solution works with most IPS, firewall, and network gear that may be already deployed at a customer to orchestrate an automated response.

There is some heavy lifting involved in deploying Invotas. Getting from informed detection to effective response requires that an organization can map out the steps required. But once that mapping has been determined, a response can be executed in seconds from detection, instead of hours or days. One demonstration that Invotas understands security operations is the way they pre-populate the system with approved change control. Mature companies with an existing Security Operation Center (SOC) and MSSPs should look at Invotas to shorten mean time to remediation. Future attacks are only going to become faster and more destructive.

Norse is one of the fastest moving new security vendors on the scene. A year ago they were unknown, focusing almost exclusively on fraud detection for large financials. But in order to collect the data they needed for fraud detection Norse had built over 30 data collection points around the globe. This vast network gave Atlanta-based Norse visibility into new threat vectors and malicious IP addresses to create a complete reputation database for the entire Internet. They are partnering with gateway security vendors and APT defense vendors to provide them with feeds and they are building their own Dark-Watch appliances to deploy when existing devices cannot handle the state memory required to apply rules to millions of addresses. For a visual demonstration of the Norse reach watch the live IPViking on their website.

Keep an eye on these pivots.

SECURITY NEVER SLEEPS, ESPECIALLY ON THREE DAY WEEKENDS

SEPTEMBER 3, 2014

As summer is drawing to an end many IT security professionals are returning to their desks after vacations and trips to drop freshmen off at their new schools. A quick check of emails, Twitter, Facebook, and news sites will reveal that security neither sleeps nor vacations.

A quick recap:

Celebrity Photo Leaks. There is an FBI cyber manhunt on for the purported "hackers" who released risqué selfies of over 100 models and movie stars on Sunday. A special subreddit was created just to track the leaks as they came out. It garnered 130,000 subscribers in three days. Security blogger Graham Cluley has the best round up of likely scenarios that explain the leaks.

One scenario that Cluley does not consider is that this was more of a peer pressure flood than a specific targeted attack on Apple's iCloud service. There is evidence that there is an underground of creepers who collect and trade celebrity nudes. One such creep leaked some pics and everyone else piled on. This theory fits the multiple leak sources and the age of the stolen pics, as well as Apple's own analysis of the leaks.

Home Depot hack. Brian Krebs is reporting that banks are seeing their customers' credit cards for sale on underground sites. The usual cross-referencing points to Home Depot as the source of the stolen credit card credentials. This may be similar to the Target breach, which had so much impact this year. There is of course a big difference between Target and Home Depot, which has had a mature security team in place for years and unlike Target has a CISO, Jeff Mitchell.

JPMorgan Chase attacks. Although details are sketchy, Bloomberg reports that the bank suffered a major breach from Russian hackers. Sensitive files belonging to senior executives were stolen.

If major Russian hacking groups have been given the go ahead to hack US financial systems, there will be other such stories breaking soon. Keep in mind that these breaches, which are apparently going further than typical cybercrime targeting account credentials, could be the reconnaissance phase of much more serious attacks, attacks that could lead to debilitating destruction of IT infrastructure.

NATO set to deem Cyber Attacks as reason to invoke Article V. When Russia engaged Estonia in massive cyber attacks in 2007, Toomas Hendrik Ilves, Estonia's President, called on NATO to invoke Article V, which calls on NATO to come to the aid of a signatory state. At the meeting in Wales of the NATO members this week the plan is to adopt a resolution that recognizes cyber attacks.

From The New York Times:

For the first time, a cyber attack on any of the 28 NATO nations could be declared an attack on all of them, much like a ground invasion or an airborne bombing.

Momentum has built for this since President Ilve's call for help. NATO's current concern over Russia's invasion of Eastern Ukraine is just one factor. A better understanding of the Law of Armed Conflict and cyber, thanks to the production of the Tallinn Manual on the International Law Applicable to Cyber Warfare, is another important step.

Fake cell phone towers? According to a secure cell phone vendor, they have discovered 17 fake cell phone towers in the US that break their encrypted connections. There are many more explanations for this than a tinfoil-hat conspiracy theory, but stay tuned for more on this.

Briefcase EMP attacks. The greatest threat to IT infrastructure (after asteroids and comets hitting the earth) is a Carrington Event-class Coronal Mass Ejection (CME) or an upper atmosphere nuclear detonation that sets off an Electro Magnetic Pulse (EMP). We usually don't include this in our Risk Management profiles because why bother? But targeted EMP attacks are plausible according to an IEEE article that you should read. Think about the isolation of data centers and sensors needed to detect this type of attack.

That should give you enough to worry about this week, if you can avoid being absorbed by the geo-political conflicts seemingly everywhere.

Oh, one more thing to be concerned about, especially if travel is an important business consideration. A series of volcanoes in Iceland are threatening a major eruption. Watch the rumblings in this great real-time data display of earthquake activity. If your people can't travel by air, there will be increased demands on your video conferencing capabilities.

SHELLSHOCK BUG IN BASH COULD SPAWN WORM

SEPTEMBER 25, 2014

By now you have heard about a new bug in one of the most popular Unix shell programs, the Bourne-again Shell, or Bash. If you run Mac OS X you probably have used Bash, as it is the default terminal app. Shellshock is a "bug" in the way Heartbleed is a "bug." It is a mistake in implementing code. Shellshock allows anyone (or anything) that has shell access to execute arbitrary code.

Robert Graham at Errata Security wrote a little test to demonstrate how he could get machines to execute ping commands. There are lots of vulnerable machines. Someone has already taken Rob's script and modified it to download malware. That's what a worm does. Note the "Thanks-Rob" in the code giving Graham credit.

This is one of the easiest exploits ever to incorporate into just about any attack scenario. Heartbleed was much more difficult to take advantage of but led to at least one damaging attack. TrustedSec has attributed the CHS breach to the presence of the Heartbleed bug in Juniper devices.

Just about every network device (routers, switches, SDN) runs on a flavor of Unix and Bash is widely deployed. Systems that are vulnerable will be those that allow components to run shell scripts, a very common short cut.

While the use of Shellshock for highly-targeted attacks on systems that you probably don't even know about within your network is the biggest long-term concern, the short-term possibilities are frightening. The code linked to above could quickly create a SQL Slammer-type Internet meltdown.

One of the thousands of systems that Graham has already discovered is induced to download a version of Graham's scanner. The infected host (probably a web server) scans for its next targets (thousands of them) and induces them to download the exploit code (via wget in the sample code), and those in turn start scanning and exploiting.

In 2003 SQL Slammer brought the Internet down in about 12 minutes. ISPs worked over the weekend to filter out the ports that SQL Slammer used. An "easy" fix like that will not be possible since Shellshock can use any port and Graham's test is using port 80 for HTTP.

SQL Slammer was bad. But the author released it late on a Friday US east coast time, giving some indication that he/she had some cause for concern. The "Thanks-Rob" worm, when it appears, could be created easily by someone without the same compunctions and get out of control very quickly. We won't have any warning.

DATA LEAK PREVENTION HAS A NEW CHALLENGE: INTRODUCING THROUGH GLASS TRANSFER

OCTOBER 1, 2014

Yesterday at the COSAC 21st International Computer Security Symposium and SABSA World Congress in Naas, Ireland, a researcher demonstrated a protocol he had devised that automates the transfer of data from any display to devices like smart phones.

COSAC is one of the longest running computer security conferences. This year it drew 60 security experts from around the world to discuss pressing issues and new developments in a congenial environment.

Presenting at COSAC is often fraught with stress for first-time attendees as they are frequently interrupted and must be prepared to address all objections, conjectures, and random observations from an eclectic crowd of very smart people.

Ian Latter presented his body of work today on two protocols he had created that effectively demonstrate the futility of 100% data leak prevention (DLP). The fact that critical data is ultimately displayed on a screen has long been the one open hole in DLP.

While solutions exist to detect critical data traversing the network or leaving the data center or control the attachment of USB storage devices (a la Snowden's thumb drives or Manning's CD drive), there has always been the possibility that a trusted employee or contractor could simply snap pictures of the display and walk out the building with critical information.

But a lot of data is most useful in file formats: software code, spreadsheets with embedded calculations, etc. Latter's new technique, in his words, treats the computer display like a bundle of fiber optic cable. Each pixel represented by a strand of data transfer capability.

Latter, an independent researcher, has written and made available on his website a very simple client agent that, once installed, converts files into a series of QR codes that are displayed in a video style (ThruGlassXfer [TGXf]). He has also made available an application for iPhone and Android that reads those QR codes and translates them back into the original file format.

Armed with the app you can download a PDF by pointing your smart phone camera at a demo video.

Thinking further about how to get his client agent on a target machine that is probably well protected, Latter devised another protocol (ThruKeyboardXfer [TKXf]), which can be used to install software from a small USB device that emulates a keyboard.

By combining the two, Latter demonstrated that a remote worker could easily gain access to and transfer any data that the user has permissions to see. The use of exploit kits could extend that capability but might trigger the protections the enterprise has deployed.

But why?

Latter explains that there is a fundamental risk, especially with remote or out-sourced workers, that has not been addressed by security architectures. By releasing his code and a 200-page paper on his research he hopes to highlight that risk and spark discussion of how to counter it.

While the risk has always been there, Latter's proof of concept of a covert channel via computer display turns a possibility into a certainty.

A DEFICIT IN SECURITY SPENDING HAS LED TO A MASSIVE SECURITY DEBT

JULY 15, 2015

Every IT department has struggled for years to justify spending on security. Various models have been used with more or less effect to encourage upper management to open the coffers. Return on Security Investment models attempt to quantify the money saved from preventing future breaches. The factors cited include: cost of lost productivity, the direct costs of notification in the case of a breach that must be reported under 45 different State laws, and the hardest to quantify of all, loss of trust or brand value.

Obviously these attempts to justify security spending are failing. How could organizations that should know better still be suffering major breaches? The theft of 21.5 million highly confidential records of government employees, past and present (and that of their families), from the Office of Personnel Management is only the latest, most egregious example.

In response to the OPM breach, on June 12 the Department of Homeland Security (DHS) initiated a cybersecurity "sprint" to identify critical assets, hunt down intruders, and remove them. What they will find is that the Federal government has to pay down a massive cybersecurity debt.

Here is what I mean by cybersecurity debt. One measure of spending is percent of overall IT budget devote to security. It is useful because it can be looked at across sectors and help identify best practices. The very best organizations spend as much as 8% of their IT budgets on security. My thesis is that organizations that under-spend on security are accumulating a cybersecurity debt that will have to be paid back. If they have been spending 2% of their IT budgets on security and the best in their sector have been spending 8%, they are accumulating cybersecurity debt at 6% per year. Of course IT budgets increase every year, sometimes by as much as 10%.

Let's look at a simple example: Five years ago a widget manufacturer had an IT budget of $1 million. Each year, as they automated plant reporting, upgraded the network, and bought new PCs, that budget increased by 10% so that after the end of five years they were spending $1,464,100 on IT. If they spent 2% of their budget on security, that would be $20,000 in the first year and $29,282 in the fifth year. If the best practice is to spend 8%, they are operating at a security deficit of 6% or $60k that first year and up to $87,846 in the fifth year, for a total of $366,306 that they did not spend on security over the five years.

To avoid the inevitable breach that shuts them down for a month, or puts them out of business altogether, they have to pay down that security debt. That means spending 25% of their IT budget on playing catch up ($336k/$1,464k). Sometime in the future they can revert to the 8%. Luckily, security technology has evolved dramatically in the past five years. Tools for continuous network monitoring, advanced multi-function firewalls, strong authentication, and even better encryption are available today at lower cost and much higher value. So, it may be possible to lock in some of that under-spending and attribute the overall savings to blind luck, the same way I once forget to renew my license plate for three months and the DMV only charged my for the remaining nine months of the year. I risked getting pulled over and suffering thousands in cost and fines and saved $35.

When you transpose these numbers to a large organization you can see where the problem arises. Government agencies notoriously underspend on security. OPM's total budget is almost $2 billion. According to recent budget justification documents, OPM spent about $51 million in 2014 and 2015 on IT, including about $7 million on salaries. At the very least, considering the sensitivity of the data OPM is responsible for, they should be spending 8% of that budget on cybersecurity, or $4 million today. Just from observing the tip of the iceberg, the fact that the breach was discovered by a vendor during a demo of their product, the fact that they still do not know the full extent of the breach or how long ago it started, or even if there have been other breaches over the last ten years, the horrible report from an internet audit, we can assume that OPM has accumulated a large security debt. Using the same model as above, I get $15 million.

Interestingly, OPM recognized the need to spend more on IT security after a breach in 2014, presumably the breaches suffered by two contractors, USIS and KeyPoint Government Solutions, as well as the March 2014 breach of OPM. The most recent budget justification

submitted in February highlighted security as the primary concern. The 2016 budget request increased IT salaries by $24.5 million (from $6.9 to $31.4 million). The increase is probably associated with the stated plan to staff a 24/7 Security Operations Center (SOC).

OPM has claimed that they learned of the latest intrusion in April 2015 and in June learned the breach extended to the background investigation records of current, former, and prospective Federal employees and contractors. Yet, OPM had already submitted a budget to pay down its security debt in February! Someone at OPM must have had a really bad feeling about their lack of security.

Going further, Gartner pegs total IT spending globally at $3.2 trillion and IT security spending at only $70 billion, or 1.8% of IT spending. The world as a whole has a lot of spending to do to pay down cybersecurity debt.

The lesson learned from OPM and other high profile breaches is that many organizations have been under-spending on security. It is time to pay down the security debt. Doing so on the installment plan is much less painful than making a balloon payment post-breach.

UPDATE: Reach the column by Chris Wysopal, co-founder and CTO of Veracode, for similar ideas of security debt for application code. Written in 2011.

DRASTIC TIMES CALL FOR DRASTIC MEASURES IN CYBERSECURITY

JULY 17, 2015

I see the White House has published a compilation of its accomplishments in the realm of cybersecurity. The timing of this self-congratulatory piece is obviously tied to the embarrassment of the Federal government for the devastating loss of background information on 21.5 million federal employees, contractors, and even job applicants. In addition to the long form background checks, apparently the attackers have made off with Social Security Numbers and a database of fingerprints.

I thought it would be interesting to examine the progress the White House declaims and compare it to my recommendations of November 4, 2008. (Please excuse my naive call on Obama to stop spying on Americans. Obviously I had no way of knowing just how big a program that was.)

Readers may have noticed that my post on security debt was my first Cyber Domain writing since October of last year. There are lots of reasons for my sparse jottings of late. Whenever I am writing a book, as I was last fall, I lose the ability to write short-form posts. With a book one has the luxury of diving deep into a topic; a 5,000 word chapter allows you to get it all out there. On top of that, four years ago I went back to school to study military history. The requirements for academic essays of 2-3,000 words, where every claim had to be backed up with exhaustive research and citations, completely destroyed my "blogger's voice."

But even more than these minor frustrations was an overwhelming sense of futility. How many times must I write the "patch all the things!" post? How many times must I denigrate risk management thinking? How many times must I warn retailers that yes, there are bad guys out there who want to steal credit card information. And most of all, how many times must I warn government agencies to get with the program and start securing their networks, endpoints, and data?

My "Letter to President Obama" was written in part to counter the *Securing Cyberspace for the 44th President* report put out by CSIS, compiled by a consortium of think tankers, professors, consultants, and industry lobbyists. It was spurred by a frustrating eight years of working with and advising government agencies, first at Gartner, then as an independent analyst.

Here are ten technical controls I suggested at the time. Read the original for higher-level recommendations.

1.   All access must be explicitly authorized.

2.   All users must be identified and strongly authenticated.

3.   All applications must be reviewed for security vulnerabilities.

4.   All network attached systems must be scanned for vulnerabilities on a schedule.

5.   All network connections must be fire-walled.

6.   All firewalls must be configured to "deny all except that which is explicitly allowed."

7.   All government networks must be mapped and understood.

8.   All data needs to be encrypted at rest

9.   All communication links need to be encrypted

10.   All intrusions need to be aggressively analyzed and appropriate responses executed.

Keep in mind that this letter was written a year before the Google Aurora attacks, two years before US Cyber Command was stood up, and four and a half years before the ground breaking APT1 Report from Mandiant.

Now let's look at the accomplishments of this White House as highlighted in a fact sheet published July 7.

Perhaps the most concrete accomplishment during the recent 30-Day Sprint is that privileged user authentication has been increased by 20% (the document does not mention a base line). Two-factor authorization is great, but "privileged users" are system administrators who can access back-end systems. What about regular users that can access, for instance, the database of security clearance information?

40,000 government systems have been scanned for vulnerabilities. I am sure that scan has discovered at least 400k vulnerabilities, probably over 4 million since much of the government still uses Windows XP. Patching those systems will take years. Keep in mind that since the 30-Day Sprint started there have been new vulnerabilities, not the least of which being three zero-days in Adobe Flash discovered in the trove of leaked Hacking Team documents.

Compared to my simple list of security controls, the Federal government as a whole gets an F. Drastic times call for drastic measures. A new list would have to put computer hygiene on a back burner and turn to immediately hunting on all networks to discover all the other systems that are currently being exploited by foreign governments, insiders, and cyber criminal organizations.

Most commercial organizations have been working for over a decade to deploy my ten controls above. Over the last four years they have learned that vulnerability management and access controls are great at reducing noise and abuse, but ineffective against determined attackers. Best practices now include continuous network monitoring for anomalous behavior and reducing response times in an effort to shut down an attack before data can be exfiltrated or systems damaged. As Richard Bejtlich, Chief Security Strategist at FireEye says (and has been saying for years): "This is why I call 'detection and response' the 'third way' strategy. The first way, 'secure your network' by making it 'intrusion-proof,' is not possible."

Federal agencies are going to have to move quickly to Bejtlich's Third Way.

To paraphrase the proverb about trees: the best time to implement a good cyber defense program was twenty years ago. The second best time? Today.

HOW POWERPOINT KICKED OFF A REVOLUTION IN MILITARY AFFAIRS

JULY 20, 2015

The following story is excerpted from *There Will Be Cyberwar: How the Move to Network-Centric War Fighting Set the Stage for Cyberwar.*

The history of China and Taiwan is short, consistent, and unresolved. When Mao Zedong finally won the Communist revolution against the Chinese Nationalists in 1949, Chiang Kai-Shek fled with his forces to the adjacent island of Formosa and established a new country, Taiwan. Since then, China's stated goal has been to reunify the two countries. Whether it will be a peaceful reunification (like that of Hong Kong in 1999) or a violent reunification contributes to the long-lasting tension between the two countries.

In 1991 Taiwanese President Lee Teng-hui angered China with his statements about reunification, leaning away from the One China rhetoric that both countries generally stuck to. Then in 1994 Lee was traveling from South America when his flight was diverted to Honolulu to refuel. The Clinton Administration, cognizant of the delicate situation, bowed to Chinese pressure and refused to grant Lee a visa, forcing him to stay overnight in the plane. Tensions began to rise in 1995 when

Lee was invited to speak at his Alma Mater, Cornell University. Congress passed a resolution requiring the State Department to grant him a visa. This was during the lead up to the first fully democratic presidential elections in Taiwan and China took a dim view of the situation. Lee spoke at Cornell in June 1995.

China announced missile tests in a region near Taiwan and began maneuvers on the mainland across the Straits from Taiwan in Fujian Province. They carried out a series of missile launches into the sea to the North of Taiwan in July. The Clinton Administration took steps to demonstrate that the United States was willing to intercede if China threatened an invasion. In March of 1996 two aircraft carrier battle groups were deployed to the vicinity.

This is where Admiral Archie Clemins comes into the story. Clemins was the Vice Admiral of the US Navy's 7th Fleet. Only two years before, upon achieving flag rank, he had been assigned to the training division of the US Pacific Fleet under Admiral Frank Kelso. He was also dual-hatted as head of N6, the information technology arm of the Pacific Fleet.

As an "IT guy," Clemins began to carry a laptop with him, an unusual sight in the 1993 Navy. It was an Apple Power-Book, probably a 160 with 4 MB of memory and a 40 MB hard drive. It was one of the earliest flip top portable computers and had a grayscale LCD screen. It weighed 6.8 pounds.

His PowerBook was his constant companion, even on trips to the Pentagon. He found that people, specifically Admiral Robert J. Kelly, Commander of the Pacific Fleet based in Hawaii, were asking him for copies of the notes he took on his portable. He was living the Information Revolution of the time. "That started the use of computers; we, at Training Group Pacific, led everybody with desktop computers," Admiral Clemins told me.

Shortly after taking on the Pacific Fleet role based in San Diego, Clemins got a call from the Navy's Assignment Officer who asked how he liked the weather in San Diego and whether he would like to transfer to the Pentagon. The previous week Admiral Kelso, head of Naval Operations, had announced a major reorganization of the Navy and Clemins had been chosen to lead the effort.

As Clemins pulled together a small team within the Pentagon he made sure that they used technology to its best advantage. Clemins credits this use of computers for the success his team had in accomplishing the Navy reorganization in 12 months instead of the 18 months originally slated for it.

Clemins was then appointed Deputy Commander of the Atlantic Fleet at Norfolk to accomplish the same reorganization. "The more I did this, the more I came to believe this [computer technology] was the way we were going."

From Norfolk, Clemins was promoted to commander of the 7th Fleet where he had served as chief of staff years before. He was determined to bring the fleet into the Information Age: "You have to remember the ships of the time, '93-94 are still moving information at teletype speed." That meant at most 80 messages a day of 40 lines each. All messages would go directly to the Commanding Officer (CO) who would route them to the appropriate department or personnel.

CLEMINS' first task was to assemble a team. He drew from surface, air, and submarine commanders. This was 1995, the year Windows 95 came out, the first commercial operating system with embedded TCP/IP networking capability. Mark Lenci, the submarine captain who Clemins tasked with retro-fitting the 7th Fleet, had little experience with networking. His only qualification: he had an AOL account. But no one in the command ranks was an expert and Clemins chose a team that could learn quickly and get things done. When Lanci reported to duty aboard Clemin's command ship, the USS Blue Ridge, he recalls Clemins saying, "Let's go take a walk." On the flight deck he explained his vision of NCW. "I don't know what a WAN (wide area network) is but I know we need one. Get the smart guys together here in the Pacific. We are going to do it." And they were going to do it with commercial off-the-shelf products (COTS).

The Blue Ridge, the command ship of the 7th Fleet, was the first to be outfitted. Lenci relates how welders were sent on board to cut out bulkheads and toss them into the South China Sea as the Blue Ridge was steaming to port. Ships of the day had stove-piped IT infrastructure; every agency or group that needed computing power deployed their own complete stack of equipment and satellite communication gear. None of the 48 systems, all running different flavors of Unix, could interoperate and none of his team knew how to run them. The satellite antenna system looked "like a pop can with a bundle of straws strapped to it," Lenci recalls.

Lenci was deployed to Washington to scrounge funds from "end of the year" money available from budgets that had not been fully spent. He returned to Japan with $4 million available for the retrofit. He and his team began to outfit both the Blue Ridge and the aircraft carrier USS Independence with a network of Windows 95 machines. Finding bandwidth on satellite comm links proved to be difficult. Most links were controlled by the intelligence agencies and they did not want to cooperate.

So Lenci, who had spent some time at SPAWAR (Space and Naval Warfare Systems Command), called a friend in Cheyenne Mountain. He asked him for a list of all satellite transponders on geo-synchronous orbits over the Pacific theater. Of the list compiled there were seven Inmarsat satellites that were being decommissioned but still had onboard fuel so they could be repositioned. He commandeered these satellites, which to this day are still employed by the US Navy.

In very short order the beginnings of a networked fleet were accomplished. All seven shore bases (including HK, Singapore, Honolulu, and Guam) could communicate via email. The technical barrier to communications had been broken down. But, as usual with change within military structures, the biggest hurdles were getting people to change. The COs could not get comfortable with everyone in their command being able to communicate with anyone on shore or another ship. They insisted that all emails be sent to them, printed out, and distributed in the old way.

To counter this, Admiral Clemins had an "Eyes Only" email sent to each of his seven one-star admirals. The email requested their presence for an important strategy meeting in Japan. It was a test to see who actually read their email. Only four of the admirals came to the meeting. After that, the COs began to read their emails assiduously.

When China began to bluster over Taiwan, Admiral Clemins' newly deployed systems were put to the test. The planning process for any Navy operation is cumbersome and time consuming. Multiple scenarios are proposed, researched, and analyzed. The process can take days and is hampered by the communication at "teletype speeds." When President Clinton ordered the 7th Fleet to send two carrier battle groups to the region, Clemins went into action. The Independence, shore bases, and the command ship were engaged in live communications with the Pentagon. Many options were discussed, even the possible need to enter a harbor in Taiwan. To support the deliberations, a young seaman was able to pull up a live feed from a webcam focused on the harbor in question. It is telling of the interagency friction and embedded processes that the intel community objected to using such open-source data. It had not gone through the intelligence cycle—tasking, collection, analysis, and reporting—after all.

At one point, and perhaps for the first time in history, Clemins used a Microsoft PowerPoint presentation, broadcast directly to the Pentagon, to help communicate the tactical situation in the region. He was interrupted by the Chairman of the Joint Chiefs who asked that a copy of the slides be expedited to the Pentagon (meaning put on a plane). Clemins instead asked the Chairman's aide for his email address. Onscreen he pulled down the <share> menu and sent the PowerPoint to the General. Within minutes an aide had retrieved a hard copy and placed it in front of the General. The Chairman of the Joint Chiefs turned to the other guys, "I want this on every joint command. Now." This was the moment when the military changed forever. Network-centric war fighting was born.*

The USS Independence was deployed to within 600 miles of Taiwan while China launched ballistic missiles into target grounds just north and south of the island nation. When the presence of the Independence did not induce the Chinese to communicate, the USS Nimitz was ordered to steam from the Gulf towards Taiwan. All of the planning and decision process took hours instead of what would formerly have taken days.

Data of the Chinese missile flights were recorded by the deployed ships. They identified the flight path and type of missile. That data was scheduled to be put on a floppy disk, flown via F-14 to shore, and from there by air transport back to Washington for analysis. In a brash moment Clemins had Lenci email the file via his AOL account—unencrypted—over Inmarsat and the Internet.

This vignette from 1996 will remind you of your own discovery of the Internet and how it changed the way your work. For the Navy and the rest of the DoD it kicked off what came to be known as RMA, a Revolution in Military Affairs. The Navy program set in motion by Clemins, called Collaboration At Sea, is still being used. The USS Blue Ridge is still there. IT21, the Navy's future plan for NCW, was born in the Taiwan Straits Crisis. The Navy Marine Corps Internet was born. Admiral Arthur Cebrowski was brought in to articulate NCW. Admiral Bill Owens, whose son served under Lenci and eventually went on to command his own submarine, became the lead proponent of NCW and the author of *Eliminating the Fog of War* a seminal book on NCW.

Today's military is still moving towards networking everything. You can imagine the issues that arise from doing that. Hindsight tells us that networking leads to attacks, and applications, devices, and platforms are invariably vulnerable.

*(The irony of a PowerPoint presentation being the killer app that sold the Joint Chiefs cannot pass unremarked. PowerPoint presentations have become the bane of military planning operations. During the protracted war in Iraq, an Air Force sortie could not launch until the obligatory briefing fueled by PowerPoint presentations. A system was devised that would take up-to-date elements of weather, geography, and terminology and centralize them in Colorado Springs so that everywhere in the world every PowerPoint would be updated with the current data and graphics. Military planners have become masters of PowerPoint. The push-back against the tyranny of bullet points has grown to the point where the newly appointed Secretary of Defense, Ashton Carter, barred PowerPoint from his briefing with "30 high-ranking military commanders and diplomats" at a meeting he called in Kuwait for February 2015.)

FIVE REASONS INTEL SHOULD
SPIN OFF MCAFEE

JULY 21, 2015

In August of 2010 Intel announced one of the most ill-advised acquisitions in IT security industry history. Intel went on to pay $7.68 billion for McAfee. At the time I was one of many who was critical of the acquisition (Intel Should Not Consummate McAfee Deal). While Wall Street was enamored of the deal because wow! Cyber!, there was never a fit. A company that dominates the silicon chip industry has no strategic reason to get into anti-virus, IPS, and firewalls.

Here are five good reasons for Intel to reverse the blunder of 2010.

1. Symantec is coming back. Symantec too has made its mistakes. Up until Intel acquired McAfee, Symantec held the record for blunders. It acquired a data center behemoth, Veritas, for $14 billion in 2004. Only recently has Symantec decided to reverse that decision.

During the last four years Symantec has been a tad rudderless. It is too bad McAfee was no longer in a position to gain market share. That opportunity was left to the other vendors in the space, Sophos, Eset, and Trend Micro, to name three. On top of that, a slew of endpoint security vendors have cropped up to address the failings of traditional signature-based AV. Cylance, Bit9/Carbon Black, CounterTack (which just announced the acquisition of ManTech's cybersecurity products, the remnants of HBGary). Even FireEye, the company Dave Dewalt went on to lead to an IPO after handing off McAfee to Intel, has made an endpoint security play with the acquisition of Mandiant.

One of the reasons I would attribute to McAfee having only flat revenue (as opposed to plummeting) since the acquisition is that its largest competitor, Symantec, has been stalled out itself. That is about to change. After Symantec finally spins off Veritas, it is coming back with a vengeance.

2. Brand confusion. Branding is important in the security space and Intel is attempting to re-brand McAfee to "Intel Security." It's a great name but does nothing for the $55 billion a year Intel brand and confuses buyers of McAfee products. Regardless of the Intel acquisition, McAfee was headed towards a branding train wreck as the weirdest character in an industry known for its oddballs, John McAfee, came out of hiding from an experimental drug retreat in Belize to make a comeback, first with a truly strange YouTube video, and now on the lecture circuit. This is a golden opportunity to spin off McAfee with a clean name.

3. The Internet of Things (IoT). There are only 3 billion or so PCs in the world and sales are dropping. At the same time, the IoT is exploding and Intel is already seeing growth in its IoT division. That is where the opportunity for Intel lies. Dumping McAfee would allow Intel to focus its resources where it can continue to dominate.

4. Finance. Sometimes large corporations make huge bets for mysterious reasons of financial engineering. Maybe the acquired company creates an off-shore tax haven. Maybe there is a patent portfolio worth more than the operating company. After four years it is hard to come up with any

financial benefit that has accrued to Intel or its shareholders from the McAfee acquisition.

The last full year that McAfee filed with the SEC it had $2.064 billion in revenue. Intel folded McAfee into its Software and Services Group (SSG) that probably had some revenue from its other products. Revenue last year for SSG was $2.216 billion, essentially flat in a market that is growing 24% according to my analysis.

If Intel had put the McAfee purchase price of $7.68 billion into an ETF based on NASDAQ it would be worth $18.6 billion today.

In its latest annual report Intel reports no adjustments for the $4 billion in goodwill it still maintains on its books for McAfee, indicating that its auditors think McAfee is still worth the purchase price. So, spinning it off may net the purchase price back. Since Wall Street is valuing other pure play security vendors at crazy multiples (Palo Alto Networks at $15 billion! That's more than Check Point Software), today would be a good day to cash in and move on.

5. Security is changing too rapidly for a division of Intel to keep up. Even people who have been active in the industry for the last 15 years are shaking their heads over what a crazy space IT security is. There are hundreds of new startups. I recently counted 1,400 vendors and I know that is a low count. Major security vendors have to evolve and innovate constantly. They do that through investment and acquisitions. Symantec is about to get back into that game. Cisco recently increased the pace of their acquisitions. Venture backing of startups is rampant. Intel Security has dabbled in acquisitions. It purchased yet another firewall vendor, Stonesoft, in 2014, but has not demonstrated that it can counter Palo Alto, Fortinet, or Check Point in the gateway security space. McAfee has to compete on many fronts, including the endpoint, network, and risk management and data security. NewCo Security, when it is released from the grasp of Intel, will have to pick up where it left off five years ago.

Most of the senior management that made the August 2010 impulse buy decision to acquire McAfee has moved on. It is time for the new leadership to take a hard look at the wisdom of holding on to McAfee. It is time to set McAfee free.

GHOST FLEET: REQUIRED SUMMER READING

JULY 22, 2015

When two experts on modern warfare get together to write fiction, I get in line to read it. Peter Singer's *Wired for War*, which tracks the rise of drones and robots for war fighting, was a primary resource for me as I attended classes at King's College. In all of my research, Singer was the only one to hint that maybe all of this automation and networking was introducing worrisome vulnerabilities. Singer's co-author of *Ghost Fleet*, August Cole, was a defense industry reporter for the Wall Street Journal. He is non-resident senior fellow at the Atlantic Council where the Cyber Statecraft Initiative addresses the future of the Internet and its impact on nation-state interactions.

I'll admit that, like many cybersecurity writers, I have been tempted to write the "Tom Clancy" for cyber (see Richard Clark's *Sting of the Drone*). I even worked with a couple of journalists to write a cyber thriller, which I will not link to. (It is currently ranked #7,851,049 on Amazon.)

For a first novel, Singer and Cole have succeeded in creating a summer blockbuster. *War on the Rocks* compared it to Clancy's *Red Storm Rising*.

By far the most important aspect of *Ghost Fleet* is the not-too-distant future they paint of disgruntled, respect seeking Chinese leadership that envisions and executes on a plan of dominance in the Pacific Rim. They solve a few fictional challenges by placing the story just far enough in the future where Google-glass, autonomous swarming drones, and operational rail guns are possible.

I am not a big fan of the multi-character, multi-plot, bestseller style. It is too hard to get to know the characters and identify with them as the story jumps around in time and location. But Singer and Cole pull it off. Perhaps I identify too closely with the main characters, a father-son team that struggle with their estrangement. I would have preferred not to be sucked into their pain so repetitively but I am pleased with how it turns out.

The secondary characters are where *Ghost Fleet* shines: the ninja-like bereaved assassin on Oahu who collects hair samples from her victims culled from the occupying Chinese forces, the insurgents who trek across the island causing mayhem, the Chinese-American electrical power scientist called on to outfit the rail gun.

That rail gun is the technological highlight of *Ghost Fleet*. The authors' build up and final release of solid projectiles for devastating precision effect will stay with this reader forever.

Summer is fading fast and August approaches. Get *Ghost Fleet* to read on the beach.

Ghost Fleet: A Novel of the Next World War goes on sale Friday on Amazon in hardback and is available for Kindle now.

THINK ABOUT IT: A THOUGHT EXPERIMENT THAT MAY SAVE YOUR CAREER

JULY 23, 2015

Sometimes it helps motivate action to perform a thought experiment. After the horrifying breach of OPM many agency heads are probably thinking, "How can I ensure I never have to face a grilling by Congress for a failure to protect critical data?" That is the thought that is prevalent today in DC. I propose a slightly different way to think about it.

If you are an agency head, CEO, or responsible for a large project that involves lots of sensitive data, take a moment to do the following.

1. Take a walk. Get away from the office. Find a quiet place to sit and think.

2. Now imagine the worst case scenario. You get a call from the FBI informing you of a breach. (Or Brian Krebs if you are a bank, retailer, or online "dating" site.) Ideally that call should come from your head of IT security, but the most poorly prepared organizations do not even know when they are breached (see Nortel). Your most valuable information has been stolen. You don't know how, you don't know when, and

you don't know who. It may even come as a surprise that you were entrusted with that particular set of data.

3. What do you do? Who do you turn to? If you are like John Thompson, Symantec's CEO from 1999 to 2009 and who got this call on the Thursday of his first week on the job, you ask, "Who is our CISO?" Thompson learned Symantec did not have one. They did on Monday.

4. You are an experienced leader, you know what to do: get a team together, gather facts, and create a plan for finding out what happened, how to fix it, and how to communicate what you are doing with your stakeholders, Congress, and the public. Here is a good list of 20 things to do if you are breached put together by David Spark for CSO.

5. OK, got all that? Did you feel the adrenaline rush from a crisis? Did you feel the confidence build as you scoped the problem, created a plan, and set it in motion in your mind?

6. Now go back to your office and make that first call. Find your CISO, or appoint someone to the role. Figure out how to discover if you are under attack today. Create a plan to ensure that you can hunt down attackers and shut off their incursions quickly. Find the budget to implement a 24/7 security operations center or hire out the continuous monitoring you have to do. Do exactly what you would do in the event of a major breach, only without the distraction of having to trek up to The Hill.

Play this scenario out in your head at least monthly. As you make progress you will find that the answers come quickly. You can even try more and more elaborate scenarios. What if your top security guy is disgruntled and goes digitally postal? What if your suppliers are breached, or your employee health data provider, or pension manager?

This thought experiment will only take a few minutes, but it may save you weeks of travail in the future. It may also save your career.

FIXING THE PENTAGON. PART I

JULY 27, 2015

What has been is what will be, and what has been done
is what will be done, and there is nothing new under
the sun.
> - Koheleth

Now that the latest, greatest, most expensive fighter jet is
coming online the critics are piling on. It's too slow! It
can't fire its guns! It can't dog fight! The software does not
work! Unlike most of these critics, I am rather hopeful that
the F-35 Joint Strike fighter will eventually be alright. It is
truly a triumph of engineering in the face of overwhelming
bureaucracy. Sadly, the cost of overcoming bureaucracy is far
greater than that of overcoming design challenges. The
Pentagon's procurement system is seriously broken. It needs to
be fixed now because in the near future the Pentagon may
have to respond to rapidly changing global threats. New

weapons platforms and technology will have to be rolled out with astounding speed to respond to innovations in war fighting. Far better to fix development processes now than during an emergency.

Despite my twenty years in the world of IT security I still maintain an interest in engineering, product design, and aerospace systems. I learned flight mechanics from an Admiral in the South Vietnam Air Force. I learned rocket design from professors who worked on the Trident I submarine-launched ballistic missile (SLBM). But most importantly, I learned how to engineer products with tight constraints for cost, weight, and timing as an engineer in the automotive world.

As the first degreed engineer working for Hoover Universal, before it became Johnson Control's Automotive Systems Group, I designed car seats for GM, Saturn, Ford, Chrysler, and Jeep. You can look up my patents on seat frame structures.

There are three rules for effective engineering product development: prototype, prototype, prototype. Build the first one out of paper. Build the next one in the shop out of materials on hand. Make temporary tools for the next prototype. Discover every problem you can, get as complete a representation of the final product as possible, before committing to production.

My job in 1982 involved running between my computer simulations, the drafting board, and various prototype shops in the Metro Detroit area. I could get anything built in Detroit back then. Practically every machine or tool shop I visited was working on the Space Shuttle or B1-B bomber at the time. I would use the same acid baths to give me multiple prototypes of different gage metal as were used to create optimally milled manifolds for the B1-B engine inlets. One shop formed the injector plate for the Shuttle main engines out of a single forged billet of Inconel 718. It was electro-chemically etched until there were 300 injectors sticking out of a four inch plate of solid nickel-chromium alloy. Each injector plate cost $2 million.

These shops were founded by what we used to call business owners, today we call them entrepreneurs. They would get their start making early prototypes and their business would thrive as space and weapons systems ramped up for production. Sadly they are all gone, along with most of Detroit's tool and fabrication plants, victims of off-shoring, the end of the Cold War, and the hiatus in manned space flight.

While I witnessed firsthand the sprawling supply chain for airframes, fuel pumps, and electronics for government programs, I worked on some of the biggest automotive manufacturing projects, including the launch of a new car company, Saturn. I even participated in the Manhattan Engine Project, a secret effort on the part of Pontiac and Chevrolet to develop the next generation four-cylinder engine.

But the program I contributed the most to was the re-design of the full-size Chevrolet sedan, dubbed GM200. You may remember how GM turned the proud, square lines of the Caprice Classic into the jelly bean shape their market research predicted would appeal to their buyers.

I was brought on to the project to prepare prototypes, first for crash testing, and then for full ride-and-handling testing. Crash-test prototypes were easy; bring in a fleet of 22 brand new Caprice Classics, carve some holes in the frames to improve crushability and add some beams to the upper fenders to reduce pitch during impact to avoid throwing the occupants up against the roof. Then I would ship them off to Milford, Michigan, where they would be instrumented with accelerometers and high speed film cameras. Then we destroyed them by hurling them into a solid concrete and steel barrier at 30 mph.

The real challenge came when I was tasked with creating full scale prototypes of the new design. I needed stampings for 250 different sheet metal parts. I needed to assemble them into a body, mount it on a modified chassis, and prepare the interior for road testing.

At the far end of the GM200 project's main design room was a glass wall, behind which was a full size mock-up of the new vehicle. Every sheet metal shape was created in clear plastic and the vehicle was assembled with plastic fasteners. Design teams would meet around the mock-up and work out real estate compromises inside the engine compartment. One day I asked someone how those plastic parts were made. They were vacuum formed. In other words, somewhere in the building was a set of wooden forms carefully machined from the CAD models. Warmed sheets of plastic would be draped over each form and the air would be sucked out through tiny holes to form the plastic into an exact shape.

I found those forms and arranged to have them moved to GM's Kirksite foundry where a small team of artisans would take impressions of each form. Using precise thicknesses of wax to represent the final sheet metal, they would create large blocks of plaster with the shape of the male and female dies required to stamp the needed shape. Using green sand they rammed these models into copes and flasks and poured molten Kirksite in the cavities they left in the sand. The final product would be a matched set of solid zinc alloy, that when put in a press could hammer out up to 2,000 components before needing to be re-worked.

I would have these tools moved next door to the sheet metal shop and request two finished stampings for each of the 250 different parts I needed. When they were done with the tools, they recycled the Kirksite.

How did I get hundreds of skilled craftsman at GM's Tech Center to work for me? I was a lone wolf that hacked the system. GM had a staff of prototype buyers that were in the process of trying to starve their internal resources by giving all the prototype business to outside shops. The story from the union guys was that the outside shops provided fine dinners, and possibly "gifts," as they vied for the work. The internal workers loved their craft and loved the fact that this crazy 28-year-old engineer in a suit was flooding them with work. I just signed work orders with a charge code that had been assigned to my project. I was done and gone before anyone in accounting ever thought to ask what I was doing.

In a union shop, engineers are not allowed to pick up a tool or handle any material. In order to get a finished part from the sheet metal shop to my final assembly buck, I was supposed to fill out a "move order." If I was lucky someone would pick my part up, strapped to a wooden pallet, and take it to the shipping dock the same day I requested the move. At the shipping dock I had to fill out a "shipping order" to have the part loaded on a truck and driven a quarter mile to the next building over. When it arrived, I would meet it and write another move order to have it taken to my team for spot welding into the vehicle.

My team, all union guys, gave me advice on how to beat the system. Pick up each part from the sheet metal shop and hand carry it between buildings. When I passed the shop steward's office I should walk slowly and pretend I was looking for someone to help me. Don't rush, don't appear to be on a mission. Amble. It may have helped that I was limping from a swollen knee.

I carried two sedans and a full-size station wagon from one building to another that summer.

After I had developed my prototype technique for the sedans, I was asked to produce the station wagon. Some of the designs for the parts had not been completed yet. I took the drawings to an outside shop that had experience making cardboard mockups for architectural models. I had them make models of the dies out of cardboard and took those to the foundry. By this time I had the system down. I assembled a complete station wagon, shipped it to Milford (where test engineers were allowed to use tools) and mounted the body on a complete chassis. I transferred all the interior trim from an existing vehicle to my prototype and handed a complete vehicle off to the test engineers. Total time from start to finish? Four weeks.

DURING THIS TIME I became fascinated with the idea of rapid prototyping and how it could be used to shorten development times. One day I read about the Chevy II, a vehicle that General Motors built in 18 months from concept to production. The project I was working on was supposed to be groundbreaking: redesigning a vehicle in 2.5 years. The first year of production of the Chevy II was 1.6 million vehicles in six configurations: coupe, sedan, station wagon, soft and hard top convertible, and differing seating options. The most popular vehicles of today barely exceed one million in production volumes.

While I wandered around the GM Tech Center in Warren, Michigan, I asked every old guy I met if they remembered the Chevy II. One of the team helping me on my builds remembered coming to work on his first day in 1960. He said, "I thought I had come to Ford's by mistake" there were so many Ford Falcons in the hallways and on the platforms. An older engineer said, "Oh that? We cheated. We copied the Ford Falcon bolt for bolt."

When I posed the question: Why is our program taking 2.5 years when the Chevy II only took 1.5? I got the answer, "Cars are more complicated today with all these regulations for safety and fuel economy." I did not buy it. We had CAD/CAM, Finite Element Analysis (my specialty), and simulators. We should be able to beat the old way.

Every new car program I was on started with a tear down of the competitive vehicles in the market. GM had a huge warehouse to hold what they called the Mona Lisa project. At one side of the cavernous space was a line of complete competitive vehicles from Honda, Toyota, and Volkswagen. Stretching away from each car were 50 yards of folding tables. Every component, tagged with its weight, was laid out for inspection. An engineer tasked with designing a new strut, control arm, or engine mount would spend a day at Mona Lisa taking notes and armed with calipers and micrometers. (I went to the Henry Ford Museum to go back farther in time so I could see the evolution of each component.)

Every new car, engine, suspension system, seat, or frame is an evolution from an earlier day. There are no pure, clean-sheet-of-paper projects. The reason for this is that no engineer can take all the variables into account. An existing component has passed all the federally mandated tests, survived 100k cycles of fatigue testing, has been through the requisite tweaks for manufacturability, and most importantly, has survived years of real world testing in every environment. Starting with an existing design and changing one or two variables, like material or gage, while adding the latest feature, is the fastest way to create a new design. Otherwise the product gets shipped and as problems are discovered, very expensive recalls and retooling ensues.

The biggest problem with Pentagon procurement is that every major project is a clean-sheet-of-paper. Designs are not allowed to evolve. Mission profiles and specifications are determined 20 years before the first system is fully operational, and those systems are expected to meet all requirements for the ensuing decades before the whole exercise is started over.

Long design and development time scales lead to costly changes as requirements are modified to meet current demand. Changes further delay production. Invariably a new weapons platform does not meet the current needs of our military.

In Part II: How the DoD has failed in major weapons platform designs. We will look at the Littoral Combat Ship and lessons learned from WWII construction of Liberty ships. Then we will look at what is proving to be the most expensive weapon system in history, the F-35 Joint Strike Fighter, and compare it to some amazing aviation successes from Lockheed Martin's famous Skunk Works.

WELCOME BACK SYMANTEC

OCTOBER 27, 2015

It has been a long road but it appears that Symantec has finally re-focused on its core business of securing its customers. Symantec announced today that it is introducing an automated malware analysis and response solution, Symantec Advanced Threat Protection (ATP).

It has been 12 years since I first heard complaints from enterprises that their anti-virus solution was not detecting targeted malware, that is, malware that was customized just so it would *not* be detected by signature systems of the day. AV clients have been augmented over the years to include white-listing and behavior-based technology, but still, they cannot keep up with the level of customization that targeted malware exhibits.

One approach that FireEye can lay claim to pioneering is sandboxing. Incoming malware, usually in email attachments, are shunted to a virtual machine where they are allowed to execute, install, and beacon home. That behavior is monitored and used to extract key indicators of compromise (IoCs), which can then be used to further inform other diagnostic and protective tools. This is what Symantec ATP does.

As of this January, Symantec will have divested itself of Veritas, the data center solution vendor it squandered its capital on in 2004. As a pure play security vendor once again, it has some catching up to do. Introducing an advanced malware defense to compete with FireEye, Lastline, and Trend Micro Systems is exactly the right first step. Doing it with internal resources is also the right approach. An acquisition may have been considered but malware defense is Symantec's core business. This new solution is merely the productization of what Symantec already does, as do all AV vendors, in its automated research to discover new versions of malware and write signatures.

Symantec ATP includes Symantec Cynic, a new cloud-based sandboxing and payload detonation service. The scale offered by a cloud solution means that a customer's OS and standard applications like Adobe and Microsoft Office can be emulated quickly and will have a higher catch rate of targeted malware. ATP also includes Synapse, which is a cross-platform correlation tool that will be able to provide intelligence on infections.

This is great news for existing Symantec customers and dire news for FireEye, which will have to compete on effectiveness, speed, ease of deployment, and price. It is also bad news for attackers who will have to invest much more in devising ways to bypass Symantec ATP.

STAY CALM AND ERASE PER POLICY

AUGUST 29, 2016

Last week, we learned that (gasp) US presidential hopeful Hillary Clinton—or her staffers—used a freeware data removal tool to purge emails from her now infamous private email server. The debate around Ms. Clinton's email practices is getting muddled, if you ask me. If she is to be condemned for hosting her State Department communications outside the State Department's IT infrastructure because that would expose it to hacking from enemy states like Russia (the most common bugaboo), shouldn't she be commended for ensuring that they were safely erased?

KEEP in mind that the State Department's email server has been hacked (purportedly by Russia) on more than one occasion. But there's no evidence that Clinton's email server was ever hacked, other than claims from the loopy Guccifer (now awaiting sentencing in Alexandria, VA).

There's a long history of policy creation on the retention of email and other documents that has led to today's norm: most organizations as part of a well-documented data retention policy have assigned useful lifetimes to all their data. This was driven by the onerous development of discovery proceedings in civil and criminal lawsuits.

To that end, the prosecution in a lawsuit can request any and all documents that could be remotely connected to their case. While US law has consistently upheld that right to discovery, there is also the acknowledgement that records do not need to be retained forever.

Most organizations such as banks, insurance companies, and yes, government agencies have instituted data retention policies that explicitly call for data to be destroyed after it's no longer useful to the operations of the organization. As breaches and cyber attacks have become more prevalent, the need to destroy data effectively has quickly come to the fore. In Europe there is even a new massive regulation, EU GDPR, which *requires* the erasure of personal data after it is no longer needed for its original purpose.

Clinton and her staff were definitely outside State Department data destruction rules when they deleted relatively recent emails. Federal data retention policies are very different than the private sector. Pretty much everything must be retained forever. In the case of the Secretary of State, everything is turned over to the Records Service Center (RSC) at the end of the Secretary's tenure or sooner if necessary. Then they are transferred to Washington National Records Center (WNRC) when they reach 5 years old. And finally they're transferred to the National Archives when they reach 30 years old, where they are kept forever.

Beyond the inappropriate erasure itself, using a freeware tool put Clinton and her staffers into a far worse predicament because it gave lawmakers and regulators the perception that Clinton's team intentionally tried to do something wrong or bypass proper data destruction procedures. And because the free erasure tool provided no proof that the data was permanently erased, there hasn't been any way for Clinton's staff to verify the method used and data that was removed as part of an audit trail. This only lends credence to the argument being floated by Trump's campaign (and its very vocal cohort of Twitter followers) that there was an intentional cover up.

When I look at everything that's occurred in this scenario —and the allegations and legal recourse that's ensued—it pains me that secure data removal only becomes a topic of discussion when it's associated with a data breach scandal. In reality, it should be a part of every organization's data protection plan.

Data destruction can involve physical shredding of hard drives and tapes. But a more economical and ecological approach is to certifiably erase that data using secure software tools. NIST SP 800-88 lays out proper procedures for doing so. It's well worth getting to know those procedures.

SOCIAL MEDIA SITES ON FRONT LINES FACE LOOMING GDPR DEADLINE

APRIL 15, 2017

Every social media site experiences security growing pains. Remember when Twitter was passing a million users and a hacker in California brute forced celebrity account passwords with a simple script? In classic reactionary mode, Twitter finally added the standard throttling to number of login attempts and eventually SMS authentication for account changes. All good—but many social media sites are still lagging far behind the threat actors. Case in point: a woman in Arizona is reporting that the Instagram account she set up for her daughter to post dance pictures has been taken over by Russian hackers. The trouble she is going through to regain control of her account is inexcusable.

Social media sites are driven to grow and rarely put thought into reducing friction for *removing* accounts. As social media becomes a primary attack vector, even challenging email, it is time for these sites to up their game.

Back in 2009 the Google Aurora attack was one of the first sophisticated campaigns to use social media. Google employees were targeted on Facebook and eventually induced to click on malicious links. The attackers gained access to

Chinese dissident and journalist Gmail accounts and along the way exfiltrated Google source code.

Today every platform is used for spam, phishing, and account theft. Who has not received a link from a Skype connection that leads to a Baidu or Google malicious URL? And it is only going to get worse.

Friday's dump of a trove of NSA exploits by the Shadow-Brokers is a portent of massive new hacking activity on the horizon. It is not hard to predict an increase in breaches over the coming months fueled by tools developed by the NSA's elite hacking teams.

Instagram, Skype, Facebook, Twitter, etc. must become proactive. In addition to their ongoing efforts to filter out hate, bullying, and fake news, they have to make it harder for attackers to take over accounts, and easier for rightful owners to regain access once it is lost. On top of that, they have to make it easier for those owners to cancel their accounts when desired. As the woman in Arizona said: "Honestly, I just want the account deleted."

There is a looming deadline for making account deletion easy. In 404 days every one of these social media sites will have to be in compliance with the new EU General Data Protection Regulation if they want to continue to do business in Europe. This means appointing a Data Protection Officer among many other requirements. Chief among those is enabling "the right to be forgotten." At a user's request all data associated with an account must be found and erased. Based on this woman's experience in Arizona, sites like Insta-gram are à long way from having this ability.

UNINTENDED CONSEQUENCES OF THE EUROPEAN UNION'S GDPR

NOVEMBER 27, 2017

The looming imposition of a new data protection regulation in the EU is already sending tremors through the legal and IT worlds as organizations wake up to the fact that by May 25, 2018, they have to comply with the most intrusive technology regulation ever.

Law firms and consulting firms are starting to use phrases like "this is Y2K all over again." You could see it coming for the last two years but nobody did anything about it. My take is that companies are waiting until the deadline is in the same budget year. That means that on January 1, 2018 there will be a mad scramble as executives and boards wake up to the fact that non-compliance could be very expensive.

GDPR applies to any company that collects data on EU residents. That means that if you want to do business in Europe, you have to invest in compliance.

Let me recap. The EU General Data Protection Regulation is a 261 page document with 99 articles and 173 "Whereases." When it goes into effect it will apply to any organization that collects or processes data on people who reside in the 28 member countries of the European Union. Some of the more visible requirements include:

- 72-hour breach notification. An organization will have only three days to disclose to the Data Protection Supervisor when they learn of a breach. I don't know any companies that can pull their stories together fast enough to comply with this. They have to 1) determine what happened, 2) put in controls to stop it from happening again, and 3) figure out how to message it.

- Hire a Data Protection Officer. This one is causing a lot of debate. Can we just give the CISO the DPO title? (No.) Can we outsource the role? (Maybe.) Where do we find someone who understands data privacy, security, and all the legal stuff? (Great question.)

- Article 17, the Right to Erasure. Any EU resident can request from any organization a complete list of all the data they have on them. On top of that, they can demand that the data be erased. The data collector/processor has 30 days to respond.

One of the overlooked aspects of GDPR is that it has some very loose statements about adequate security around privacy data. Terms like "state of the art" are bandied about, a litigator's dream.

What about the fines for non-compliance? Think about this: Twenty million euros or four percent of global revenue, whichever is greater. Just to put that in perspective: 4% of Amazon's revenue (2016) would be $5.44 BILLION, of Google's $3.6 billion, Facebook's $1.1 billion, and Netflix, a mere $352 million. You can do the math on your own company.

So what could the unintended consequences be of imposing a massive new regulation on the healthiest component of the global economy, the digital market? For one, expenses go up so profitability goes down. Lower profitability means lower investment, fewer startups, and slower growth.

Another consequence could be that GDPR severely

restricts access to technology for EU residents and companies. The technology industry is practically defined by the Two-People-in-a-Garage trope. The vast majority of the 3,122,110 apps in the iTunes AppStore 1) are created by small companies and 2) collect a lot of personal information. Every internet startup dreams of getting their first million users and they get there by going viral with inexpensive, often free software. Their model is collect info and use Big Data to extract value.

But now they will fall under GDPR because they will have personal data on EU residents. The definition of personal data includes IP address, geolocation, home address, email address, and on and on.

One way to avoid the cost of compliance, of hiring a DPO ($150k), building in controls, and creating a 72-hour breach notification ability is just don't collect data on EU residents. Make them click a button asserting that they do not reside in the EU before installing. Or use geolocation to block them altogether.

This means the EU will be cutting itself off from the latest and greatest technology. Want to install the newest secure communications app? Sorry. How about that new business app for managing contacts, or accounting? Not available in the EU. That new VR/AR game that is taking the world by storm? Sorry, only people outside the EU get to experience it.

I predict even tech startups based in the EU will choose to sell only to foreign markets when they launch.

This is a major problem for the EU. It will be disruptive in the extreme and add new digital borders that the internet does not need. GDPR will accelerate the trend towards digital mercantilism.

HOW 5G IS GOING TO CREATE A SECURE INTERNET IN 5 STAGES

DECEMBER 6, 2017

Always look at infrastructure changes to make easy predictions about the future. You could get very rich.

A decade ago I attended meetings around the world where the topic was "how can we, as a country, join the Internet revolution?" Brazil and Columbia stick in my mind. Don't even get me started on Australia and their wasteful endeavor to create a National Broadband Network (NBN). I never had the floor but I wanted to stand up and shout "deregulation!" That is what sparked the internet revolution in the United States. In 1993, here in Michigan, it cost 8 cents a minute for telephone calls that went outside your immediate area code. You could be a mile away from your ISP's nearest POP (Point Of Presence) and see outrageous phone bills that ratcheted up quickly at $4.80 an hour. At RustNet we sold internet access for $19.50/month. If we wanted to get customers in a different area code we had to put stacks of dial-up modems in an office in that area code. Then we backhauled the traffic to our main office and sent the packets out to the internet through our upstream provider in Chicago. (Anyone remember Net99?)

The big break up of AT&T had occurred in 1982 and the regional telephone companies (Baby Bells) started to compete for your business after the 1996 telecom deregulation. Per minute charges went away just in time to fuel the rapid growth of internet subscribers. By that time the telcos offered their own backhaul so you did not need to maintain huge stacks of modems in every POP. You just paid for a T1 to the telephone company's Central Office (CO) and they delivered the calls to you.

In 1995 I published a business plan for How to Start an ISP. It gave me great visibility into the wave of deregulation that was sweeping the world. As each country figured out that per minute charges were holding them back they would deregulate, encourage competition, and I would see sales of the plan going to that country. South Africa and Mozambique used my plan as a starting point. The internet took off. By 2005 you could tell which countries still had per minute charges. They had Internet Cafes because people could not afford to dial in.

Of course 4G spelled the end to all that. Now you can get internet on your phone and, if you can tether your phone to your computer, you use that for internet access. I can get 95 Mbs over Verizon 4G.

Well 5G is going to explode many things. And it is coming fast. Ericsson predicts there will be one billion 5G subscribers in six short years.

What is different about 5G? It is very, very fast. Huawei has tested 5G connections at 70 gigabits per second. Gigabits. At that speed even immersive experiences like SecondLife will work. No wonder people are excited.

But what could this do for security?

5G introduces new networking paradigms. It is going to have dramatic effects on the Internet of Things (IoT) as very small, low power radios will be able to connect. That will pose an opportunity for data theft and continue the weekly news cycle of privacy violations that we have come to know and love.

But think about what these speeds will do to your typical enterprise (and SMB) networks. Why would anyone use the pokey internet connection at work when they get 5G at home and on their smart devices? Businesses have already moved the critical tools they need to the cloud: email to Office365, document sharing to Microsoft-hosted SharePoint or Google Docs, or Dropbox, HR systems, Salesforce, etc. They don't need your network at all. And if you force them in through a VPN they are going to be tunneling through your pokey network to get access to those mission-critical services.

One company, Zscaler, saw this coming and started addressing the issue of protecting mobile connections a decade ago. They plan to IPO soon. Timing will be great for the early investors. 5G opens up some new business models that will compete directly with Zscaler's offering of hosted network policy enforcement and traffic scrubbing.

Ever see the scene in *Gettysburg* where General Buford rants about how clearly he can see what will happen in the morning?

The hardwired connection is dead for office use. Sure, every firewall vendor will add 5G radios to their UTM devices for remote offices and HQ, just as they have added 4G. But going through a gateway means dealing with the slow Wifi in the office. It will be faster for users to jump on the 5G network themselves. So they will.

Goodbye cable triple play. We won't need twisted pair, CAT5, or fiber to the home anymore. All home devices, including your TV, will connect directly to the internet via 5G.

New, very fast growing businesses will start up to address these problems.

Here is what happens next.

Stage 1. A startup that is probably already out there will introduce a policy overlay to the carrier networks. An enterprise will just enroll all employ devices and manage what they can do over the network. It will be like a virtual UTM. They will encrypt traffic, filter content, and apply firewall rules. Managed Service Providers will do that policy work for SMBs.

Stage 2. The carriers will recognize that they have created a monster as every enterprise starts cancelling their lease line subscription. Seeing the opportunity they will start to develop their own service offerings for security.

Stage 3. One carrier, late to the game, will acquire the fastest growing 5G security management platform from Stage 1.

Stage 4. All the other carriers will cut off that 5G management platform for their own networks and make their own acquisitions.

Stage 5. All carriers will bundle security into their offerings. Network security will finally be part of the internet.

This whole timeframe will play out by 2030.

Thank you, technology.

CYBER PEARL HARBOR VERSUS THE REAL PEARL HARBOR

DECEMBER 7, 2017

December 7 is a good day to re-think the implications of a "cyber Pearl Harbor." Leon Panetta famously used the term in 2011, when it seemed like all of our generals had become cyber experts overnight.

"The potential for the next Pearl Harbor could very well be a cyber-attack," the CIA Director testified before the House Permanent Select Committee on Intelligence.

At the time Keith Alexander was in the midst of standing up US Cyber Command, which achieved operational readiness on October 31, 2010, months before Panetta's statement.

Panetta, and just about anyone else inside the Beltway, uses the term "Cyber Pearl Harbor" to imply a disabling attack on critical infrastructure. Yes, our power grid, communications, and traffic lights are very poorly protected from hackers. Yes, an attack similar to that in Ukraine over Christmas 2015 would not be difficult to achieve. But would it be strategic? What purpose would it serve a foreign government to shut down the power in the United States? Would China want to damage the economy of its biggest market?

Would Russia risk the blow back?   Perhaps Iran or DPRK would figure they had nothing to lose?

Regardless, an attack on critical infrastructure is something for the Department of Homeland Security to worry about. The DoD has bigger worries.

Back before the wars in Afghanistan and Iraq, before military thinkers and policymakers became obsessed with counterinsurgency, the idea of the day was the Revolution in Military Affairs, or RMA, a doctrine that emphasized modern information, technology, and communications. It was sparked by Soviet analysis of the West's move towards more reliance on precision targeting and coordination as demonstrated in Operation Desert Storm.

The reclusive and enigmatic "Yoda" of the Pentagon, Andrew Marshall, was pouring through Russian language journals and presumably secret communiques. He was intrigued by the Soviet identification of a "Military Technical Revolution." Europe throughout the Cold War occupied the center of the chessboard. On one hand, grand strategy revolved around a massive preemptive blitz of tanks and troops supported by air and even tactical nuclear weapons, emanating from the Soviet bloc, and on the other hand, arms buildup and nuclear deterrence from the West.

When Russian and Chinese thinkers witnessed an actual invasion using massed weapons and troops, supported by air and stand-off cruise missiles, as a US-led coalition easily pushed Iraqi forces from Kuwait, they believed they saw the future of modern warfare. A combination of precision-guided weapons, networked intelligence, surveillance, and reconnaissance (ISR), and modern command and control would be a force multiplier while eliminating the fog of war.

Arthur Cebrowski was the chief proponent of the new network-centric warfare (NCW). His 1998 paper, *Network-Centric Warfare: Its Origin and Future Proceedings*, written while he was still director for Space, Information Warfare, and Command and Control, is imbued with the excitement of the halcyon days of the internet boom. Reading it today, one is struck by the enthusiasm for networking that was the dot-com boom:

We are in the midst of a revolution in military affairs (RMA) unlike any seen since the Napoleonic Age, when France transformed warfare with the concept of levée en masse. Chief of Naval Operations Admiral Jay Johnson has called it "a fundamental shift from what we call platform-centric warfare to something we call network-centric warfare," and it will prove to be the most important RMA in the past 200 years.

In his Pentagon briefing upon taking the director of Force Transformation role, Cebrowski said: "If you are not interoperable, you are not on the net. You are not benefiting from the information age." Cebrowski was the Scott McNealy of the Pentagon.

When modernized militaries next engage in combat, expect a debilitating cyber-attack giving the adversary an asymmetric advantage. The move to network-centric warfighting by the US military set the stage for an inevitable Cyber Pearl Harbor.

The tenets of NCW, once again, are eliminating the fog of war through a sensor grid and a combination of precision-guided weapons, ISR, and command and control. The US military, and other militaries around the world on both sides, were late to the computer and networking game (now dubbed "cyber") but determined to catch up. A global information grid was sketched out. Satellites for reconnaissance and communication were launched. Precision GPS systems deployed. Drones for ISR and weapons delivery to targets were built in ever increasing numbers. A high altitude drone, the Global Hawk, was deployed not only to replace the '50s vintage U2 platform but to add a layer to the ISR and command and control from land, sea, and air systems.

But, while weapons systems were being networked, the operational networks of the Pentagon crawled along at a pace much slower than in the commercial space. Transformation encompassed putting PCs on every general's desk and empowering operations and planning personnel with PowerPoint tools. By 2008 most enterprises had already discovered and addressed the disruptive nature of "being networked." Viruses spread by floppy disks and then the internet were addressed with anti-virus software. Worms such as Code Red, SQL Slammer, and Nimda had had their impact. Firewalls were locked down to "deny all except that which is explicitly allowed." Intrusion Prevention was deployed to block worms and network-based attacks. To avoid data loss, endpoint controls were established to block the use of unauthorized USB devices. Vulnerability and patch management systems were almost universally deployed.

The Pentagon had its wake-up call, according to William Lynn, then Assistant Secretary of Defense for Cyber, in 2008 when the Agent.btz worm spread from a forward operations base in the Middle East throughout SIPRNet, the top-secret military network. The cleanup effort, labeled Buckshot Yankee, took nine months and involved re-imaging millions of PCs at a cost of $1 billion. We can learn a few things by reading between the lines. In 2008 the Pentagon did not have device control systems deployed. We also know this from the way Bradley Manning exfiltrated the State Department cables from a SCIF in Iraq by burning them to a Lady Gaga CD via USB port. In addition, we know that the Pentagon did not have the ability to remotely update its PCs as the operation was accomplished locally at each facility.

Note that the commander in charge of the Joint Functional Component Command for Network Warfare (JFCC-NW) that first saw Agent.btz crossing SIPRNet was Keith Alexander. As the military and federal government caught "cyber fever" and scrambled to shore-up defenses, there was also a land grab to claim the cyber domain. Then-Secretary of Defense Robert Gates addressed the scramble, directing the Air Force and Navy to stand aside and then combining JFCC-

NW and the Joint Task Force- Global Network Operations (JTF-GNO, also led by Alexander). Gates eventually appointed Alexander to head US Cyber Command in addition to the NSA.

But the parallel between the Pentagon and the measures that industry has been taking to address the rise of cybercrime, espionage, and attack continues. The Pentagon came to the game late and reacted with uncommon speed to the threats that accompanied a move to NCW, but with one glaring omission.

Software assurance, the practice of designing and testing software to exclude vulnerabilities, has been apparently neglected completely by the Pentagon and the defense contractors that supply it with precision weapons, ISR, and command-and-control capabilities. With the famous Trustworthy Computing Memo written by Bill Gates, Microsoft embarked on a massive SA effort in 2002 when it became apparent that vulnerabilities in Windows and its applications represented an existential threat to its market. Software development was halted for a full year as every engineer was trained in the methods of code scanning and secure software design practices. While not perfect, that effort paid off eventually. Fifteen years later, the latest versions of Windows are relatively good.

The Pentagon made a mistake common to many manufacturers. They assumed that because their systems were proprietary and distribution was controlled, there would be no hacking, no vulnerabilities discovered, and no patch-management cycles to fix them. This is security by obscurity, an approach that always fails over time.

Evidence of the lack of software assurance within the defense industrial base abounds. Drones in Iraq and Afghanistan sent their video feeds in the clear, something discovered when insurgent laptops were captured with drone videos on them. There is apparently no verification of GPS signal authenticity as drones have been captured by both Iran and North Korea by overwhelming GPS signals with spoofed information. And encryption keys are apparently accessible on those captured drones.

In one experiment run by the Air Force, three million lines of proprietary code were scanned for vulnerabilities. They found one "software vulnerability" per eight lines of code, one "high vulnerability" per 31 lines of code, and one "critical vulnerability" per 70 lines of source code.

Modern precision weapon systems rely on software for target acquisition and flight control. The F-35 Joint Strike Fighter, the most sophisticated weapons platform ever built, contains 9 million lines of code with another 15 million lines of code in the logistics support system required to supply it with spare parts. Apply the above number for vulnerabilities and there are potentially 128,000 critical vulnerabilities in the most expensive fighter jet in the US's arsenal.

Does security by obscurity hold for weapons platforms? Not if the adversary is actively engaging in cyber espionage to get copies of software source code. According to Ellen Nakashima, sources provided the Washington Post with a confidential report to the Pentagon that itemized over a dozen weapon systems that had suffered from Chinese cyber espionage. These included: the advanced Patriot missile system (PAC-3), the Terminal High Altitude Area Defense (THAAD), the Navy's Aegis ballistic-missile defense system, the F/A-18 fighter jet, the V-22 Osprey, the Black Hawk helicopter, the newly minted Littoral Combat Ship, and yes, the F-35 Joint Strike Fighter.

Just as hacking of vulnerable systems has moved from widely deployed and relatively inexpensive Windows PCs to medical equipment, automobiles, and industrial control systems, the weapons platforms that are the basis of NCW are surely vulnerable and surely going to be targeted. When modernized militaries next engage in combat, expect a debilitating cyber-attack, giving the adversary an asymmetric advantage.

So imagine a future altercation between the US Navy and that of China, perhaps in the contested South China Sea, or maybe in the Taiwan Straits. Further imagine that China uses GPS spoofing to misdirect the carrier-based fighters sent out on sorties; or creates a fog of war by inserting conflicting comms into secure channels; or directly targets vulnerable weapons systems. The result could be a disaster. A military defeat via cyber-attack.

This would be a Cyber Pearl Harbor.

* Much of this article was derived from a column in Cicero Magazine and from *There Will Be Cyberwar*.

THE INTERNET OF IDIOTS: HOW
WE ALL PARTICIPATE IN LIKEWAR

OCTOBER 2, 2018

Deep inside Peter Singer and Emerson Brooking's new book, *LikeWar: The Weaponization of Social Media*, is a great quote attributed to Colonel Robert Bateman: "Once, every village had an idiot. It took the internet to bring them all together."

Reading *LikeWar* will help you to avoid being part of this Internet of Idiots (IoI). As much as nobody wants to admit that they get sucked in by confirmation bias, we all fall prey to it. The constant barrage of messages we get through Facebook, Twitter, our favorite sub-reddits, YouTube, and Instagram subtly impact our world view. Only constant questioning and filtering will protect us from being part of the problem.

Like any viral infection, information offensives work by targeting the most vulnerable members of a population—in this case, the least informed.

Cyberwar is proving to be a fertile topic for journalists, researchers, and academics to write books about. I try to read them all. *LikeWar* is among the best, and it is the first to meld the fields of strategic studies, the history of warfare, and the rising tide of online conflict.

Singer and Brooking are policy wonks and historians. Both write prolifically and bring their expertise together to walk us through the history of the internet and how we got to the present day, when nation-states, including China, Russia, the United States, and the UK, have started to incorporate information warfare into their arsenals.

The book is packed full of stories–because there are so many–of actors as diverse as the members of 4chan to teenagers in Macedonia to Barack Obama's campaign to Russian operatives, as they developed the tactics to disrupt the truth in service of their aims.

"Online battles are no longer just the stuff of science fiction or wonky think tank reports, but an integral part of global conflict."

If you lived through the internet era, many of *LikeWar's* stories will be familiar to you: the story of Liu in Weifang, China, who sought to destroy the internet to prevent embarrassing pictures (of him folk dancing) from being disseminated by destroying cable boxes; or Bruce Stirling's story of the mysterious "Japanese guy" who dropped off a bunch of 2400 baud modems at a Czech university in 1989, fueling revolutionary fires.

The Color Wars as former Soviet States underwent democratization and the Arab Spring and Iranian elections are all related in *LikeWar*. All of these stories have an element of social media weaponization to them.

The still hard-to-grasp story of election interference in the UK's Brexit vote and the US's 2016 election are the reason this book had to be written, and the reason it had to be written by these two authors. They bring the perspective needed to understand the new face of conflict. *LikeWar* applies a historical perspective to an emerging threat, one that we are just now learning to face even as the realization dawns that we have a problem.

Information warfare is a rapidly developing field with a long history. Writing a comprehensive history is a daunting task that Singer and Brooking have accomplished even while new information appears every day. Only this week have we seen Bellingcat, the Open Source Intelligence (OSINT) team that *LikeWar* depicts piecing together the downing of MH17 by Russian forces in Ukraine, dramatically tracing and identifying one of the "Russian tourists" that poisoned the Skripals in Salisbury. But armed with this book we are able to fit new information into what is now a consistent framework.

While students of history, strategic studies, political science, and international relations will all find *LikeWar* on their required reading list, anyone else who wishes to understand the world we live in must add *LikeWar* to the top of the pile on their nightstand.

THE THREE STAGES OF CLOUD TRANSFORMATION: APPLICATION, NETWORK, SECURITY

FEBRUARY 15, 2019

From mainframe, to client-server, to web, to cloud, IT architectures have evolved to support the way people demand to work. In a sense, everything old is new again: Modern cloud-computing technology shares user commonalities—specifically, the ability to connect remotely —with a mainframe architecture, except the cloud is considerably more highly-distributed, scalable, and resilient.

Early computing architects could never have imagined the limitless size, breadth of scope, and always-on availability of today's cloud computing. Infrastructure-as-a-Service platform providers like Amazon, Microsoft, and Google have invested heavily to be able to offer elastic, pay-as-you-go cloud services. Those same services have effectively displaced on-site computing and even private data centers. The cloud is no longer a playground for IT experimentation but rather an operational mandate for enterprises of all sizes.

There are three stages to the enterprise cloud transformation journey: Application, Network, and Security.

1. Application Transformation

Innovative software providers like Salesforce ushered in

the era of Software-as-a-Service (SaaS). Salesforce's CRM offering quickly displaced incumbent enterprise internal-hosted contact management systems. (Anyone remember Siebel? Act!?) Similarly, Microsoft moved its Microsoft Office suite of email and productivity tools to the cloud with Office 365.

SaaS offers enterprises several advantages to shrink-wrapped alternatives:

• Subscription pricing instead of software licensing.

• Scalability: One-size-fits-all from five users to thousands.

• Availability: Maintenance, support, and uptime are all the responsibility of the provider.

• Dynamic upgrades: Users log on Monday morning and discover significant upgrades that have been made over the weekend. They can start to use them right away, without having to wait for the IT team to test the updates, schedule downtime, and roll them out.

Cloud transformation also provides enterprises with an ideal opportunity to better manage corporate applications. Most enterprises have embarked on migrating internal applications to the cloud in three tranches:

1. Lift & Shift: Take internal apps that are already web-enabled and host them in the cloud.

2. Partial Refactoring: Move elements of an application stack, usually the front-end, to the cloud. Leave legacy data-processing and storage in the corporate data center (for now).

3. Refactoring: Re-write applications for the cloud. Host the entirety of the application—front-end, middleware, and database—in the cloud.

2. Network Transformation

In the old world of legacy hub-and-spoke corporate networks, applications were hosted in the data center, and users accessed them via the corporate network, and—always —within the confines of the perimeter-based firewall. To connect, users logged on via a VPN (over SSL or IPSec), connected to a VPN concentrator back at HQ, and traveled via (expensive) MPLS circuits to their desired application destination.

Cloud computing breaks the legacy network model. MPLS hair-pinning degrades the user experience, particularly when users are accessing cloud applications like Office 365. Users demand to connect directly to internet and cloud resources from home, the coffee shop, or on a plane. Hub-and-spoke networks constrain that growing traffic, routing it over a spotty VPN to the local hub, filtering it through a stack of (expensive) security hardware appliances, out through a secure web gateway to the cloud. Cloud access requires bandwidth, and enterprises struggle to keep up with bandwidth demand (and to pay for it).

Users connecting directly to cloud resources via local internet breakouts represent the promise of network transformation. The approach is supported by Software-Defined Networking (SDN) capabilities that recognize traffic destination and route it to the corporate data center or out to the internet. And that broadband internet connection is considerably cheaper to manage than leased MPLS lines.

3. Security Transformation

Legacy network security models protected the entire corporate network. But how can an enterprise protect users bypassing the old network on the way to the cloud?

Security transformation should start with deploying zero-trust networking, an approach that establishes a default-deny posture for all network data and traffic interactions. Second, move on from legacy security to dynamic, continuous adaptive trust and threat mitigation.

The legacy castle-and-moat network security model relies on IP address for authentication. That's a start, but with today's threat landscape, it's not secure: Go to any website. You can quickly determine the IP address. You can try to log into the page multiple times. You can try different ports for FTP, Finger, or telnet. A hacker can attempt cross-site scripting or SQL injection attacks. A nation-state can intercept the connection and inject their own malware to infect the end user's computer or smartphone.

In an SDN-enabled zero-trust environment, the corporate application (whether hosted in a data center or in the cloud) is never exposed to the open internet. It is discoverable only to authorized users. Cloud-based inline security—a security check post—identifies the user requesting access and authenticates access privileges. This check post informs the application which then connects the user device to the resource.

The cloud-based inline security check post uses a granular policy engine that can enforce each user's access to each application. Traffic goes through multiple filters much like a UTM device, except the architecture is multi-tenant and scalable. And each user benefits from the threat-intel derived from all user traffic.

The implications of cloud transformation are readily apparent. More efficient IT leads to more efficient business processes which lead to higher enterprise productivity. Better security is delivered at a lower cost.

Similar to how SaaS spells the end of licensed, on-prem enterprise software, the new cloud security architecture signals the demise of the overburdened network security hardware stack in front of the data center and its cumbersome refresh cycle. The internet has replaced the corporate network. The cloud has replaced the corporate data center.

THE CLOUD IS CREATING HEAD WINDS FOR SECURITY APPLIANCE VENDORS

MAY 13, 2019

As the market for cloud-based services heats up, every vendor of traditional security products is struggling with its cloud strategy. Network security appliance vendors face particular challenges.

Symantec's newly appointed interim CEO, Rick Hill, acknowledged this trend in his May 9 earnings call for the 4th quarter, 2019. In addition to the general malaise of sales across all of Symantec's business lines, he had this to say:

The ProxySG business, which is the Blue Coat hardware Proxy bundle, has fallen off quicker than we anticipated, and as a result, we've not experienced as large a refresh cycle as we expected. The cause is clear. The move to the cloud was much quicker than thought. We were behind with our product offering...

In other words, Symantec's security appliance business, which they acquired for $4.65 billion in 2016, is continuing to show signs of weakness and the reason given is *faster adoption of cloud services.*

Symantec has a wide portfolio of products in its enterprise and consumer divisions, but they are primarily in the endpoint protection business, which has its own challenges. Endpoint protection solutions have to demonstrate better efficacy and value in the face of good-enough anti-malware from Microsoft bundled with Windows 10.

Proxy appliances provide protection by terminating network connections and applying filters to protect web traffic. Content URL filtering (to control where employees can go on the internet) is a must-have feature and Blue Coat was already losing market share to the other security appliance vendors such as Fortinet and Palo Alto Networks that simply bundled that feature into their UTM or Next-Gen Firewall appliances.

In a cloud world, applications are delivered from the cloud to users who could be anywhere and on any device. They are not on the corporate network. An expensive security hardware stack in the data center is not even positioned to provide protection. It should be no surprise at all that Symantec is experiencing this shift and it is impacting their revenue.

Many organizations have tried and failed to morph their software solutions to the cloud. Compare the rapid growth of cloud-delivered applications like Salesforce, Workday, and Okta, to those of the once dominant leaders like Siebel, PeopleSoft, and Netegrity (acquired by CA in 2004), despite efforts to maintain relevance.

The reality is that established legacy vendors with large install bases will survive but they will struggle to hold on to market share. They will not ward off the rise of companies with products that are "born in the cloud." These products take advantage of the reliability, easy deployment, and elastic architecture of the cloud to create multi-tenant solutions that can scale quickly and gain market share at a lower Total Cost of Ownership.

Look to cloud-first solutions to challenge legacy on-prem software and hardware solutions.

Microsoft is the rare example of a tech vendor that has successfully moved products to the cloud, most notably Exchange to Office 365. Its customers have reaped the benefits of moving to a scalable infrastructure with frequent feature enhancements, reachable from anywhere on any device.

What are the challenges for security appliance vendors?

Network security gear is designed to handle millions of packets a second. In the corporate data center throughput and low latency are king, so these boxes have specialized silicon to handle the loads. Individual appliances can cost hundreds of thousands of dollars in the data center. All corporate traffic is consolidated from locations around the world and filtered through these appliances.

The cloud is replacing the corporate data center while the internet is replacing the corporate network. In an effort to stay relevant in this new world, security appliance vendors strip out the hardware acceleration they invested so much in and virtualize their software so it can be deployed in a VM in the cloud. These are single tenant solutions. Each customer deploys their own copy of the application. They still have to update each instance and maintain complicated security policies based on IP addresses.

The acknowledgement by Symantec that the move to the cloud is hurting its security appliance business is just the beginning as a twenty-five-year-old industry enters a phase of upheaval.

SANDWORM BOOK REVIEW

NOVEMBER 2, 2019

Andy Greenberg's *Sandworm* has achieved what I thought was no longer possible: it scares me. *Sandworm* is the story of the Russian GRU hacking team that has evolved in a few short years into the most methodical, persistent, and destructive intelligence agency cyber warriors. After reading *Sandworm* you will not doubt those superlatives. You certainly cannot dispute "most destructive," since Sandworm is responsible for NotPetya, a viral scourge that caused over $10 billion in real damages around the world in June 2017.

You have probably read Greenberg's Wired article about the NotPetya attack against Ukraine that spilled over into much of the rest of the world. From his early writing here at *Forbes*, where he covered technology and the internet and morphed into a security journalist (Andy was the one who invited me to become a contributor to Forbes), to his long form reporting at *Wired*, Greenberg has become a valuable source of original reporting. In *Sandworm: A New Era of Cyberwar and the Hunt for the Kremlin's Most Dangerous Hackers*, available November 5, 2019, Greenberg hunts down the researchers on the front line who experienced the trail of destruction left by these hackers, and provides their personal stories. He makes the irrefutable connection to the GRU, the intelligence arm of the Russian military, the same unit that CrowdStrike identified as infiltrating the DNC, although not the ones who eventually stole and leaked the emails. That was a group dubbed FancyBear.

NotPetya gets most of the attention in the enterprise because it impacted so many companies, from Maersk, the shipping giant, to Merk, the pharma company, to TNT in Europe. Greenberg adds to our understanding of the destruction NotPetya caused, including to US medical centers, many of which relied on a medical transcription service that was disabled for weeks, causing havoc for patients and doctors.

By far the scariest attacks attributed to Sandworm are the two attacks on Ukraine's power grid, the first just after Christmas 2015, and the second in 2016. After his research and reporting, Greenberg assigned himself the sobriquet of Cassandra. He puts himself in the same camp as Rob Lee, founder of Dragos, and Michael Assante at SANS, both of whom rang the alarm after the Christmas attack on Ukraine that shut off three separate power distribution companies. The long predicted "attack on critical infrastructure" had occurred, yet DHS and the White House did not give it the attention it deserved.

IT security people, who often say they don't care to know anything about threat actors and their motivations, just the attacks and how to thwart them, may change their perspective after reading *Sandworm*. Knowing that there is a large team of experienced hackers that are willing to release a destructive worm on the world just to disrupt an adversary causes you to re-think your risk models. Certainly, the founder of M.E.Doc, the financial accounting software company in Ukraine that was used as an intermediary in the NotPetya attack, did not think a state-sponsored hacker would infiltrate them over the course of a year and then use their update servers to wreak havoc on the world through its customers. It's the "I am not a target" mentality that mirrors the "I have nothing to hide" stance that many people take when presented with the threats that surveillance poses.

In addition to taking us on a journey of understanding of the events around multiple attacks by Sandworm, Greenberg takes a stab at answering these bigger questions. What motivates the Sandworm hackers? Why is the response from those in charge of protecting critical infrastructure so tepid? What lessons have we learned?

Greenberg's *Sandworm* has earned a position beside Cliff Stoll's *Cuckoo's Egg*, and Kim Zetter's *Count Down to Zero Day*, both in university curricula and your bookshelf.

GARTNER HAS IT RIGHT. PALO ALTO NETWORKS HAS IT WRONG.

DECEMBER 9, 2019

This past August, Neil MacDonald, Lawrence Orans, and Joe Skorupa at Gartner published their seminal report titled *The Future of Network Security Is in the Cloud*. In it they correctly identify the tsunami of change that is hitting the network security industry as cloud-delivered apps are consumed by users on mobile devices.

The vision as laid out by these renowned analysts is straightforward. The legacy "data center as the center of the universe" network and network security architecture are obsolete and have become inhibitors to the needs of digital business. They describe the underpinning shift to cloud infrastructure, a digital transformation that has been underway for ten years. They also point out that the corporate network cannot protect end users who consume cloud applications from any location and any device without the contorting, expensive, backhaul of traffic through the corporate data center.

Gartner coins a new term for the future of security and networks, SASE (pronounced *sassy*), Secure Access Service Edge. This architecture is not new because there are already

several vendors executing well on it. But Gartner's categorization helps to lend clarity. So, what is a traditional on-
prem, hardware-accelerated, all-in-one security appliance
vendor to do? SASE is a direct challenge to multi-million-
dollar stacks of multi-gigabit throughput hardware appliances. What is the one component of SASE, which includes
the concepts of Identity Based Perimeter and Zero-Trust
Networking, that resonates with a hardware vendor? The
SD-WAN component. Branch offices still need to connect to
the internet and you still need a piece of hardware to do that.
Let's face it, SD-WAN is just a fancy name for a
programmable router.

Fortinet (where I had a role in 2006-8) has always been a
switch and WAN router company, like Cisco with its market-
dominating ASA. Switches for internal segmentation and
multiple WAN ports for load balancing and high network
availability were required features for all-in-one appliances,
along with wireless access points, and even backup connectivity over cellular networks. These companies will have a role
to play in the SD-WAN market. But both will face fundamental challenges to build out Gartner's vision for the future
of network security. Palo Alto Networks is a leading security
vendor by market cap with a valuation of $22 billion. They
are not blind to the opportunity in the cloud. They have been
expanding into cloud capability with multiple acquisitions,
including Evident.io for cloud configuration management and
Twistlock for container security, assembling a portfolio. But no
amount of marketecture will turn a collection of capabilities
into a made-for-the-cloud replacement of datacenter security
stacks.

Palo Alto's recent product press release on Prisma Access
falls far short of SASE, despite their claims. It appears to be
virtual instances of PAN's firewall spun up in various data
centers around the world with traffic routed to them by hardware versions of PAN's firewall in each branch office and the
data center. In other words, "Don't replace your expensive

firewall infrastructure for the next generation, just buy more of what we offer!" As Gartner puts so well:

In a modern cloud-centric digital business, users, devices and the networked capabilities they require secure access to are everywhere. As a result, secure access services need to be everywhere as well.

I have written elsewhere about what this looks like. Because of the difficulty of creating a flat service offering with granular policies for millions of users connecting to thousands of apps, SASE must be built as a cloud-native multi-tenant architecture. There is a policy control plane that sits on top of the whole infrastructure which allows a customer company to define granular policies for every user and every app they want to use. There is an enforcement engine that applies filters to decrypted traffic to prevent malware and attacks from spreading. Unknown executables can be sequestered while they are detonated in a sandbox and observed to determine if they pose a threat. Finally, there is a logging component that either stores all the logs per customer or directs them to a destination of the customer's choice. The network infrastructure requires peering relationships with the major cloud and app providers that gets a user's traffic to its destination as efficiently as possible. The move to Office 365 by most large enterprises is driving the need for what I term an enterprise internet.

The two separate components that do not have to be built into SASE are SD-WAN, the physical part, and identity management, which should reside with Azure AD, Okta, Ping Identity, or the multitude of new cloud identity platforms. Because the security policies are managed and enforced in what amounts to a reverse CDN, this is justifiably called edge computing. The "edge" is not on-prem; that is the old model.

Speaking on Mad Money, Zscaler founder and CEO Jay Chaudhry responded to PAN's claims of cloud superiority with: "To do cloud security right you need to have purpose-built architecture. You can't take the legacy boxes and stick them in a cloud and say it's cloud security," Chaudhry chided. "That would be like taking DVD players and putting them in a data center and calling it a Netflix service."

SASE is about creating a ubiquitous, resilient, and agile secure network service—globally. This means that the SASE platform can serve all business users everywhere and that customers don't have to be aware of the inner working of the service itself. Simply put, customers should be isolated from the locations, capacities, capabilities, and service continuity considerations of the service. In PAN's world, customers still think "my cloud-based appliances," still think "user allocation to appliances in specific locations," and still think "how the failover will work." This isn't SASE, this is someone else's appliance stuck in the cloud.

Shlomo Kramer at Cato Networks objected very politely to Palo Alto's claims of dominating the very space that threatens its core business. In an opinion piece at Network World he states that PAN mistakes virtual appliances for a cloud-native architecture and he is right.

It is clear that Palo Alto Networks is starting to recognize a major challenge. It has the expertise and resources to build a Secure Access Service Edge, but that would mean investing tens of millions and a minimum of three years to introduce a product that will directly undercut their existing sales teams, partners, and install base. No major security vendor has ever succeeded in pivoting to a new model fast enough to succeed.

Cloud-native companies like Cato Networks, Zscaler, and startup Perimeter 81 are well positioned to win in this new market. We saw a similar disruption of on-prem software incumbents like PeopleSoft and Siebel Software at the hands of young cloud-native companies like Workday and Sales-force. You know who won that war.

SOC STAFFING IS A GOLDEN OPPORTUNITY

DECEMBER 16, 2019

In 2012 I visited the Security Intelligence Center of Lockheed Martin. My goal was to understand how the previous year Lockheed was able to identify a breach in process. We had learned of it from news stories that Lockheed had shut off remote access to all 80,000 employees. Anyone who needed to get on the corporate network was told to go to an office.

Remote VPNs were authenticated with RSA SecurID tokens. The shutdown occurred only weeks after RSA itself had been penetrated and its file of secret seeds for those tokens had been exfiltrated. SecurID tokens are ubiquitous in the corporate world. The little devices generate an 8, 10, or more digit code every minute to 90 seconds. Thanks to a shared secret, the authentication server produces the same code at the same time. Only someone in possession of a registered token can login.

The breach, attributed to China, affected all 60,000 RSA customers. Including defense contractor Lockheed Martin. Researchers had tried for years to extract the secret seeds from these tokens. They would take them apart and etch the silicon chips. They would put them in a microwave oven, hoping to get the poor little things to cough up their secrets. Occasionally a researcher would report success, but invariably they destroyed the device in the process. Much has been written about third party and supply chain risk. The theft of RSA secret seeds is the most impactful of all such breaches. RSA had to replace many of the millions of devices in their customers' hands. So how in the world did Lockheed Martin detect an attempt by Chinese hackers to login remotely with full privileges via an authenticated session? I'll tell you.

Lockheed had built an SOC to track the continuous hacking attempts against their systems. Don't forget that Lockheed probably has more experience being targeted than just about any commercial operation. Lockheed owned Sandia Labs, which was where Shawn Carpenter worked when he discovered what came to be called Titan Rain, the systematic attempts by China to engage in cyber espionage dating back to at least 2003. Lockheed is one the largest components of the so-called Defense Industrial Base (DIB), which we learned was massively breached in 2007-8 and terabytes of design data for two dozen advanced weapons systems were stolen, including for the F-35 Joint Strike Fighter.

By 2010 Lockheed's SOC (which they called an SIC) had been built up to 80 people. There were malware analysts who would capture and reverse engineer the malicious code samples directed their way. They maintained a data store of thousands of samples that were unique to Lockheed. They also captured network traffic and monitored endpoints. Lockheed described to me how they recruited puzzle solvers to staff their SOC. They did not look for people with cybersecurity experience, they looked for smart people in their IT department that had the ability to put together disparate data from endpoints, malware analysis, and network traffic and build a story. They used the Cyber Kill Chain as a framework for reporting the activity of hacking teams they identified.

When I saw Lockheed's capabilities, I had one of those moments when the future becomes clear. Every highly-targeted enterprise would need to build the same capability—members of the DIB, government agencies, and large financial institutions. The next tier, those that just see the run of the mill attacks, ransomware, DDoS, etc., would acquire a new range of tools for security analytics to give them similar capabilities. And finally, small organizations that could not build and staff an SOC would outsource to a new generation of managed security service providers. This service has become known as MDR, managed detection and response. eSentire in Ontario was one of the very first to provide MDR services.

There is also a broad spectrum of service providers that will provide "SOC as a Service," a dedicated team in their facility to provide these MDR capabilities. Of 113 Managed Security Services Providers I identified while researching Security Yearbook 2020, seven identified themselves as SOC as a Service providers. These companies are NRI Secure Technologies in Japan; Expel, Binary Defense, Perch, and Clearnetwork, in the US; The Cyberfort Group in the UK; and Cyberhat in Israel.

Another service is provided by firms that will build and staff a SOC for you. They can maintain it as an outsourced service or eventually transition the operation and its people to the client. But where are they going to find the staff?

Ryan Craig, author of *A New U: Faster + Cheaper Alternative to College*, is a successful investor in companies that source and place people with technical skill sets. He is on the prowl for such a company in the SOC-augmentation, -creation business. Working with him this year we have discovered that the cyber skills gap is a many-to-many problem. The shortfall in experienced, trained people is disbursed across every organization. Other than US Cyber Command perhaps, there are no large concentrations of demand. And there are no concentrated sources of people to fill these roles.

Thousands of colleges have cyber programs. They often have classes on ethical hacking that prepare students for their CEH certificate. But employers demand experience. Where is a student going to get that experience? Craig believes they will get it through a new channel provided by SOC staffing companies. This new breed of staffing organization will be an intermediary between colleges and employers. It will hire smart puzzle solvers out of school and put them to work as Level 1 SOC analysts where they will get exposed to the everyday workflow of poring through data, responding to alerts, and escalating to Level 2 and 3. In the meantime, they will be subjected to intensive classroom training to get the skills and certifications they need. In as little as a year they will be experienced, certified, cyber workers. The firm that trained them can then place them at their customers that are transitioning to managing their own SOC.

Lockheed Martin had to build an advanced SOC because they were on the front lines. No one had ever had to respond to such a sophisticated barrage. Every organization needs the same capability to some degree. This opens up tremendous opportunities for graduates and the intermediaries that can hire them, train them, and place them.

THE DEMISE OF SYMANTEC

MARCH 16, 2020

I am picking up on disturbing news about Symantec. First, a reseller from Colombia who I was chatting with at the recent RSA Conference in San Francisco informed me that he was there to find a solution to fill a gap created by Symantec abandoning all but its top resellers. Second, another industry veteran told me that Symantec is abandoning all but its most profitable 2,000 customers. That will leave over 100,000 Symantec customers looking for alternatives. It's a good time to be CrowdStrike, BlackBerry Cylance, or Carbon Black.

Symantec's evident strategy—post Broadcom acquisition —is insane and doomed to failure. Historically, this move is only matched by the tremendous blunder that Symantec made under John Thompson when it acquired Veritas.

Let's look at Symantec's history and its place in the cyber-security industry eco-system. Much of the following is excerpted from my recent publication, *Security Yearbook 2020*.

Anti-virus products predated the internet. The 1980s were a time when viruses were transferred from machine to machine via floppy disks. The original anti-virus vendors grew from companies that provided a variety of utilities for the nascent PC industry. File storage, system optimization, disk cleaning, data erasure, backup and recovery, and anti-virus made up bundles sold by software companies that primarily addressed the consumer market. As PCs invaded the workplace, so did viruses. And as networks became predominant in the '90s, viruses began to spread over the wire instead of through dirty diskettes. As viruses became more and more virulent, the importance of AV grew, as did the AV market.

The Symantec name came from a small software company founded in 1982 by Stanford grads to create a database program for the new IBM PC. It was acquired by a smaller competitor, C&E Software, in 1984. The combined company retained the Symantec name and shipped its first major product, called Q&A, in 1985. Sales that year were $1.4 million.

Under its CEO at the time, Gordon Eubanks, Symantec embarked on a strategy of acquiring niche products and taking them to market. In 1987 Symantec acquired tools for project management (Timeline), presentations (ThinkTank) and compilers for the Macintosh (THINK C and THINK Pascal), and an email system called InBox.

Symantec went public in 1989 and its stock took off, giving it the currency to continue to acquire companies including Peter Norton's PC software company, Norton Utilities, for $60 million in stock. Symantec also acquired a C++ compiler and pcAnywhere for remote desktop management. By 1993 Symantec even got into the contact management business when it acquired the makers of ACT! from Contact Software International.

In October 1993 Symantec finally entered the AV market when it acquired Cleveland-based Certus International Corp. Five years later it acquired the AV products of both Intel and IBM. Symantec also acquired Fifth Generation Systems, which had a contract with a small company in Jerusalem called BRM, for anti-virus software. That acquisition gave BRM the capital to invest in Check Point Software.

Eubanks stepped down from Symantec in 1999 to be

replaced by John W. Thompson, an executive from IBM. Thompson had a 28-year career at IBM, rising to the role of General Manager of the Americas. He had little experience with security products, but was tasked with growing the enterprise security business of Symantec. He embarked on divesting the company of non-security products like the Internet Tools division and the Visual Café product line, as well as ACT! He then started acquiring security companies such as Axent Technologies, a firewall vendor, L-3 Network Security for vulnerability management, and Seagate's Network Storage Management Group. He also looked briefly at Finjan Software. He passed on that investment, but was so impressed with Finjan's CTO, Ron Moritz, that he later hired him as Symantec's CTO. Moritz defined Symantec's acquisition strategy, which he termed the NSSSM strategy: networks, systems, storage, and security management.

Very early in his tenure, Thompson relates, Symantec suffered a breach on a Friday. He asked, "Who's our CISO?" They did not have one. By the following Monday morning Symantec had appointed its first CISO.

Under pressure to keep Symantec's stock price up, Thompson continued an aggressive acquisition strategy, culminating in 2004 with the largest acquisition in the software industry for the time: the $13.5 billion purchase of Veritas, a data center software and storage company. The best evidence that this was a major blunder for Symantec is the valuation for the Veritas division when it was spun out to investors led by the Carlyle Group in 2015 for $8 billion.

Under John Thompson Symantec continued to grow through acquisitions. It played an important role in the overall industry, offering an alternative to an IPO to many high-flying startups with good technology. The big paydays for investors and founders fueled more startups and more investments.

Sygate, acquired on August 16, 2005, had a series of desktop tools including a popular PC firewall which Symantec discontinued after the acquisition. It also gave Symantec a Network Access Control (NAC) product.

Altiris was acquired on April 6, 2007, for $830 million. It produced system and asset management software. At the time Thompson told analysts, "Added to our portfolio, (Altiris) makes us infinitely more competitive with the likes of a Microsoft."

Vontu, a data loss prevention (DLP) company, was acquired November 5, 2007, for $350 million.

PC Tools, another PC utility company focused on security, was acquired August 18, 2008. PCTools was run as a separate company until Symantec killed it in May 2013.

AppStream, a provider of application virtualization software, was acquired on April 18, 2008.

MessageLabs was one of Symantec's larger acquisitions. It paid $695 million in November 2008 for the online messaging and web filtering company.

PGP was acquired June 4, 2010, for $300 million. The Pretty Good Privacy software was originally a free encryption solution that mirrored RSA's encryption algorithms. It was created by Phil Zimmerman. The technology was acquired by Network Associates and then spun out to PGP Corporation, formed by Phil Dunkelberger and John Callas. The acquisition, along with Guardian Edge announced at the same time (an additional $70 million), gave Symantec an endpoint encryption solution.

The Verisign certificate business was acquired August 9, 2010, for $1.28 billion. It was the end of an era for the first certificate authority to sell SSL certs recognized by the major browsers. Versign, which eventually got out of the security business, had decided to focus on its remarkable cash cow of maintaining the top level domain servers and collecting a fee for every .com, .net, and .name domain. Symantec later spun this business off to DigiCert in November 2017 for $1 billion.

RuleSpace, acquired in January 2010, provided content URL filtering services for many ISPs.

Clearwell Systems was acquired May 19, 2011, for $390 million. It provided ediscovery solutions for legal firms.

LiveOffice, a cloud email and messaging archiving company, was acquired on January 17, 2012. Price: $115 million. The products were already integrated with Clearwell's discovery solutions.

Odyssey Software for device management including mobile devices was acquired March 2, 2012. It was followed by Nukona, acquired April 2, 2012, which was a mobile application management solution.

NitroDesk, a nine-person shop with application container technology for Android devices, was acquired May 2014.

Then came the divestiture of Veritas under new CEO Michael Brown. Splitting off Veritas in 2015 was the first acknowledgement that Symantec was suffering and was in need of restructuring. The following year Symantec acquired Blue Coat, the manufacturer of secure web gateway appliances, for $4.65 billion. It was almost a reverse merger as the CEO of Blue Coat, Greg Clark, became the CEO of the merged companies.

Blue Coat had had its own troubles over the years. It was initially launched as CacheFlow in 1996. In early 2002 Cache-Flow's CEO Brian Nesmith took the company public. Its stock jumped almost five fold on opening day. Nesmith then pivoted the company into secure gateway appliances and renamed it Blue Coat.

Blue Coat quickly became the largest vendor of content URL filtering appliances. Every large organization needed a way to block employee access to inappropriate or time wasting websites. Adding a category for malicious websites made these devices security products and gave rise to the category of secure web gateways. Blue Coat had a problem though. A gateway appliance that sits in the data center is very expensive. It has to handle tens of thousands of simultaneous sessions.

In the early 2000s large distributed enterprises like retail stores, distribution centers, car dealerships, and restaurants were moving to local internet breakouts. Instead of back-hauling all the traffic from the remote location to HQ over very expensive MPLS circuits, each location would go directly to the internet over low-cost broadband. To provide security they needed to replicate the stack of security gear found at HQ, but without the million dollar price tag associated with datacenter-grade equipment.

This gave rise to the inexpensive, all-in-one security appliance industry led by WatchGuard, SonicWall, and Fortinet. They each added content URL filtering as a subscription service to these devices. At price points of $1,000 or less, Blue Coat could not compete.

Blue Coat stopped growing, and in February 2012 was taken private by Thoma Bravo for $1.3 billion. Considering the $4.65 billion Symantec paid for Blue Coat, this was a good outcome for Thoma Bravo. But not so good for Symantec.

Shortly after Greg Clark took the reins in November 2016, Symantec acquired consumer credit protection company Life-Lock for $2.3 billion. Combined with the Norton consumer AV business, this represented $2.2 billion in annual revenue for the consumer division.

But growth was lackluster under Greg Clark and he stepped down in May 2019. The announcement caused a 15% tumble in Symantec's stock price.

The newly appointed interim CEO, Richard Hill, soon announced a sale of the company to Broadcom, but it fell apart in July. It was later restructured and on November 4, 2019, Symantec's enterprise security business was acquired by Broadcom, while its consumer business remained a public company called NortonLifeLock. This spells the end of Symantec as a security behemoth. It is likely that it will not play the same role in the industry as it has in the past.

There are 255 endpoint security vendors listed in the directory portion of *Security Yearbook 2020*. They run the gamut from anti-virus, to encryption, to the control of physical devices and their ports.

Now that Symantec has effectively left the field, which vendors are stepping in to fill its role? Cisco and Palo Alto Networks are the remaining large acquirers. But it appears that we are entering a new era of Private Equity taking on the role of fueling growth by acquiring promising technology companies. The trouble with Private Equity is that they lack strategy. Much like Broadcom, which is in essence a PE play, they look to financial gimmicks to turn a quick return on investment.

The cybersecurity industry is not prone to cash cows that can be bled of profits to pay down debt financing. Cybersecurity is driven by innovation, channel development, and customer growth. Private Equity has yet to demonstrate it knows how to do any of those things.

Current Symantec enterprise customers should be looking at replacing the multiple Symantec products in their portfolios. Look for cloud delivered solutions that can accelerate your efforts to transform your security architectures while saving money.

Symantec is bleeding people, down 2.311 since September 2019. Startups should be targeting the Symantec install base which is already being abandoned, while hiring the Symantec sales teams and partners which have been cast adrift.

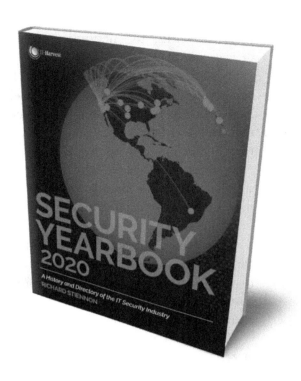

Security Yearbook 2020: A History and Directory of the IT Security Industry

Available at www.it-harvest.com/shop

The first, and only, history of the cybersecurity industry, written by Richard Stiennon, Chief Research Analyst, IT-Harvest. Includes a directory of 2,336 vendors by category and country.

Hard cover, 328 pages.

Curmudgeon: How to Succeed as an Industry Analyst

Available on Amazon, June, 2020

An essential guide for industry analysts and those who are thinking of pursuing a career as an industry analyst.

Soft cover and ebook.

www.ingramcontent.com/pod-product-compliance
Lightning Source LLC
Chambersburg PA
CBHW071231050326
40690CB00011B/2069